Lonely planet

EPIC
SNOW ADVENTURES
of the
WORLD

Experience the world's most thrilling winter adventures

© Roberto Caucino / Shutterstock

© Adrienne Pitts / Lonely Planet

© Ondrej Prosicky / Shutterstock; Donn Tardif / Getty Images

❄ ❄ ❄
Easy Harder Epic

INTRODUCTION

Anyone who loves getting outside in winter automatically has double the opportunities for adventure each year. Where others see dreary wet weather, you're thinking about all the light fluffy powder coming down up high. While others are preparing to hibernate, winter lovers are tuning up their fat bikes, skis and snowboards; shopping for season passes at their favourite ski resorts; or getting in shape for something even more ambitious that might involve sharp metal things such as ice screws and crampons.

Meanwhile, there are several bucket-list adventures that are only possible in winter, like ice skating at New York's Rockefeller Plaza or spotting Polar Bears in the Arctic. Some say adventuring in the cold snowy months is only for the most hardcore among us. But, as with adventures like those, you do not need to be a skier, snowboarder or climber to access the beauty of winter. You only need the urge to step out of your comfort zone. The beauty of this book is the low barrier to entry, full of winter adventures that are family-friendly, cold by day but cosy by night, or even downright luxurious. You'll find winter adventures that are easy, but also exhilarating, like spending the night in a hotel made of ice or making eye contact with a grey wolf.

Of course, many winter fanatics are passionate about skiing and snowboarding, which is why we've also created the ultimate insider's guide to several of the greatest ski resorts around the world, such as Val d'isère, Cardrona, Portillo and Palisades Tahoe. In fact, in a few cases, our 'insiders' are big names in the skiing and snowboarding world, such as Olympic gold medallists Jonny Moseley, Bode Miller and Sage Kotsenburg; champion freeskier Arianna Tricomi; and iconic pro snowboarders Victor de le Rue and Bryan Iguchi.

There's actually never been a better time to be a skier or snowboarder. Today's ski passes – including Ikon and Epic – are like Willy Wonka's Golden Ticket. A fairly reasonable price of admission opens the door to Valhalla, a vast network of ski areas, all over the world, for as many days of skiing as your legs will allow, and for a surprisingly reasonable fixed cost. Whereas retail tickets at the ski resort window do still feel like highway robbery, today's season passes allow you to do the robbing. The more skiing or riding you do, the cheaper each day gets.

For a truly epic winter adventure, combine the experiences featured in this book: Ski Jackson Hole Mountain Resort one day,

Yellowstone for a winter wildlife safari the next. Ski Portillo in Chile all week and cap the trip off with a day of dogsled mushing.

On the far other end of the adrenaline spectrum will be a hardcore few who will target epic mountaineering or ski-touring objectives, so you'll find a few of those in here as well. Meanwhile, serious snowbirds will get their midsummer fix by going so far as swapping hemispheres.

It must be said, there is a lot of talk about the state of winter – specifically, how weather extremes are posing some challenges for those going in search of snow. Organisations such as Protect Our Winters (POW) have become incredible resources for activism on that front. In the meantime, this book offers something of a workaround: go where the snow is. Many parts of the western US just had their snowiest ski season ever, while a different kind of record was being broken in Europe, with the driest winter seen on the continent in years. This isn't a rant about global warming, it's a rant about how, if you are a true snowbird, all it takes is a bit of travel to find the goods.

HOW TO USE THIS BOOK
The main stories in each chapter of the book feature first-hand accounts of exciting winter adventures in that region of the world, including the United States, Canada, the Southern Hemisphere, Europe and Asia. Each includes a Directions toolkit to help plan the trip – the best time of year to hike, how to get there, any special equipment required. But beyond that, these stories are likely to inspire other ideas. We have started that process in the 'More Like This' section following each story, which offers other ideas along a similar theme, or in the same region or country. On the contents page, the adventures have been colour-coded according to their difficulty, which takes into account not just how long, remote and challenging they are, but their logistics and local conditions.

It's important to note that winter adventures, in particular, do require solid planning and a solid awareness of your own skillset. Many of the adventures in this book are challenging, but even some of the easier ones can go from safe to scary quite quickly. Whether you're a seasoned skier or a novice embarking on your very first snowy adventure, please ensure that you're adequately prepared and have taken appropriate safety precautions to help prevent dangers to yourself and others.

Clockwise from left: Jackson Hole-based pro snowboarder Bryan Iguchi; bisons and thermal springs in Yellowstone, Wyoming; a bluebird day at Jackson Hole Mountain Resort. Previous pages, clockwise from left: embarking on a descent of the famous Vallée Blanche above Chamonix, France; endangered European bison; snowball fights – no skill required; the Tatras mountains of Poland

UNITED STATES

COLORADO'S BEST BASE CAMP

The 10th Mountain Division hut network in Colorado is a state treasure. There is no finer backcountry ski-touring experience in Colorado – or any other state, for that matter.

Sometimes it's best just to say yes to a thing, even if you don't think you can do it. It's what I find myself doing a lot when hanging out with my brother, Karl. Last winter, Karl invited me along on a backcountry ski trip to one of Colorado's famous 10th Mountain Division huts, a network of remote wilderness cabins built to commemorate a World War II battalion that trained in the Rocky Mountains.

Most of Colorado's 10th Mountain huts are bare-bones wooden shelters situated well above 10,000ft (3000m) elevation, equipped with simple bunks, a wood stove and an outhouse, no running water or electricity. You reach them by skiing or snowshoeing several miles up steep, rugged trails through remote wilderness, while carrying a heavy pack (loaded with all your food, drinks, clothes and bedding), in unfamiliar gear.

Karl, his wife and a group of super-fit locals have been going on these hut trips for years, and I'd often dreamed of joining them. But the trips are pretty hardcore and I am not hardcore. Karl's friends are the type to bicycle 50 miles (80km) over high mountain passes before breakfast. I live at sea level, I'm a *good* downhill skier, but that's when there are chairlifts involved. I worried that I'd fall behind, get lost and freeze to death in the woods, or that I wasn't fit enough to make it up the trail at all. It was so intimidating, I almost turned down the invitation. Until I reasoned that, if I ever wanted to do it, this was the year. I had been living at high elevation for a couple of months because of the pandemic, and the hut in question was supposed to be relatively accessible. Sisters Cabin sits at an elevation of 11,445ft (3500m), so I was pretty sure it wouldn't be easy. But 3.7 miles (1.6km) sounded reasonable.

The challenge of a hut trip actually begins a year in advance, when you attempt to book your hut. 10th Mountain huts are reserved through a lottery system, and Karl's group lucked out this year: they scored a three-night reservation at Sisters Cabin. This is the newest and fanciest hut of the bunch: high ceilings and timber beams, picture windows, real mattresses on the bunkbeds, a woodstove in the living room, *indoor bathrooms* with composting toilets, even a wood-burning sauna. And from what I'd heard of Karl's past hut trips, I could also look forward to three nights of gourmet dinners, fancy whiskey, fluffy slippers, Bluetooth speakers and unlimited bacon.

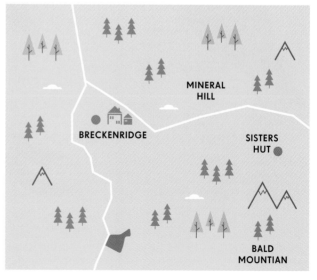

When we arrived at the trailhead on the morning of the trip, people immediately started duct-taping their feet to protect against blisters. We did some stretching, went to the toilet, and then strapped on our skis and packs. It didn't take very long for my first mistake to catch up with me. I had ignored Karl's advice to rent backcountry or splitboard skis and boots, which have both a free-heel and fixed-heel mode (needed when there will be as much down or traversing as up). Instead, I'd brought my nice comfy, lightweight free-heel-only Nordic touring setup, which I already owned (one hut-mate called them death sticks). I'd even had a set of skins cut to fit them. These are like long furry slippers you stick to the bottoms of your skis; the backward-pointing hairs grip snow on the ascent while allowing you to slide on downhills.

For the first mile or so, the going was easy, considering the 10,300ft (3100m) starting elevation. The track followed a nice, wide roadbed to Sallie Barber Mine. From there, we turned sharply uphill onto a singletrack mountain bike trail called Nightmare on Baldy. I was still feeling pretty good, following the little blue diamonds marking our path from one switchback to the next through beautiful snowy woods. It even started snowing.

It took me a little over four hours to reach the hut. Part of this was the altitude, part was the pack, and part of it was the novelty of skinning uphill, while balancing a heavy, tippy backpack, which can be surprisingly taxing when your feet are locked into ski position. On a steeper section, I watched someone with a proper splitboard touring setup flip a riser up on the ski to offset the angle and ease calf pressure. No such gizmo on my Nordic setup. The last mile or so was a major struggle, and I was exhausted by the time I finally limped into the mudroom of the hut.

On hut trips, it is as important to go with good skiers as it is good cooks and bartenders. This crew had been planning hut trips for 20 years and they had things dialled. The minute I arrived, Andrea stripped the skins off my skis and hung them on the drying rack by the fire, which was already roaring, thanks to the fitter skiers in the group. My sister-in-law produced a round of cocktails. Throughout our stay, people took turns sharing snacks, adding wood to the fire, heating the sauna, getting water from the cistern or a snowbank.

There's something magical about waking up in the morning to a fresh dump of snow, frosted trees sparkling in the sun, and the only thing you have to do all day is make tracks through untouched pillows of perfection. Every morning began with a pot of coffee and a lot of calories. Then we'd head out to get some turns in, either on the ridge above the hut or in the meadows around it. In the afternoons, we'd hang our damp socks and skins up to dry by the fire and transition back to slippers or hit the sauna.

Serious hut trippers will talk about meal planning the way they do dropping into a complex couloir. The hard part, Tim explained, is measuring your ingredients precisely enough that you have just what you need to feed the group without adding too much extra weight to your pack. I don't know how much their packs weighed, but the culinary wonders that emerged from within were impressive.

HUT HISTORY

The 10th Mountain soldiers used the inhospitable alpine terrain around Camp Hale, Colorado, to prepare for battle in the mountains of Italy. During World War II, they discovered Europe's system of mountain huts; afterwards, some of the soldier-mountaineers returned to their training grounds, nostalgic for those European huts. By the early 1980s, 10th Mountain veteran Fritz Benedict had envisioned a plan for a string of rustic ski huts in the mountains between Aspen and Vail, roughly 6 to 8 miles (10 to 13km) apart, connected by backcountry trails. The first two were finished in 1982.

Clockwise from top: Sisters Cabin is one of the newer huts in the 10th Mountain Division network; exclusive access to the Colorado backcountry. Previous page: Some use the huts as a base for backcountry skiing, while others lounge, cook, eat and repeat

Tim and Erica served a meal of homemade ravioli, steak, green salad and a smoked salmon starter. Rob and Andrea countered with a gorgeous, complex *pozole* (spiced soup) the next night.

During downtime, I'd perch in a window nook by the woodstove, reading or watching the sun set over Breckenridge ski resort. At night we played drinking games or did puzzles. Karl observed that the Sisters Cabin might be too luxurious to count as a real hut trip.

It's not uncommon for people to suffer on hut trips, though. However, it's usually the overly ambitious sea-level out-of-towner working too hard, or those who underestimate the exponential effect altitude can have on a hangover. **BO**

"There's something magical about waking up in the morning to a fresh dump of snow, frosted trees sparkling in the sun, and the only thing you have to do all day is make tracks through untouched pillows of perfection"

DIRECTIONS

Best time to go // January to March (most huts are open November to April).

Gear required // Splitboard or backcountry ski setup with skins, ideally with free-heel mode for climbing and fixed-heel mode for downhill. Sleeping bag, warm clothes, swimsuit.

Nearest town // Breckenridge, Colorado (best nearby beer and food: Outer Range Brewing in Frisco, CO).

Getting there // From I-70, take Hwy 9 south to Breckenridge. Then take CR 450 (Huron Rd) to Reiling Rd (CR 460). Take Reiling Rd to French Gulch Rd (CR 2) and go 3 miles (5km), past day-use parking for French Gulch Trailhead and on to Sisters Cabin parking (permit required).

Where to stay // Lodging in Breckenridge is expensive, but the Bivvi Hostel strikes a good balance between upscale-hostel and a woodsy, log-cabin feel. Book ahead.

Things to know // Parking permits required for each car. Four-wheel drive and good snow tyres recommended.

*Opposite: There are roughly 30
10th Mountain Division huts in
the state of Colorado*

MORE LIKE THIS
TOP 10TH MOUNTAIN HUTS

CONTINENTAL DIVIDE CABIN

This family-friendly cabin along the Continental Divide has the shortest and easiest approach of all the huts in the 10th Mountain Division network, at less than a mile. An ideal introduction to hut trips for kids and newbies, it's equipped with lots of toys, a portable cot and high-chair, and a covered wooden walkway to the outhouse (so you can scurry out there in your hut slippers). The cabin is privately owned but can be booked through 10th Mountain and sleeps eight, with two private rooms and four beds in the main room. There are 15 miles (24km) of easy cross-country ski trails surrounding the hut. There's a full kitchen and an outdoor grill, but you can also ski to an extravagant dinner at the nearby Tennessee Pass Cookhouse. The cabin is also open during summer.

Nearest town // Leadville

PETER ESTIN HUT

One of two huts in the 10th Mountain Division network that are known specifically for being surrounded by excellent skiing, the Peter Estin was built in 1985 and is in many ways the quintessential Colorado mountain hut. With 16 beds across two floors, and an expansive deck with epic views, the hut is perfect for larger groups who are eager to get some turns in. An alpine ridge above the hut provides famously great downhill skiing, and there are also networks of trails branching out in all directions. The hut is linked by trails to the Gates Hut and the Polar Star Hut, for those interested in hut-to-hut adventures. Its namesake, Peter Estin, was a New Yorker cartoonist and author as well as being a dedicated skier.

Nearest town // Vail

EISEMAN HUT

The Eiseman Hut is generally regarded as having the best skiing of any of the 10th Mountain Division huts. You earn those turns, though, with one of the longest and most challenging treks of the bunch. The views aren't too shabby once you get up there: among other rugged peaks, you can see Vail Ski Resort, whose founder, Pete Seibert, himself fought as part of the 10th Mountain Division during World War II. The sleeping arrangements here are in the 'sleepover' vein – there are two small private bunk rooms, but most of the 16 beds surround the fireplace in the common room. But who cares about that when you have endless powder stashes within a mile of the hut's front door? Ambitious and skilled backcountry skiers may choose to aim for the chutes (narrow routes between rock walls) on 12,400ft (3400m) Goat Peak.

Nearest town // Vail

JONNY MOSELEY ON PALISADES TAHOE

Twenty years ago, gold medallist Jonny Moseley was winning everything, helping to reinvent freeskiing while he was at it. His home resort in California's Lake Tahoe made it all possible.

There are plenty of junior ski programmes around the US, but the one at Palisades Tahoe seems to produce an inordinate number of great skiers. Just look at like the Alpine World Cup right now – I think six of the skiers are from this mountain. And it all starts with the Mighty Mites kids' programme. Palisades Tahoe really takes care of its little guys. I was one of them.

I was actually born in Puerto Rico. My dad, who was from northern California, had moved there for work and met my mom, who was from Pennsylvania and there on vacation. They ended up having me and my two older brothers there. But my dad had been there for 10 years and started to really miss skiing. Things were great for him in Puerto Rico – he'd be off sailing to St Croix on the weekends – but he clearly missed skiing enough to say goodbye to that. He moved us to Marin County, just north of San Francisco.

From the moment we arrived in Marin, we were going to Palisades Tahoe every weekend. The mountain is beautiful – it's a horseshoe valley and when you pull up, the peaks rise straight up around you. The formations on Tram Face alone are stunning. Once I started travelling more for skiing competitions, I saw there's no other place like it. And the mountain is just so addictive – it gets in your blood. My family has been religious about the place ever since.

My parents immediately put me and my brothers in the race programmes. I started in is what is now called Shooting Stars and, after only a few lessons, the woman there – Pat, who only recently retired – was like, 'He's ready; he can go to Mighty Mites.' Eventually, it made sense to have a more permanent base near the slopes and, in 1985, my folks bought a house on the main road in what's called Olympic Valley. It was a shack; it might have been only the 13th house built in the valley. I was racing every weekend.

The big thing in the 1980s was a movie called *Hot Dog* (Peter Markle, 1983), which was set at Palisades Tahoe. It came out when I was nine and felt like the heyday of freestyle skiing. They filmed that movie at the resort and all the athletes who did the stunts were top-level freestyle skiers from the area. I would consider this the beginning of what was known as the 'Squallywood' era (Palisades Tahoe was known as Squaw Valley for nearly 70 years, before the name was changed to something more culturally sensitive).

Freestyle was getting hot – there were dual mogul contests (where skiers race side-by-side over mogul bumps) everywhere – and that's

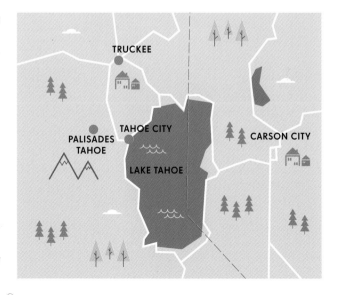

© Emma McIntyre / Gettyimages

how we got into it. My brothers and I were all on the race team at first. But when we saw freestyle skiing, we were like, 'This is for us – we want to jump.' By the time I was entering mogul contests, freestyle skiing was just being considered for the Olympics. One ex-World Cup freestyle skier started a team and we joined within a year. I think all our coaches back then had done the stunts in *Hot Dog*.

I started becoming enamoured with ski films, starting with Warren Miller, who has been making them since the 1950s. That's when I was exposed to extreme skiing pioneers like Scott Schmidt and Glen Plake. I was probably about 13 and my best friend, Trevor, who was also a ski team kid, got really into filming. He got a Sony handycam for his birthday and we started filming each other. Funny enough, about five years later, one of my own first filming experiences was when I got a small part in a Warren Miller film.

But there was an important second wave of the whole 'Squallywood' thing, with guys like Shane McConkey, Kent Kreitler and the Gaffney brothers, who were pushing things even further with freestyle skiing and filming. I really admired all those guys; most of them were about five years older, so I was more a fan than part of that crew. They all hung out at a bar called Le Chamois – or Shammy – but I wasn't old enough to drink then. Plus, there's a big divide between the skiers who are travelling, competing in the World Cup in racing or freestyle, and the guys who are living full-time in the valley. And for a while I was at Palisades Tahoe less and less because I was on the World Cup tour.

When I was a sophomore in high school, I won the junior national title in freestyle skiing and, shortly after that, I was selected for the World Cup team. It took a while, but I started winning World Cup events, and that's when I was selected for the Olympic team. In 1998, I went to Nagano, Japan for the Winter Olympics and I won the gold medal, mostly because of the 360 mute-grab, which was almost a snowboarding-inspired move. There were a handful of us pushing the boundaries, but I just so happened to be the one who nailed the trick in a high-profile competition. That was a watershed moment for freeskiing. That year was nuts – I ended up winning the gold, nine World Cup mogul events and the national title in 1998.

After 1998 I could barely look at a pair of ski boots. I was pretty burned out and I didn't feel like abusing myself in the moguls any more. But I didn't stay away from events for long, as I was just starting to get into more informal competitions like the X Games. This was a really creative time for me. I ended up winning silver at the 1999 X Games with a new trick that I had created called the 'dinner roll', which is basically an off-axis 720. Then I won the slopestyle event at the US Open with the same trick.

It all ties back to Palisades Tahoe. See, they never had a 'level of difficulty' rating in freeskiing. But, being from this resort, I personally felt you should always be trying to do the most insane trick. You need to always be progressing; it's instilled in you. At that time, I felt like my sport – simple moguls – was stagnant. I wanted to bring new tricks like this into this old sport.

TAHOE TWINS

One of the most anticipated developments in the US ski industry has been connecting Palisades Tahoe and neighbouring Alpine Meadows. At one time, 'Squaw' and Alpine Meadows were two of Lake Tahoe's greatest ski resorts, sitting in stunning adjacent valleys. Squaw Valley bought Alpine Meadows, to become Palisades Tahoe. After years of negotiations with a landowner there is now a gondola connecting the resorts that allows you to ski and ride both mountains in a day.

"That mountain is just so addictive – it gets in your blood"

I ended up qualifying for the next Olympics and wanted to do that trick. I had to submit the 'dinner roll' to the International Skiing Federation to get it approved and for them to assign a degree of difficulty. Even so, it wasn't quite enough and I came in fourth. The next year they ended up changing all the rules and actually gave the 'dinner roll' a higher level of difficulty, which I feel opened up inverted (off-axis) tricks to future competitors.

After I won the gold medal in Nagano and competed in the 2002 Olympics, all sorts of opportunities started popping up – commentating, hosting *American Ninja Warrior*, *Saturday Night Live*, and the MTV show *Real World/Road Rules Challenge*. They were all great gigs but it wasn't skiing. But Palisades Tahoe was

Clockwise from top: Palisades Tahoe is a freestyle funhouse; an aerial tram carries skiers – and sightseers – from the base village to High Camp at 8200ft (2500m). Previous page: Olympian Jonny Moseley at the 2016 Deer Valley Celebrity Skifest in Park City, Utah

DIRECTIONS

Best time to go // December through April is reliable. In a big snow year, the season will run to 4 July.

Gear required // Solid all-terrain skis or snowboard, designed for steeps, powder and moguls.

Nearest town // Truckee is Lake Tahoe's historic epicentre, with a great variety of bars and restaurants. Olympic Village at the base of Palisades Tahoe also has plenty of options.

Getting there // Reno airport is 40 minutes away; San Francisco airport is three hours.

Where to stay // Staying in Truckee or Tahoe City will require a car. Make the most of your trip by renting a condo in Olympic Valley or staying at The Village hotel.

Things to know // Palisades Tahoe hosted the 1964 Winter Olympics. Soak up the atmosphere at Le Chamois pizza place and bar, a popular hangout for the past 50 years and the epicentre of the Squallywood scene.

particularly generous and gave me something I really wanted: a lifetime ski pass. It also named a run after me, and I was given the coveted Wildflour Baking Company lifetime cookie pass – you only get one if you've won a gold medal and there are kids in that valley who will enter the programme just for that. In 2012, I approached the resort about becoming an ambassador; Palisades Tahoe was going through a bit of a reinvention and I really liked its vision.

Plus, the resort really started to support local athletes – stars like Cody Townsend, Jeremy Jones, Michelle Parker, Ross Tester and JT Holmes (who is a legend). We established a real athlete programme; we brought champion ski racer and freestyle skier Daron Rahlves back to help coach the race team, which is freaking ridiculous! That guy is so good. Palisades Tahoe is just constantly progressing and changing. There's always a bit of tension between tradition and pushing boundaries and that's a good thing. It's the mountain that creates these athletes – the intensity of the mountain and the level of skiing spits out diamonds. **WC**

MORE LIKE THIS
FREESTYLE FAVOURITES

MAMMOTH MOUNTAIN, CALIFORNIA

Mammoth Mountain stands at the heart of the steepest, tallest, most remote part of California's Sierra Nevada mountain range – it takes a good five hours to get there from Los Angeles and even longer from elsewhere in the state. And yet the terrain and scale are so good, people flock there. Mammoth Lakes ski resort sits in the middle of some of the country's most famous backcountry terrain, which is why the mountain gets such a high number of skilled skiers and riders, who will regularly add uphill hiking to their daily ski routine. The gondola delivers you to 11,050ft (3370m) – higher than any other resort on the West Coast – and the gateway to the mountain's 3500 skiable acres (1400 hectares) and 3100ft (940m) vertical drop. While the resort could easily just let mother nature do all the hard work, Mammoth Mountain's terrain park crew (responsible for creating and maintaining manmade features) is one of the best in the country, with a halfpipe and park that is Olympic-level.
Nearest town // Mammoth Lakes

MT BAKER, WASHINGTON

There is a string of 10 active volcanoes that runs from the northern part of California to Canada. All but three rise above 10,000ft (3000m) and the Mt Baker ski area sits on one of those volcanoes. The ski area itself isn't huge, but it punches way above its weight. Mt Baker itself is only 10,700ft (3300m), but it rises more than 8000ft (2400m) from the area around it. The resort tops out at just 5000ft (1500m) elevation, yet somehow gets over 50ft (15m) of snow per year (it had 72ft/22m a few years back). Locally owned since 1953, Mt Baker still only has 1000 skiable acres (400 hectares) and yet skiers and riders gush over the variety of terrain and consistent snow conditions. Two hours and 45 minutes north of Seattle – or two hours and 15 southeast of Vancouver – it has a local vibe and a very talented pool of riders and skiers, without ever feeling particularly crowded.
Nearest town // Vancouver, British Columbia, Canada

MT BACHELOR, OREGON

Mt Bachelor is also a volcano, but dormant. It sits right between Seattle and Portland, rising out of the flatlands. With little to break up the storms that rip across the Pacific Northwest, these volcanoes get hammered – which means loads of snow, but also some pretty adventurous skiing and riding at times. Mt Bachelor's size and scale are accentuated, especially when you consider that the lifts allow access to 4320 skiable acres (1750 hectares) on *all* sides of the mountain. The summit chair plops you right onto the tippy top of the volcano, at 9000ft (2700m), which affords dramatic views of some of the other volcanoes of the Pacific Northwest. The backside feels like pure wilderness, but the resort has a cleverly placed trail at the bottom of the backside bowls and west bowls that will funnel you back to a lift. Plus, the place just has soul, especially among snowboarders, with classic annual events like the Dirksen Derby.
Nearest town // Portland

Clockwise from top: Mammoth Mountain ski area is the highest on the West Coast of the US; stepping out of bounds at Mt Baker; the Cascade Mountain Range in Central Oregon, near Mt Bachelor

TO HEAVEN IN A HELICOPTER

Valdez, a tiny seaside hamlet in the Chugach Range of Alaska,
is the reigning champion of global heli-skiing.

I was sleeping in a cramped RV parked on the side of the Richardson Highway in Alaska with three guys who hadn't showered in days. The camper smelled like bacon grease, stinky ski boots and mildew. But none of that mattered. Because I believed I was about to have the best damn ski day of my life.

And that was saying a lot. I was 28 at the time and working as an editor at a ski magazine in Colorado, which meant I was having a lot of best-ever ski days in some of the snowiest, most legendary spots on the planet. My salary was minuscule, but I was skiing weeks in a row without a single day out of my ski boots and my goggle tan was fierce. I was also competing in telemark freeskiing competitions at

the time and filming for indie ski movies. All of which is to say: I was a ski machine back then.

Even so, Alaska was the pinnacle, a steep skier's paradise with a layered history. Alaska was a place I'd wanted to go ever since I'd picked up my first ski magazine. Then my friend Jonah, who made backcountry ski movies, invited me on a spring ski trip to Valdez to be in his next movie, which would include a day of heli-skiing. I convinced my boss it was a work trip and immediately expensed a flight to Anchorage.

I met Jonah, the filmer, plus Jake and Paul, who would be athletes in the film, at the airport in Anchorage. We rented an RV and picked

CHUGACH NATIONAL FOREST

VALDEZ

MOUNT DIMOND

CHUGACH MOUNTAINS

PRINCE WILLIAM SOUND

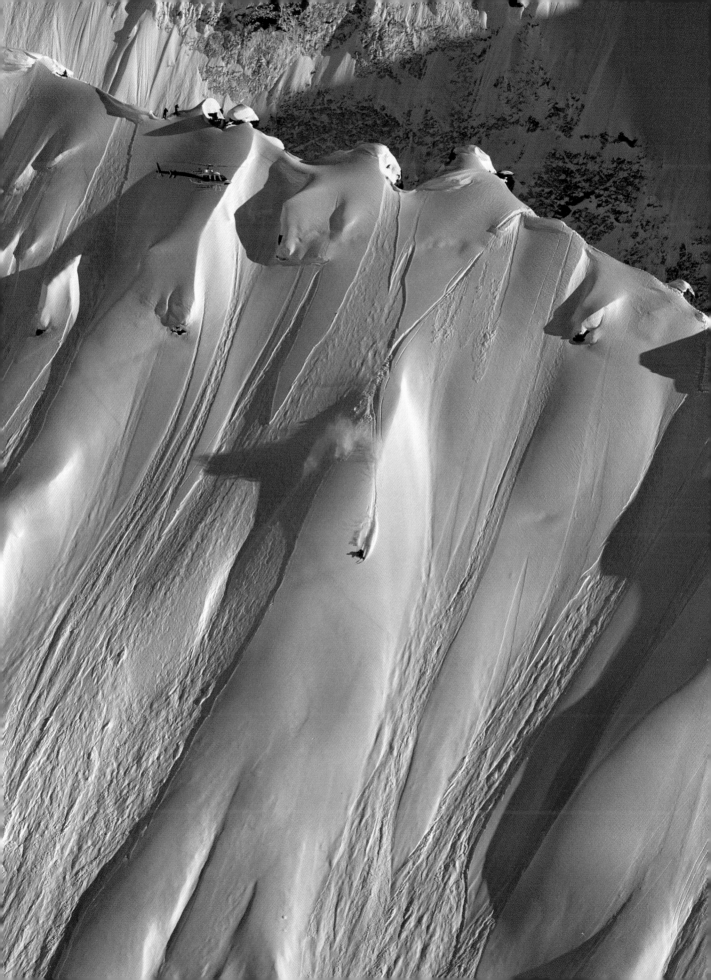

up groceries before making the six-hour pilgrimage to the ski bum's mecca of Valdez, the heart of heli-skiing in Alaska. This wasn't some flashy ski movie with a huge crew (or even any crew). Jonah's film was more of a bootstrapped project, one guy with a camera and a tiny budget cobbled together from a few small ski-industry brands. His film would tour mountain-town bars and ski shops for small but passionate audiences.

Heli-skiing is an absurdly opulent corner of ski culture, an environmental catastrophe that costs thousands of dollars per day and is typically reserved for the ultra-rich. That said, it's also arguably the most fun experience on the planet. It's euphoria on skis, the kind of adventure you'll dream about long before it happens and long after it's over. However, heli-skiing was also always something that had felt way out of reach, financially. And here I was, in the land of heli-skiing with barely enough money to afford a single day.

Our plan was to spend several days backcountry skiing without the use of a helicopter, skinning up (going uphill) from the road as far as our legs could take us. We'd all saved up enough cash for a one-day splurge of heli-skiing with one of the most respected outfitters in the area. Jonah had also made a deal with Valdez Heli-Ski Guides for one day in a chopper, in exchange for some footage.

The town of Valdez isn't much to look at – an old mining and fishing outpost, population 3900 – but it's on the shores of the stunning Prince William Sound. Drive the Richardson Highway from town up Thompson Pass and towards the top of the pass; the roadside is dotted with four or five heli-ski lodges and outfitters that promise the best powder skiing you've ever had.

It was the spring of 1987 when an Alaskan pilot named Chuck McMahan flew over Thompson Pass and thought, 'That looks like good skiing if we could fly to it.' He started bringing his friends up in a Super Cub plane carrying skis, charging just $15 per flight. Soon, McMahan and his friend Michael Cozad bought the Tsaina Lodge, a rundown roadhouse on Thompson Pass, and it soon became ground zero for a motley crew of some of the best skiers in the world. To kickstart business, Cozad came up with the idea of hosting an extreme skiing competition. Among the 37 invited skiers were now-legendary names like Seth Morrison, Kim Reichhelm, Dean Cummings and Doug Coombs, and in April 1991 Coombs won the first World Extreme Skiing Championships.

Coombs, who hailed from Wyoming, was hooked on the area and in 1993 he and his wife, Emily, founded Valdez Heli-Ski Guides, which used the Tsaina Lodge as its home base. It was the first heli-ski outfitter in Alaska, and in the years that followed, other operations opened along Thompson Pass, establishing Valdez as the epicentre of awesomeness. Skiers came from around the world to see what all the fun was about.

Times have changed. Doug Coombs died in a ski accident in France in 2006. The old Tsaina Lodge fell into disrepair. New owners eventually rebuilt it, reopening as a boutique 24-room hotel in 2012. But one thing stayed the same: the epic ski terrain. At Valdez Heli-Ski Guides you have access to a colossal 10,000 sq miles (26,000 sq

"The helicopter ride alone is a thrill, as the Chugach Mountains spread out like a real life IMAX movie"

km) of terrain, including iconic lines like 6200ft (1900m) Mt Dimond, a towering monolith that drops 5500 vertical feet (1300m). Add to that exceptional terrain an average of 500in (1270cm) of snowfall a year and a relatively stable snowpack and you've got a place that people dream over on the pages of magazines.

For the first six days of our trip we slept in the RV on the side of the road, woke before the sun was up and climbed into the mountains on our own power, skinning and bootpacking up steep couloirs for the camera and for the adventure of it. We would ski-tour and film all day, returning to the camper exhausted, to make burritos and pass out in our bunks. I appreciated the simplicity of it all, as well as the hard work. But each day, as we heard the buzz of helicopters overhead – zipping hyped-up clients to and fro – I fantasised about what it would be like to skip the gruelling climb to the summit and instead be dropped there by a whirling engine. Soon, I thought, that'll be me.

Finally, the day arrived when Jonah, Paul, Jake and I didn't have to hike for our turns. I'd barely slept the night before because I was

Thompson Pass averages around 500in (1270cm) of snow a year. This is also the place that once held the record for the biggest annual snowfall in the US, set in 1953 at a whopping 974in (2474cm) – that's 81ft (25m) of snow. In short, this place can get buried.

Clockwise from top: the most expensive chairlift in the world; Valdez, Alaska sits on Prince William Sound. Previous page: the slopes and spines of Valdez have appeared in more ski films than any other terrain

DIRECTIONS

Best time to go // Heli-ski outfitters in Alaska usually operate from February into early May, but March and April are prime for the most stable snow and best ski conditions.
Gear required // You'll need an avalanche beacon, shovel and probe, plus powder skis. You can rent all of that from the outfitter (bring your own ski boots). Many outfitters loan you an avalanche airbag backpack and harness.
Nearest town // The coastal village of Valdez.
Getting there // Fly into Anchorage, then hop a short one-hour flight from Anchorage to Valdez. Otherwise, it's a five- to six-hour drive from Anchorage.
Where to stay // Stay on Thompson Pass in the newly renovated Tsaina Lodge, or stay in Valdez at the upscale Totem Hotel, a 40-minute shuttle ride from the helipad.
Things to know // You'll get between six and 10 runs a day, depending on conditions, and you'll need to be an advanced to expert skier or snowboarder.

so excited. That morning, our guide – a fast-charging Utah skier by the name of Dylan Freed – prepped us on getting in and out of the helicopter (move slowly and methodically) and gave us an update on weather and snow and avalanche conditions. We loaded into the heli and lifted off in a blast of wind and snow. The helicopter ride alone is a thrill, as the Chugach Mountains spread out in front of the glass window like a real-life IMAX movie. The pilot dropped us on a narrow ridge like it was no big deal, then zoomed off, leaving us alone in stillness. The only thing left to do was ski.

The very first run is the one I'll never forget. When I dropped into the steep face, snow billowed around me like a cloud – light and translucent. I floated down the slope, arcing big turns for 3000 vertical feet (910m), with snow moving behind me like a waterfall. I heard someone hollering with joy, then I realised it was me.

All day, Dylan guided us down steep chutes and open bowls, one dream-like untracked powder line after another. I watched as my friends descended to the bottom of each run, snow caked onto their smiling faces, in disbelief that this day was real. **MM**

*Opposite: British Columbia is one of
the top three heli-skiing destinations
in the world*

MORE LIKE THIS
LEGENDARY HELI-SKIING

CANADIAN ROCKIES, BRITISH COLUMBIA

Canada is where heli-skiing got its start and it's still one of the most dependably good places to go in search of powder. At Mica Heliskiing in the western Canadian Rockies, you'll base out of a luxury backcountry lodge with 500 sq miles (800 sq km) of mountainous terrain to explore by day. To get there you'll take a six-minute heli-flight from the ski town of Revelstoke into the remote Mica Heli Lodge, where each day begins with a heli-lift to a snow-slathered nearby peak. With an average of 60ft (18m) of snowfall per year, this place is powder heaven. The lodge, which is perched high above the Columbia River, has a rooftop hot tub, chef-prepared meals, a full bar, and striking views of the Selkirks and Monashee Mountains from the massive windows. You'll come for the skiing, of course, but the lodge is a worthy destination of its own.

Nearest town // Revelstoke

RUBY MOUNTAINS, NEVADA

You may not expect extraordinary skiing in middle-of-nowhere Nevada, but that's exactly what the Ruby Mountains deliver. The Rubies are an under-the-radar range, 90 miles (140km) long, about 10 miles (16km) wide, and with 50 peaks that top out above 10,000ft (3050m). As you're driving Interstate 80 across Nevada, you'll spot the spiky, snow-capped mountains that rise like magic from the desert floor. There's no developed ski area out here, and just one heli-ski outfitter: Ruby Mountains Heli Experience. A former ski patroller from Utah, Joe Royer, opened Ruby Mountains Heli in 1977. These days, it's still Nevada's only heli-ski outfitter and is still run by the Royer family. The terrain ranges from steep, above-treeline bowls to low-angle tree skiing through aspen groves. The 10-room Ruby 360 Lodge – named for the panoramic views of the Great Basin – opened in 2017 as a base for heli-ski guests, with the helipad outside the door.

Nearest town // Elko

SAN JUAN MOUNTAINS, COLORADO

Colorado is proof that you don't have to travel to Alaska or British Columbia to have an epic heli-ski experience. And you don't have to commit to a full week-long, wallet-draining, all-inclusive trip of a lifetime to ski out of a helicopter. In the San Juan Mountains of southern Colorado, you can sign up for a day of heli-skiing with Telluride Helitrax and get yourself six mind-altering runs, totalling up to 14,000 vertical feet (4300km) in a day. This is a day-trip experience – no overnight lodging or meal plans included – and although it's not cheap (you're still spending more than $1,500 for a day of skiing), it's slightly more affordable than the Alaskan equivalent. Telluride Helitrax opened in 1982 and continues to be one of the state's most trusted heli-ski outfitters, with access to over 200 sq miles (520 sq km) of terrain. The season here is long by comparison: you can ski powder from late December and spring corn (granular snow caused by warm days and cool nights) in couloirs well into April.

Nearest town // Telluride

HIGHLAND BOWL

Hiking 'the Bowl' at Colorado's Aspen Highlands leads to some of the best off-piste terrain in the world — and is a high-elevation rite of passage for any hardy skier or snowboarder.

t's just an 860ft (260m) climb, but it happens to pierce through that 12,000ft elevation (3700m) threshold that floors you. The summit of Aspen's Highland Bowl sits at 12,390ft (3780m), to be exact – there's a small wooden sign saying so – but honestly, the burning quads, the dizziness, the runner's high, the view – it's pretty obvious that you're standing atop one of the highest points in this part of Colorado.

A lot of great ski resorts in the Rockies have some legendary hike-to terrain – basically any run that requires a hike or ski upwards to ascend beyond the chairlifts and crowds – but Aspen's Highland Bowl is among the best in the world. And it is world-class skiing that makes you feel like you are in the backcountry, but with the security of resort avalanche mitigation. Most Highland Bowl hikers are savvy enough to carry a beacon, shovel and probe, but the resort will close the terrain if they deem it unsafe. The snow staircase that gets carved from the top of the Deep Temerity lift is set by the devoted locals as soon as there is enough snow to drop in.

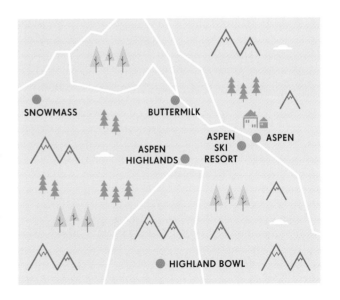

SNOWMASS

BUTTERMILK

ASPEN HIGHLANDS

ASPEN SKI RESORT

ASPEN

HIGHLAND BOWL

⛷🎿 AVALANCHE CONTROL

Although Highland Bowl has been part of the ski area boundary permit since Aspen Highlands opened in 1958, the terrain didn't officially open to the public until 2002. For a number of years in the 1970s, the ski area would charge an extra fee for those who wanted to hike up and ski the bowl. The slopes weren't controlled for avalanches, so skiers did so at their own risk. Brave skiers would hike the ridge, ski down to Castle Creek Rd and hitch a ride back.

"The hike up to the top of Highland Bowl is the great equaliser"

Aspen Ski resort doesn't suffer the same bottleneck that resorts like Vail and Breckenridge do – it's only about four hours from Denver, but slightly out of the way. Aspen is known as a celebrity hotspot, a skier's retreat for the ultra-famous and excessively rich. That's partly what makes Highland Bowl such an anomaly. This climb isn't some elite club for the one percent. There's no champagne on ice up here, nobody to valet your gear to the top. It's a ski bum's paradise and – assuming you can make the trek and safely handle the descent – everyone is welcome. The hike up to the top of Highland Bowl, or 'The Bowl', as the locals call it, is the great equaliser.

For one, if you're anything like me, you'll probably make quite a few mistakes on your first time up and suffer the consequences. I remember that day, moving a little too fast, trying to keep up with my friend Will, who was charging ahead up the knife-edge ridge. I also carried my skis over my shoulder until my gloved hand, which was clutching the hard, metal edges, became cold and numb.

But there's a ski patrol shack at the top of the Deep Temerity lift, where you can not only get the scoop on what conditions are like in

the Bowl, but also buy a canvas strap that allows you to essentially carry your skis on your back instead of in your hands (the lifties are happy to give you instructions on how to use it). Meanwhile, the rest of my body began overheating from all the exertion and I was sweating through all my layers.

Fit, acclimated skiers and snowboarders can get to the top of Highland Bowl in about 45 minutes (a speedy enduro athlete from Aspen named John Gaston has done it in a record-setting sub-15 minutes; Gaston also holds the current record for 11 Bowl hikes in a single day). But simply doing two back-to-back bowl hikes in a day is a very worthy accomplishment for mortals. The Boston Marathon has its Heartbreak Hill, and Highland Bowl has its own version. Aspen's Heartbreak Hill (which sometimes gets called Heart Attack Hill) comes towards the end, when the summit is in sight, but a steep, sustained pitch lies between you and your finish line.

As I watched Will disappear ahead, I continued pushing upwards, trying to ignore my cold hands and hot everything else. And then I felt it. The 12,000ft (3700m) mark. The thin, breathless air, but also

the immensity of the snow-covered summit. Colourful Tibetan-style prayer flags blew in the wind, dangling from an old double chairlift that sits on the summit as a bench to rest on. The panoramic views of the Maroon Bells and 14,025ft (4275m) Pyramid Peak stretch out to the south, while Aspen Mountain lingers in the east. The views from the top are spectacular, overlooking all four ski resorts that make up Aspen Snowmass. There's a wild ruggedness that Colorado's Rocky Mountains consistently deliver – craggy summits, steep slopes, cold powder – that's simply hard to find anywhere else.

And, of course, there's a pretty good reason so many skiers and snowboarders suffer through this legendary climb: the 2500ft (800m) drop into some of the most sustained, steep pitches in the Rocky Mountains. Every slope that drops away from the summit sits between 35 and 48 degrees. The Bowl has roughly 270 acres (110 hectares) of mostly north-, northeast- and east-facing terrain. From the top, nothing is groomed in preparation for skiers (snowcats can't even drive up terrain this steep). In other words, there is no *easy* way down. Of the 18 named routes off the summit, not one is a bad choice. On a powder day like this, I knew to go for instant gratification by dropping fall line from the peak into Ozone or Be One (if those are tracked out already, venture skiers head right to the north-facing G Zone for sneaky lines through the trees like G-2 or G-3). I dropped off the summit, still chasing my friend Will, as he sliced up shin-deep powder.

So I made a few mistakes on my first time up the Bowl. But I learned from them. And I've been back up there over a dozen times since. One interesting thing I learned rather soon after that first hike was that the free-of-charge snowcat starts running at 10.30am and will deliver skiers about a third of the way up, cutting off a good 15 to 20 minutes from your bootpacking time. But you'll also quickly learn that a Highland Bowl purist never uses the snowcat. **MM**

From left: Highland Bowl from afar; fresh tracks can be had for days after a storm. Previous page: the journey is the destination

DIRECTIONS

Best time to go // January to mid March has the most reliably good snow. The Bowl usually opens in late December, snow permitting, and closes by early April.
Gear required // You'll want powder skis. It's a good idea to bring an avalanche beacon, shovel and probe, and know how to use them. A backpack or a carrying strap will make it easier to haul your skis. Warm layers and sunblock.
Nearest town // The high-end resort town of Aspen.
Getting there // Either fly to Denver and drive (or take a shuttle) four hours to Aspen, or fly directly into Aspen. A free bus picks you up around town and goes to all four ski areas: Aspen, Highlands, Buttermilk and Snowmass.
Where to stay // The Limelight Hotel has locations in both Aspen and Snowmass. Or the historic Mountain Chalet Aspen has bunks in a shared room for a fraction of the price.
Things to know // If you're not comfortable skiing black diamond terrain, this zone isn't for you.

Opposite, clockwise from top:
sidecountry at Alta, Utah; a skier
scouts his line at Bridger Bowl,
Montana; going rogue at Washington
State's Crystal Mountain

MORE LIKE THIS
TOP INBOUNDS
HIKE-TO TERRAIN

SILVER KING, CRYSTAL MOUNTAIN, WASHINGTON

Silver King – which locals simply call the King – is the crown jewel of Crystal Mountain, the highest point in the ski area at 7010ft (2140m). To get there you'll ride Chair 6 to the top of Silver Queen, then hike along a bony ridge over a zone called the Throne. Yep, it's a real kingdom up here. There are plenty of ski lines down, but push onwards until you get to the proper summit of the King. The views of Mt Rainier are worth it. It's about a 20- to 30-minute hike to the top. The resort calls this zone the Southback – it's inbounds and controlled for avalanches, but it feels backcountry-like, with fewer crowds and more hiking for your turns. From the top, the north-facing bowl offers steep chutes or mellow glades – take your pick. For lodging, overnight RV camping is allowed in designated parking lots, a Pacific Northwest tradition. Otherwise get a condo at the base of the ski area. Seattle is about two hours away.
Nearest town // Enumclaw

MT BALDY, ALTA/SNOWBIRD, UTAH

Mt Baldy is the 11,070ft (3370m) peak that straddles the border between the two neighbouring ski areas of Snowbird and Alta. You can access the peak from either resort when the terrain is open, and both require a hike – plan on 20 to 45 minutes to reach the crest, depending on which side you're coming from. Check to make sure the terrain is open before you go – ski patrol or mountain signage should tell you. (Keep in mind, snowboarders still aren't permitted at Alta.) From the Snowbird side, ride the aerial tram to the top of 11,000ft (3350m) Hidden Peak, wrap under the tram via a groomed track, then follow the road towards Baldy. Soon, you'll reach a gate where you'll switch over to bootpacking (hiking with skis on your shoulder). Enjoy the view of the Wasatch Range from the top. For the descent, North Baldy has served as the venue for many big freeskiing contests and the amphitheatre-like terrain is strewn with chutes and cliffs. From Alta, take the Sugarloaf lift to a stout bootpack up the ridge. Main Chute is the least technical way down and it's still an elevator-shaft-like 44 degrees.
Nearest town // Salt Lake City

THE RIDGE, BRIDGER BOWL, MONTANA

Bridger Bowl is unlike any other ski area. For starters, it's a community-driven ski hill that feels like a throwback to another era. Skiers and snowboarders come here for deep powder, steep lines and a friendly, nostalgic vibe. The best skiing on the mountain isn't accessible by chairlift. You've got to hike for it. Avalanche beacons are required (you can rent one from the rental shop at the base), and a shovel, probe and partner are recommended. This zone is expert only and backcountry awareness is critical – there is no easy way down and it's very easy to get cliffed out. So ski with caution. You'll ride the Bridger lift – check in at the ski patrol shack at the top if you have any questions – then follow the bootpack straight up 600ft (180m) to the Ridge. From there you'll hike along the Ridge in either direction, heading to North Bowl or South Bowl for a line of your choosing. There's no lodging at Bridger Bowl, but Bozeman – and its various hotels and vacation rentals – is less than a half an hour away.
Nearest town // Bozeman

GOING WITH THE LAVA FLOW

Volcanoes are awesome ski-mountaineering objectives with a challenging ascent, ridiculous views – and wide-open slopes on the descent.

Who better to ski down a volcano with than a geologist? A geologist who has remembered all his ski gear. Today, I'll have to settle for my friend Seth. Normally a very prepared backcountry skier, he has somehow forgotten his ski pants. Which means our crew is standing around in a parking lot very early in the morning at the base of California's towering 10,460ft (3190m) volcano, Lassen Peak. The objective was to climb and ski it, though we weren't so sure any more. We discussed what Seth could wear instead.

Seth settles on long underwear bottoms covered by his stretchiest jeans. After tucking the jeans into his ski boots, we tell him he'd better make up for his ridiculous outfit by dropping geologic knowledge about the volcano on our way uphill. Turns out, there's nothing a geologist would like to do more. Seth is employed by the state of Nevada, and he knows a lot about rocks and volcanoes.

Lassen Peak, the southernmost active volcano in the Cascade Range, is part of what's called the Ring of Fire – a collection of volcanoes around the rim of the Pacific Ocean. From northern California stretching into Oregon and Washington, this series of spiky volcanic peaks rises dramatically from the flatlands and makes up a geologic landscape unique to the Pacific Northwest.

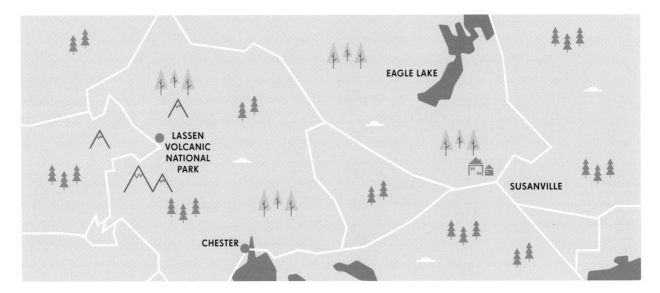

EAGLE LAKE

LASSEN VOLCANIC NATIONAL PARK

SUSANVILLE

CHESTER

They also make for a rare opportunity for the mountaineers who hope to climb them (you can also climb most of these volcanic peaks in the summer months, with far less snow, as a less technical approach).

Lassen is considered an entry-level 'ski mountaineering objective', which means it's a good first volcano to ski. But it'll still require some 4000ft (1200m) of climbing at high elevations to reach the top. Mt Shasta, 100 miles (160km) to the north, is a good next objective, then you'll start working your way north on the Cascade Range, ticking off one volcano after the next, building your way up to rowdy mountaineering missions like Mt Rainier in Washington. The Ring of Fire will have you hooked in no time. But you've got to start somewhere, and Lassen Peak, with its low-grade consequences and relatively mellow approach, is a great somewhere to start.

We begin our ascent from a zone called, eerily, the Devastated Area. This is where, in 1914, Lassen Peak stirred after 27,000 years of inactivity. It began with a steam explosion that blasted out of a small crater at the summit, but that led to nearly 200 more explosions over the next year. Hot rocks the size of cars blew from the summit and blocks of lava ended up 20 miles (320km) away.

All of which is to say that when my friends and I start up Lassen Peak on skis in an area that was once decimated by a violent eruption, I am viscerally aware that this mountain is a live beast and it could erupt again at any time. (Though, Seth reassures me, scientists will likely warn us when that's about to happen.)

In reality, our biggest threat today isn't scalding hot lava. It's the technical feat of ski mountaineering, which will involve skinning uphill for several thousand vertical feet, followed by bootpacking with crampons on our feet and ice axes in hand, so we can self-arrest in case of a fall. Avalanche danger and rockfall are also concerns (if these skills aren't in your expertise, there are great guiding services on all the volcanoes of the Pacific Northwest).

This is not a ski resort; there is no ski patrol, avalanche mitigation, or chairlifts. But a developed ski area did once exist in California's Lassen Volcanic National Park. Originally a seasonal gathering place for the Atsugewi, Maidu, Yahi and Yana tribes, white settlers arrived in the area during the California Gold Rush of 1848. A local blacksmith and Danish immigrant named Peter Lassen developed the Lassen Trail using the volcanic peak to orient emigrants, and the mountain was later named after him.

Congress designated this area a national park in 1916, after the last big eruption. Today it's one of the lesser visited and least developed national parks – Lassen Volcanic National Park has around 500,000 visitors a year, just 10 percent of what California's Yosemite National Park gets. When there's still snow on the ground that means even fewer visitors, since the roadways are mostly closed and hiking trails are buried under snow. Mt Shasta, to the north, receives far more traffic since it's bigger and considered more of a bucket-list objective.

"I am viscerally aware that this mountain is a live beast and it could erupt again, at any time"

SNOW MOUNTAIN

The site of the former Lassen Ski Area's warming hut is now the Kohm Yah-mah-nee Visitor Center, which is open year-round near the southwest entrance to the park. *Kohm Yah-mah-nee* is the Maidu phrase for 'snow mountain', which is what the Native people call the peak.

Clockwise from top: skinning up the northeast bowl of Lassen Peak; Lassen is part of California's 'ring of fire'; the mountain sits within Lassen Volcanic National Park. Previous page: the peak has snow year-round

The Lassen Ski Area opened in the 1920s with a rope tow and a warming hut near the southwest entrance of the park, followed by a chairlift in 1982, but the operation closed in 1993. These days, the only way to ski the slopes of Lassen is to climb them yourself.

Most backcountry skiers climb and ski Lassen in the late spring, whenever the Lassen Peak Highway – the roadway through the national park – finally gets ploughed to the Devastated Area, about 10 miles (16km) from the park's northwest entrance. Seth informs us that Lassen is a lava dome volcano, which as far as I understand means it's a bit more rounded and mound-shaped than the pointy and cone-like volcanoes you see in picture books and movies.

Now, the climb itself is certainly an adventure, but is perhaps even more like an endurance event. Our trudge to the top is relatively uneventful and quick, as our metronomic slide, step, slide, step motion propels us upwards. We started at 6am, a relatively leisurely start for mountaineering. Some peaks require alpine starts in the very early hours, such as 2am or 3am. But Lassen takes around four hours to climb, so we're still at the summit at a respectable 10am.

Another great thing about volcanoes is that they are solitary peaks and the views are incredible. The only other mountain blocking our view is Lassen's neighbouring volcano, Mt Shasta, in the distance. From the top, we ski down the popular northeast-facing bowl, passing right by the 1915 eruption vent – and are already making plans to take on Shasta. **MM**

DIRECTIONS

Best time to go // The National Park Service road crew begins clearing in March or April, depending on snow conditions, so plan on May or June for the best time to ski.
Gear required // You'll need an avalanche beacon, shovel and probe – plus the knowledge of how to use that gear – touring skis or a splitboard, crampons and an ice axe.
Nearest town // The small city of Susanville.
Getting there // In the snowy months, enter the park through the northwest entrance, an hour east of Redding or an hour west of Susanville via remote roadways. The nearest airports are in Redding, Sacramento or Reno, Nevada.
Where to stay // Susanville has hotels and guesthouses. Otherwise, stay in a cabin or B&B in tiny Shingletown, about 20 minutes from the park entrance.
Things to know // This is a challenging climb, followed by steep, technical skiing. Hire a mountain guide and research current conditions before you go.

Opposite, from top: a day out on Mt Adams, Washington; splitting the two-day trip up Mt Shasta, California

MORE LIKE THIS
SKI-FRIENDLY VOLCANOES

MT ST HELENS, WASHINGTON

With a summit elevation of just 8363ft (2550m) – the fifth highest peak in Washington – Mt St Helens is among the easier volcanoes in the Cascades to climb and ski, with roughly a 5000ft (1500m) climb to reach the crater's rim. Most people climb and ski the south-facing Worm Flows, the most direct winter route, named after the worm-like paths of rocky lava that dot the trail along the southeast face of the mountain. You don't have to worry about crevasses on that route. You'll park at the Marble Mountain trailhead and start by following a marked winter hiking and snowshoeing path. Climbing permits are required and you may also need a parking permit – check for permitting restrictions online with the Mt St Helens Institute before you go. The best ski conditions are found between April and May. The Mt St Helens Institute does offer a limited number of guided climbs to the summit during the winter and summer, but none are on skis.

Nearest town // Cougar

MT SHASTA, CALIFORNIA

Once you've tackled Lassen, Mt Shasta should be the obvious next item on your volcano to-do list. It's bigger and bolder, though. You'll climb over 7000ft (2130m) to reach the 14,179ft (4320m) summit, and like Lassen, you'll want an ice axe, crampons, plus ski-touring and avalanche safety gear. Shasta Mountain Guides leads guided climbs and ski descents of the mountain. The most popular route up is called Avalanche Gulch, which starts at a parking area and trailhead known as Bunny Flat. You can sleep overnight in the parking lot or stay in a hotel or rental house in the mystical town of Mt Shasta, 20 minutes down the road. Plan on a very early, pre-dawn alpine start (bring a headlamp). You'll need a permit to climb the peak – get one from the ranger's station. Mt Shasta is said to have its own spiritual energy vortex and visitors come from far and wide to seek it out. If you find it, you'll know.

Nearest town // Mt Shasta City

MT ADAMS, WASHINGTON

Mt Adams is another good stepping stone volcano, a 12,276ft (3740m) glaciated stratovolcano (a volcano built of layers of lava) near the Oregon-Washington border and the Columbia River Gorge. It has routes on the south side that are free of hazardous crevasses. The third highest peak in the Cascade Range, the summit has outstanding views of other peaks in the Ring of Fire, including Mt Rainier, Mt Hood and Mt St Helens. The South Rib is the standard ski descent, though there are other less-travelled routes if you prefer that. On the way down, enjoy over 8000ft (2440m) of vertical drop with slopes ranging from 35 to 40 degrees. Alpine Ascents and Northwest Mountain School offer guided ski descents of the peak. Like all of these volcanoes, Mt Adams is best skied in the late spring or early summer months for easier access and a more stable snowpack, and you'll need a permit from the Forest Service to climb above a certain elevation.

Nearest town // Hood River

SILVERTON: THE ANTI-SKI RESORT

A little over 20 years ago in southwest Colorado, a ski couple followed their dreams and opened one of the most unconventional ski resorts in the world.

My day at Silverton Mountain started the way all days at Silverton start: signing waivers in a yurt, checking avalanche beacons, then listening to my guide deliver the safety speech that had everyone in my group of eight second-guessing their skills. This is not how a day at a typical ski resort begins – there is nothing typical about Silverton Mountain.

Sure, there's a lift, it has a ski patrol and even a 'lodge' – if you consider a canvas yurt that houses the mountain office, swag shop and bar a 'lodge'. But that's where similarities to a typical ski resort end. Sandwiched in the middle of Colorado's San Juan Range, not far from Telluride, Silverton Mountain consists of a solitary double chair lift, rising from a forgotten winding road in the middle of a premier backcountry zone. Once at the top, skiers have access to 1819 acres (736 hectares) of expert-only terrain, or another 22,000 acres (8900 hectares) available by bootpack (hiking with your skis over your shoulder) or short helicopter ride. Needless to say, very few come here just for the lift-accessed acreage.

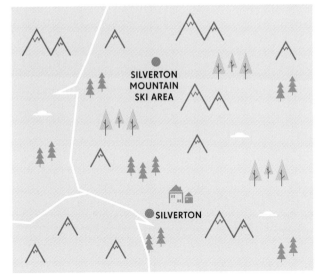

"Even though you catch a lift to access the goods, every turn has an isolated, backcountry feel to it"

After the chair drops you off at 12,300ft (3850m), everything is difficult. There are no groomed trails, no excessively gladed trees, no mellow pitches – nothing for intermediate skiers at all. Instead, it's all cliffs, bowls and chutes, and 400 annual inches (1000cm) of snow. It is big mountain skiing at its finest, a slice of Alaska in the lower 48.

But skiing Silverton is as much about the vibe as it is the powder. This operation is full of purist charm, from the yurt that serves as the base lodge/front office/ticket window/merch store to the chair lift that was saved from a California scrap heap. The old school buses that shuttle you around the base of the mountain feel like they were originally part of Colorado's state penitentiary fleet. There's no running water. No indoor plumbing. You park on the side of the road and eat a packed lunch somewhere on the mountain between runs. Naturally, après activities are out of the trunk of your car.

While the rest of the ski industry is going bigger, with heated gondolas and mega passes and on-mountain latte bars, Silverton has managed to stay true to its roots and focus on the principles that the operation was founded on in 2002. 'We felt the industry was leaving out hardcore skiers and boarders,' said Jen Brill, one of the founders of Silverton. 'We were passionate snowboarders who didn't care about all the real estate amenities, we just cared about the skiing.'

It's that no-frills reputation that got me interested in the mountain in the first place. Consider the gumption of the helicopter, in particular. Instead of adding lifts to expand the operation's terrain, Silverton added a chopper. And then made

those heli-rides affordable. It was a brave move that helped put the mountain on the map.

After the beacon checks, our group took a short lift ride through a thick, evergreen forest at the base of the mountain to the bald, glistening ridgeline that towered over everything. We exited the lift and bootpacked to the first turns of the day – a practice run on Cabin Bowl, a wide-open concave slope full of wind-crusted snow that funnels you into the trees a few hundred feet below. Our guide had us drop one at a time so he could assess what kind of skiers he was leading. The powder wasn't deep, but it was soft, allowing me to get comfortable, sinking into my turns. Even my bad turns were memorable though, simply because I had the entire bowl to myself. I wasn't one of hundreds or thousands carving up the slope – it was just me and half a dozen of my ski partners. Silverton makes sure of that; the number of people allowed on the mountain on any given day is limited, so even though you catch a lift to access the goods, every turn has an isolated, backcountry feel to it.

After another practice lap, this time to the west side of the ridge for steeper trees, I found myself kneeling in the hardpacked snow and watching a helicopter approach to take me on my very first 'heli-bump'. I had serious doubts about the decisions that led me to this 12,500ft-high (3800m) landing zone. On the one hand, this is a dream come true; heli-skiing has been on my bucket list since I was a teenager. But Silverton is the anti-resort, so you don't have to be a millionaire to go heli-skiing here. You just need a couple of hundred bucks and the ability to ski hard terrain.

PLAY LIKE A PRO

Energy drink
manufacturer
Red Bull built a
private half-pipe
for one of its
sponsored athletes,
snowboarder
Shaun White, in
the backcountry
of Silverton
Mountain, so White
could perfect his
signature tricks
before the 2010
Olympics. Want to
feel like White?
You can rent the
entire mountain
for a day for less
than $10,000.

*From left: skiing Silverton; tower of
historic old City Hall in Silverton,
Colorado. Previous page: lift, hike or
heli to access endless 'sidecountry' at
Silverton*

The flight was short, no more than three minutes in the air in total, but it saved us hours of traversing. Next thing I knew, I was peering over the lip of what might be the steepest face I'd ever skied. Again, we dropped in single file, partly because of avalanche safety protocol, but also because everyone deserves to ski untracked powder after a heli-bump. We each skied a few feet to the side of the person who dropped in front of us, careful to preserve as much powder as possible for the next in line. When it was my turn, I started slow, hesitant as always, but quickly decided to trust my skis and my legs. The powder was knee deep and I gave into the rhythm of the process, sinking and rising through the snow, getting bouncier as I gathered speed. It was maybe 200 vertical feet (61m) of pure joy and it completely reset my approach to the day.

After a few more pitches of trees, my heli-run ended with our group shooting a narrow gully towards the bottom of the mountain. Heavy snowfall had coated the small drainage into a sinuous natural half-pipe that curved and twisted for maybe a quarter of a mile. At the bottom, there was a bus stop where a dozen skiers or so stood waiting for the shuttle bus to take them back to the base of the mountain. The scene stood in stark contrast to the typical lift line chaos you find at most resorts. Instead of grimacing through the long line and shuffling forwards every few seconds like zombies, we stood like a bunch of little kids happily waiting for the school bus, each talking excitedly about the fun we had just had in Silverton's backcountry. **GA**

DIRECTIONS

Best time to go // Between December 29 and March 12, the only way to ski Silverton is with a guide. Between March 15 and April 15, you can ski the mountain on your own. Heli-skiing runs from the end of November to April. February and March are typically the snowiest months.
Gear required // Powder skis are a must for Silverton. The hike-to terrain is mostly bootpack, so skins aren't necessary. You also need an avalanche beacon, shovel and probe to ski at Silverton, all of which can be rented at the mountain.
Nearest town // Silverton, Colorado.
Getting there // Durango is 90 minutes south. From Denver, Silverton is a 7.5-hour drive.
Where to stay // The Wyman Hotel, in a refurbished historic building on Silverton's Main Street.
Things to know // On guided ski days, Silverton lumps skiers into groups of eight with one guide. The lift opens at 9am and closes at 3pm; après happens in the parking lot.

Opposite: the best in the Midwest, Mt Bohemia

MORE LIKE THIS
BACK-TO-BASICS SKIING

THOUSAND PEAKS RANCH, UTAH

Thousand Peaks is a family-owned ranch tucked into the Uinta Mountains, where Utah, Wyoming and Colorado meet. During the summer, its 40,000 acres (16,200 hectares) is dominated by sheep. But come winter, powder hounds take over. Local business Park City Powder Cats runs daily cat-skiing trips (guided backcountry runs using a fully tracked snowcat vehicle) throughout the ranch's four distinct bowls, which offer steep chutes, sublime glades and deep powder thanks to the average 500in (1270cm) of snow a year. The terrain tops out at 10,800ft (3300m) and the biggest lines offer 2000ft (610m) of vertical drop. And, of course, there are no lines. Take an 'intro to backcountry' clinic, knock out a full day of cat laps, or follow a guide on skins to earn your turns; regardless of the adventure, you'll feel like you have the entire ranch to yourself. And it's just 30 minutes outside Park City.

Nearest town // Park City

MT ASCUTNEY, VERMONT

Defunct ski resorts can be found all over the mountains, but when Ascutney Mountain Resort shuttered its lifts in Vermont, local non-profit Ascutney Outdoors took it over and started managing it as a backcountry access area with a single T-bar lift. That T-bar takes you about halfway up the mountain so you can either lap the lower runs from there, or carry on skinning to higher, steeper terrain when conditions allow The mountain tops out at 3100ft (945m) and the descents from near the summit cover every bit of that.

Nearest town // Brownsville

MT BOHEMIA, MICHIGAN

Mt Bohemia is the fifth highest point in the Keweenay Peninsula, and yet it is still just a mere 1500ft (457m) high. But it is also perhaps the most high-quality low-elevation resort in the world. Located in Michigan's rugged Upper Peninsula, Mt Bohemia features 620 acres (250 hectares) of terrain serviced by a couple of lifts and a shuttle bus. None of the terrain is groomed and 90 percent of it is black diamonds – the Mt Bohemia trail map actually says 'no beginners allowed'. Cliffs, tight trees and fast chutes are the norm. There's also a sister operation, Voodoo Mountain, that's cat-skiing only.

Nearest town // Lac La Belle

GLIDE THE APPALACHIAN TRAIL

The most famous long-distance hike in America is summer-only to most.
Local skiers, however, wait for winter storms and then they pounce.

I never thought I'd die this close to a Waffle House, but it was hard to deny the pickle we were in. It was pushing midnight, maybe -14°C (7°F), and a buddy and I were trying to cross-country ski a two-day section of the Appalachian Trail. Here, we were crossing a grassy knob, but the snow was falling so fast, and the wind was blowing so hard, I couldn't see a foot in front of my face. With my headlamp on, it was like I was trudging through a white wall. My ski partner and I had to scream to communicate over the wind. I kept reaching out and touching his shoulder to make sure we were still together. You hear about people getting turned around in epic conditions like this to dire consequences – that dude in Jack London's short story, *To Build a Fire* (1908), died in the same kind of storm – but it's not like I was in Alaska. I was at the top of a mountain in the relatively tame Southern Appalachians. I had passed a Waffle House on my way to the trailhead.

The Southern Appalachians are not the Rocky Mountains. While the Rockies rise to 14,000ft (4270m), the southern Apps rarely top 6000ft (1830m) in elevation. These mountains also get a fraction of the snow that their taller cousins out west enjoy. Winter is unreliable for skiers down here, with precipitation coming in the form of a cold drizzle more often than not. And yet it does snow here and occasionally it snows enough to pull out the skinny skis from my garage and kick and glide through the woods.

The western border of North Carolina traces a long chain of 5,000 and 6,000ft (1500 and 1830m) mountains that suck up the majority of moisture from winter storms coming from the south and west. The Appalachian Trail follows that same ridgeline as it makes its way 2000 miles (3220km) north, giving you access in the form of trailheads and the opportunity to ski the most famous footpath

in the world. A few spots along that chain offer the right combo of terrain and access, but the best skiing might be on and around Roan High Knob, a 6286ft (1916m) mountain on the North Carolina/Tennessee border that offers a mix of high-elevation grassy meadows and dense, evergreen forest. It's one of the snowiest locations in the south, pulling down more than 100in (250cm) a year. At one point, it even supported a full-service Nordic centre.

There is some seriously fun winter terrain to be explored in this part of the US, particularly along the Appalachian Trail, which traces a 2000 mile (3220km) squiggly line across some of the highest peaks in the eastern United States. With enough snow on the ground, you

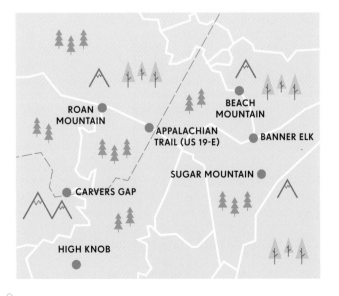

*"The impermanence
of our snow situation
makes southern skiers
more appreciative of
what we have"*

⚡🎿 GRASSY BALDS

The high-elevation balds that punctuate the Southern Appalachians are a bit of a mystery. Ecologically speaking, the mountain tops should be covered in trees like their neighbouring peaks. Some scientists believe the grassy mountain tops originated thousands of years ago, the result of grazing mastodons and woolly mammoths. In recent history, herds of goats have been used to maintain the high-elevation grassy balds along Roan Mountain.

can find yourself skiing anything from a mellow forest road to steep hairpin switchbacks through hardwood forest, to open meadows on a high-elevation grassy bald. It all depends on what you consider 'fun', and how willing you are to get in over your head.

My ski buddy and I were in over our heads, mostly because of poor planning. We'd had a late start because this particular storm had developed rapidly throughout the day, and if you want to cross-country ski in the Southern Appalachians you have to drop everything and meet the storm on its own terms. In this particular case, that meant clicking into our skis well after sunset. So there we were, skiing blind until we found a side trail that took us off the exposed ridge into the woods where the wind and snow were broken up enough for us to see our way to a suitable campsite. We did our best to clear a spot for the tent, but we ended up pitching it on a layer of packed snow. And my sleeping bag was a vastly insufficient -1°C (30°F) affair. I woke up with what I would later learn to be mild frostbite on my big toe.

The next morning was beautiful. The sun was out and there was shin-deep powder on the ground and nobody around. We left camp and took the access trail to the AT (Alpine Touring) shelter and found a patch of woods with a mellow grade and beautifully spaced trees. It was casual glade-skiing, just steep enough for us to put together a handful of shaky tele-turns. We lapped the woods for an hour, taking different lines each time. This was cross-country skiing at its best. The snow was deep enough to cover imperfections on the ground, the forest was quiet and empty of other skiers, and the landscape was gorgeous.

The impermanence of our snow situation makes southern skiers more appreciative of what we have. While western skiers wait patiently for a base to build, we have to pounce on every wayward storm. If a storm is brewing on the radar, I pack my ski gear, try to get all my business in order and wait. It doesn't always pan out.

The skiing starts at Carver's Gap, a trailhead for the Appalachian Trail off Tennessee 143. Ski south on the gated forest

From left: a backcountry base camp along the Appalachian Trail; sunset from Round Bald along the AT; sunrise at Roan Mountain. Previous page: a whitetail buck roams the Great Smoky Mountains in winter

DIRECTIONS

Best time to go // Winters are hit or miss, but the most consistent snowfall comes in January and February.

Gear required // Opt for lightweight cross-country gear. If you want to stick to the forest roads, long skinny skis work best, but for winding off-trail, a shorter cross-country ski with a little shape will serve you well.

Nearest town // The tourist hub of Banner Elk is about 45 minutes east of Carvers Gap and is the closest town.

Getting there // Asheville has the closest airport, roughly 80 miles (129km) south of Carvers Gap. It's a 2.5-hour drive from Charlotte's international airport.

Where to stay // The Pineola, in tiny Newland, has a lodge, cabins and even spots for your RV in the heart of North Carolina's High Country.

Things to know // You'll need to bring your own gear because finding rental cross-country ski gear in the Southern Appalachians can be tough.

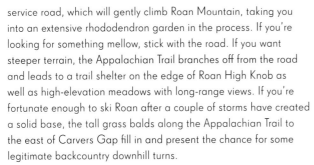

service road, which will gently climb Roan Mountain, taking you into an extensive rhododendron garden in the process. If you're looking for something mellow, stick with the road. If you want steeper terrain, the Appalachian Trail branches off from the road and leads to a trail shelter on the edge of Roan High Knob as well as high-elevation meadows with long-range views. If you're fortunate enough to ski Roan after a couple of storms have created a solid base, the tall grass balds along the Appalachian Trail to the east of Carvers Gap fill in and present the chance for some legitimate backcountry downhill turns.

Knowing what to ski is the easy part though. Knowing when to ski is a little trickier. The fleeting nature of the snow is frustrating, but I've come to realise that part of the joy of cross-country skiing in the Southern Appalachians is about capitalising on the conditions and hitting them at their peak. There is no 'tomorrow' when you ski cross-country in the Southern Appalachians. There is only today. **GA**

MORE LIKE THIS
CROSS-COUNTRY SKIING
IN THE SOUTHEAST

CLINGMANS DOME RD, GREAT SMOKY MOUNTAINS NATIONAL PARK

Mountains rise to well over 6000ft (1830m) in Great Smoky Mountains National Park – which straddles North Carolina and Tennessee – and collect good snow during most winters. The park's main thoroughfare, Newfound Gap Rd, gets ploughed, but Clingmans Dome Rd is closed to vehicular traffic and spared the plough. It's seven miles (11km) from Newfound Gap to the peak of Clingmans Dome, a 6643ft (2025m) peak with a concrete observation tower at its summit offering long range views that stretch for 100 miles (161km) on clear winter days. Skiing to the top of the observation tower (a swirling concrete ramp makes this possible) and having it to yourself is a winter-only treat. The AT parallels the road and passes Mt Collins shelter halfway to the dome. The Dome Road gets so much cross-country love, it's spawned the Great Smoky Nordic Ski Patrol, an all-volunteer unit that has patrolled the Dome, keeping skiers safe for decades.
Nearest town // Gatlinburg, Tennessee

BLUE RIDGE PARKWAY

The Blue Ridge Parkway is a 469 mile (755km) two-lane asphalt road running from Shenandoah National Park in Virginia to Great Smoky Mountains National Park in North Carolina. Much of the road is gated in the winter, closing it to vehicles, and doesn't get ploughed, turning it into a cross-country skier's dream. A number of sections of the Parkway can be skied, but the 7 mile (11km) slice that includes the Linn Cove Viaduct, a high-elevation bridge, is particularly stunning. The Viaduct is an engineering marvel, built to protect the sensitive ecosystem of Grandfather Mountain, which is punctuated by granite outcroppings and stands of evergreens. The concrete bridge seems to hover over the terrain as it curls around the side of the mountain.
Nearest town // Blowing Rock, North Carolina

MAX PATCH

The Appalachian Trail strolls right across the 460-ft-tall (1400m) Max Patch, a grassy bald in Pisgah National Forest that collects good snow with storms coming from the south and west. High-elevation balds like Max Patch are rare, but an integral part of the Southern Appalachian ecosystem and give hikers and skiers a chance to experience an 'above the treeline' summit experience. You can pick your mileage, from a mile-long out and back from the nearest trailhead to an endless romp along the AT as it moves north and south from the grassy summit. Many skiers will simply run laps on the steepest slopes of Max Patch, getting a couple of hundred vertical feet of downhill turns with each lap. Regardless of how you ski it, you'll have 360-degree views from the top of the bald knob.
Nearest town // Hot Springs, North Carolina

Clockwise from top: the Blue Ridge Parkway in all its winter glory; icy falls along Newfound Gap Rd to Clingmans Dome; taking a breather on top of Max Patch, along the AT

CHRISTMAS IN THE BIG APPLE

If New York City were a house on your road, it would be the excessively illuminated and bedazzled one with animated reindeer and spinning candy canes.

Before we start: forget about words like 'hip' and 'edgy'. No, there is nothing 'underground' about this. It's definitely not a 'cult favourite' or 'off the beaten track'. This is a winter adventure that is about pure wonder – the kind of wonder you used to feel when you were seven years old, before you knew what was cool and uncool, before you worried about long queues and high prices. It's Christmas at the iconic ice-skating rink beneath the tree in Rockefeller Center in New York City and people are having a blast.

Whether or not you actually celebrate the holiday, Christmas in New York is a bucket-list item for a reason. The city's famously hard edge gets softened with a sprinkling of frost. People smile more. Shopfronts glow. The city even *smells* good: hot sugared almonds from street cart vendors, fancy candles wafting out of Soho boutiques, fir trees for sale on the lots that pop up seemingly 30 seconds after Thanksgiving ends.

Ice-skating in Rockefeller Center is perhaps New York's most beloved Christmas tradition. The rink in the outdoor plaza has been open seasonally since 1939, creating a famous backdrop for photos and films. Skaters twirls (and fall) in front of *Prometheus*, Paul Manship's 1934 cast bronze sculpture of the Greek Titan stealing fire from the Gods. Behind that is the legendary tree – a Norway spruce, sometimes as much as 100ft (31m) tall, lit with great pomp the Wednesday following Thanksgiving. It's a tradition that dates to Rockefeller Center's construction during the Great Depression, when workers put up a much humbler version and decked it with cranberries and tin cans.

Your admission ticket gets you an hour on the ice, which may seem short, but, believe me, doesn't feel short at all, especially on a very cold afternoon when the wind is slipping down the back of my neck, despite my heavy wool scarf. There is plenty of time to do dozens of turns around the rink, gazing up at the art deco buildings, stopping to snap pictures. These days I see that kids can rent a skating aid shaped like a giant penguin. Since the rink only holds 150 people, the line was overwhelming at first – the closer to Christmas, the longer they are. I am told that weekday mornings are quite nice but, remember, the hassle is part of the experience.

Amateur and first-time skaters from all over the country are falling over and giggling wildly. They're holding hands. There is something delightful about people from all over the world coming

SNOW BUSINESS

New York isn't known as a snow mecca, but in 2016, 27.5in (70cm) was dumped on Central Park, the highest snowfall since records began. White Christmases – defined as an inch or more of snow on Christmas Day – are even rarer than blizzards; one occurs approximately every six years. The last White Christmas was in 2009. The coldest winter temp on record was -29°C (-20°F), back in 1934, turning the Hudson River into an ice canal.

together to try something they've always wanted to. This isn't cool, but nobody cares. Everyone's just enjoying themselves and each other, and the bright cold December sun.

But it can be fun to consider your time on the Rockefeller rink as just the beginning of a quintessential Christmas in New York tour. For me, the first stop post-skating is always Rockefeller Center's outpost of La Maison du Chocolat, which serves unbelievably expensive – and unbelievably delicious – little cups of thick rich French hot chocolate. It's the ideal jolt of warm sugar and caffeine to energise you back into the cold New York streets. A 10-minute walk downtown leads me to Bryant Park, where December means Holiday Village time. Nearly 200 vendors set up in little glassed-in kiosks, where I can step in from the chill to look at handmade pottery, art prints, jewellery, ornaments and all sorts of other crafts. And there is food too – gooey raclette sandwiches with French ham and pickles, fluffy Chinese pork buns, spiked cider, Italian doughnuts stuffed with oozing Nutella. Oh, and there's another skating rink – less iconic, sure, but much bigger. (It's free if you bring your own skates.)

"People smile more. Shopfronts glow. The city even smells good"

Afterwards, I hit Fifth Avenue and walk south for some of the city's primo window displays. No, I cannot afford and also do not want any gemstone jewellery from Tiffany & Co, but I definitely do enjoy gawking at diamonds dripping from robin's egg blue faux Christmas trees and dollhouse-size city dioramas sparkling in the lights. I then cut over to Herald Square for the mother of all window displays at Macy's, the department store that basically invented the tradition. Since 1870, it has been trimming its windows with trees, animatronic woodland creatures, elaborate streetscapes, faux falling snow and more. It takes some 200 artists and designers nearly a month to create the enchantment. Families – or just people who are mad for Christmas – head all the way inside for the 8th-floor Santaland, a 13,000 sq ft (4000 sq m) indoor North Pole village, complete with snowcapped mountains, gingerbread-trimmed houses, singing snowpeople and busy elves. It's chaotic, overstimulating and, yes, magical (the chaos is part of the deal, remember?) But if you want to see old Saint Nick himself, make reservations online.

I recently stumbled upon an add-on to this tour that you might describe as off the beaten track. But it is New York, so I doubt it will be for long. Across the East River, a more local-oriented scene unfolds in Brooklyn's Dyker Heights. Unlike most of the rest of the city, this neighbourhood is mostly single homes, built for wealthy families in the late 19th and early 20th centuries. At Christmas, homeowners attempt to outdo each other with the most splendiferous holiday displays. Many hire professional decorating

companies to smother their Tudors and Victorians with twinkling lights and make their yards into reindeer-and-sleigh parking lots. Individually, they're beautiful. Together? A sight worth trekking to Brooklyn for. The best displays are usually on 11th Avenue to 13th Avenue and from 83rd to 86th Street. Go before 9pm, since some owners turn the lights off for the night.

Whether you've made the detour or not, this tour ends where it began: Rockefeller Center for another Christmas in New York activity that some may (unfairly) dismiss as a cliché: the Rockettes Christmas Spectacular at Radio City Music Hall. The Rockettes are a nearly 100-year-old women's dance company with gravity-defying high kicks. Their Christmas Show is the stuff of generations of holiday memories, with all the dazzle you would expect and can handle, set to classic Christmas songs like Jingle Bells, Let it Snow and White Christmas.

My own Christmas evenings in New York never feel complete until I've had a nightcap at Lillie's Victorian Establishment, a 10-minute walk west of Rockefeller. With crystal chandeliers, red velvet banquettes and gilt-framed pictures of bygone queens, it's themed and goofy – a lot like the rest of my day. **EM**

Clockwise from top: the famous Radio City Rockettes perform; snow in Central Park; Saks Fifth Avenue puts on quite a show during the holidays. Previous page: the ice rink at Rockefeller

DIRECTIONS

Best time to go // Give the city a week to recover from Thanksgiving (the last Thursday in November) and Christmas activities will be in full swing.

Gear required // New York in December is cold – temperatures usually range from 0-4°C, although it's not unusual for things to swing lower or higher. Dress in layers.

Getting there // New York is served by two major airports – LaGuardia and JFK, as well as Newark Airport, across the river in New Jersey.

Where to stay // New York hotels are pricey, especially in Manhattan. Staying in outer boroughs is often cheaper, but make sure you're close to public transport. But if there was a time to splurge, this is it: the St Regis, with giant nutcrackers guarding the door, goes all-out for the holidays.

Things to know // Everyone loves New York at Christmas, which means crowds. Plan for the most popular activities (like ice-skating) on weekdays and/or mornings.

Opposite, from top: Christmas time in Amsterdam with the Rijksmuseum at twilight; the Biltmore Estate in Asheville, North Carolina

MORE LIKE THIS
CHRISTMAS IN THE CITY

AMSTERDAM, NETHERLANDS

Amsterdam is perhaps most itself during an extra-cold winter, when the canals freeze and your cheeks go red the moment you step outside. Much like the Rockefeller rink, Ice*Amsterdam is situated in front of one of the city's most iconic buildings, the Rijksmuseum. The museum's red bricks and turrets make a stunning backdrop to an afternoon of winter ice-skating, followed with a beer and a pot of fondue at the adjacent cafe. In Dam Square, a 66ft (20m) tree is lit in mid-December, in a ceremony that includes carol singing and vendors hawking traditional winter treats like *oliebollen* (doughnuts). And to combat the winter darkness, the annual Festival of Lights brings artists to create light installation pieces across the city. They're not necessarily holiday-themed, but their glow certainly creates a festive ambience, reminding us why humans have always gravitated towards light at this time of year.

Nearest town // Amsterdam

ASHEVILLE, NORTH CAROLINA

The desperately charming art deco-era city of Asheville, North Carolina sits atop a Blue Ridge peak like a crown. It glows most enticingly during the holiday season, when every shop, museum and home in town puts out a wreath and a metre (or 10) of fairy lights. Kick off a Christmas trip with a gander at the National Gingerbread House Competition entries at the 1913 Grove Park Inn, which looks like a giant elf house. The entries are mind-bogglingly complex – imagine gingerbread castles, complete with turrets and drawbridges – and smell good to boot. Afterwards have a cocktail by the fireplace at the Inn's bar as the surrounding mountains go inky black. Nearby, the Biltmore Estate, America's largest family home, dresses up like an enormous Christmas present, with seemingly thousands of miles of ribbons and wreaths, bows and swags, lights and trees. Follow an afternoon visit with a snowy hike in the Blue Ridge.

Nearest town // Asheville

ALMONTE, CANADA

You may not know where Almonte is, but chances are you've seen it on TV. Although Canadian – it's about 40 minutes from Ottawa – Almonte frequently plays an all-American town in made-for-TV Christmas movies. Visit and you'll see why: the postcard-pretty 19th-century downtown of craft shops, bookstores and local bakeries; the vintage diner; the tranquil riverfront. In winter, the charm cranks up to 11, with decorations on every available surface. In early December, the Light up the Night festival draws crowds for an open-air Christmas show of music and fireworks – bundle up. When the temperature drops low enough, the small waterfall under the old mill freezes into bulbous shapes; stroll across the stone bridge for the best views. As the holidays near, the farmer's market in the handsome town hall converts into a Christmas market, so stock up on local treats and crafts. And don't miss the sweet, small town Christmas parade on a weekend night in early December.

Nearest town // Ottawa

SAGE KOTSENBURG ON BRIGHTON

Sage Kotsenburg became a household name when he won snowboarding's first ever Olympic slopestyle gold medal. But these days he looks for glory on his favourite hill in Utah.

You wake up and you just know when it's a Brighton Day. When you get to the lot you can smell the strong whiff of the 1990s and early 2000s snowboarding culture. Everyone gets up early on storm days and heads to Brighton. They are grilling in the parking lot, drinking coffee, each with their rituals, getting ready for the lifts to open. I'm usually with at least 30 buddies, all of us just psyching on riding a powder day at Brighton. We've had so many epic days this season already. By mid-January the resort had received 450in (1140cm) of snow and it looks like we're on track to hit the 500in (1270cm) winter average by February.

I'm originally from Coeur d'Alene in Idaho but I've been coming to Brighton for almost 20 years. My brothers and I watched all the snowboard movies and Brighton was this legendary snowboard destination in the Wasatch Mountains, where all the pros filmed. It was the first resort in Utah to allow snowboarding, and one of the earliest in the country. Plus, legendary pros like JP Walker, Jeremy Jones and Mitch Nelson were all based here. They'd film their video parts in the resort and build all these crazy DIY features and out-of-bounds jibbers among the trees.

I was about nine or so when I first came. I travelled here with my older brothers, who would also go on to become professional

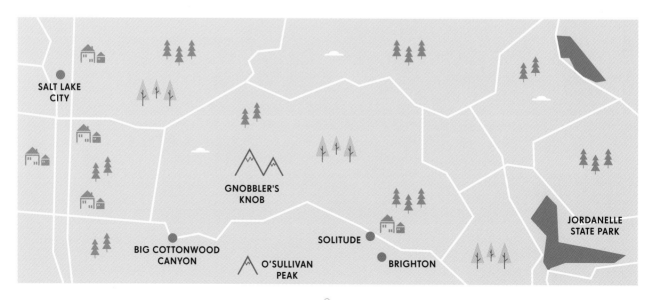

⛷️🎿 UNDER LIGHTS

With 22 lighted runs, including the new, long-awaited lights at Snake Creek and the terrain parks, Brighton Ski Resort boasts the largest amount of night-skiing terrain available anywhere in Utah. For those with afternoon arrivals or daytime plans in the city (as well as fanatics who can't be bothered to stop just because the sun sets), night-skiing is an excellent way to sneak in some extra laps. Pack another jacket and a clear goggle lens.

Clockwise from top: there's a map, but getting lost is half the fun; sunset over Brighton Ski Resort; Kotsenburg slashing turns. Previous page: Kotsenburg at the Air + Style competition at the Rose Bowl in Pasadena, California, 2015

snowboarders, to compete in junior events. The thing was, we were competing in the park and pipe, and the facilities back then, and through my teens, were terrible. They are sick now, but back in the day all we wanted to do was finish the competition so we could hit the resort and the backcountry. What I liked about it was that it had a locals' resort vibe to it. While things have changed, it still has those fundamentals today.

However, as much as I love Brighton's legacy and vibe, it is the terrain that makes it my all-time-favourite resort. The mountain is just naturally designed for snowboarding. It's a kind of bench mountain, with these cliffs and poppers and not a sustained downhill the whole time. That means you can find these creative features, be it trees, rocks or pillows, and it's so well suited for snowboarding. I think you can tell people from Utah who have grown up riding Brighton. There are little features in their style and approach that have been shaped by riding there, and I include myself in that. You can hit 40ft (12m) cliffs, or little features in trees, but you have to remember where they are and they are so hard to find. You have to mentally map the zones.

The resort was crucial when I made a big career switch a few years back, from slopestyle competition to backcountry riding. I'd reached the peak of competitive snowboarding and won the first Olympic gold medal in slopestyle, but I wanted to focus on what made me happy. I also needed to find something where I was uncomfortable. I spent the next few years focused on learning and honing my craft when it came to backcountry riding and especially safety. A lot of that was done at Brighton. You can cover every aspect of snowboarding there, which is unique.

Now, I live in Park City, so it's only a 45-minute drive from my home up through the Big Cottonwood Canyon to Brighton. I've had a dozen days up here already this winter. It's my go-to riding and filming destination when I'm not doing trips overseas or competing at the Natural Selection Tour. It's the zone I feel most at home and where I ride with all my friends. It's also where I've met so many cool people who I have so much in common with.

I love that there's no real town at Brighton itself, just a few cabins, and so it's a journey to get there. You gather at the mouth of the canyon, car-share up, turn the tunes up and it feels like

> *"It is the terrain that makes it*
> *my all-time-favourite resort"*

you are part of a unit. In terms of my ideal day, it would start with getting first lifts up either the Crest or Milly quad chairs. We'd usually peel off into squads of four for the quickest chairlift times. We'd lap the off-piste runs until all the powder was gone.

Once the powder was stripped, I'd rip the resort and the groomed runs, before heading back to the lot for lunch. Fed and watered, we'd then grab the backcountry packs for some out-of-bounds action. Unlike in most resorts, you can do short hikes to access incredible terrain in relative safety. Another unique advantage of Brighton is that all of the out-of-bounds riding funnels back down to the base.

There'd be time to shape a feature and have a session, before heading back to the truck at the end of the day. Back in the lot you'd talk to everyone you chatted to in the morning and see what they all got into. It's this shared stoked experience that I love. It's timeless and I can go there and turn everything off. I ride with my friends and whether we hike out-of-bounds or stay in the boundary lines, Brighton is where I have had some of the best days of my life on my board. **BM**

DIRECTIONS

Best time to go // Every lift-serviced resort area is typically open by Christmas, with the season closing in mid-April.

Gear required // Dedicated powder equipment and proper backcountry packs. There is a ski rental shop at Brighton's base, but a wider range in Salt Lake City.

Nearest town // Solitude Resort and its on-mountain accommodation is a 15-minute drive away. Salt Lake City is just a half-hour drive down the Big Cottonwood Canyon.

Getting there // Fly into Salt Lake City International Airport (SLC) and it's a 40-minute drive to Brighton Resort.

Where to stay // The one hotel option is the rustic, upscale Brighton Lodge. Off-site, the nearest lodging is at Solitude.

Things to know // The resort is divided into two sides: Majestic and Millicent, aka Milly. The Millicent side is serviced by one lift and is largely for advanced and expert riders. The Majestic side has terrain for beginners and intermediates, as well as tree-skiing for advanced riders.

*Opposite, from top: tree riding at
Killington, Vermont; Oregon's iconic
volcanic ski resort, Mt Hood*

MORE LIKE THIS
SNOWBOARDING'S ROOTS

MT HOOD MEADOWS, OREGON

Oregon's Mt Hood and Brighton share an uncanny number of similarities. The biggest of the three Mt Hood resorts, Meadows doesn't have any lodging on-mountain. That makes it a very different experience from the typical cookie-cutter destination American ski resorts. Like Brighton, it does feature interesting terrain, both alpine and below treeline, and thus offers plenty of variety for all levels of skiers. Its solid 426in (1082cm) of average snowfall doesn't quite match the Cottonwood resorts, but it does make up that difference with skiable terrain. The 2150 skiable acres (870 hectares), serviced by 11 total lifts, 85 named runs and a 2777ft (846m) vertical rise, is further topped by an additional 1700ft (520m) of vertical for ambitious skiers and riders who want to hike. It is also close to the other Mt Hood Resorts of Timberline and Ski Bowl, while summer camp options exist on the Palmer Glacier.

Nearest town // Portland

KILLINGTON, VERMONT

Jake Burton, considered the father of snowboarding, hailed from Vermont, so there's no shortage of snowboarding history in New England. Mt Stratton was the first resort in the US to allow snowboarding, and while Killington took a little while to follow, it soon became a snowboard hotspot. Killington – known as the 'beast of the east' – summits at 4241ft (1292m) with a base elevation of 1165ft (355m), giving it the largest vertical drop in New England. The mountain is home to an extensive trail system that spans seven mountains across four bases. With its abundant natural snowfall and the most extensive artificial snow-making system in the world, it also has a long season that usually runs from late October into May. Its terrain parks and pipes are considered world-class, while The Stash, designed by Jake Burton himself, is an exceptional organic terrain park stacked with more than 65 natural features, including log rails, wall rides and rainbow trees.

Nearest town // Killington

CRYSTAL MOUNTAIN, WASHINGTON STATE

Southeast of Seattle in the mighty Cascades, Crystal Mountain treats snowboarders to some of the West Coast's best powder. The resort, the state's largest, has more than 50 runs spread across 2600 acres (1050 hectares), each with an unobstructed view of Mt Rainer, one of the largest active volcanoes in the country. The 468in (1189cm) of annual snow falls on a diverse range of terrain, ranging from competition venues for big mountain skiers and snowboarders, to beginners and family-friendly slopes. Plus, there are four different freestyle terrain parks. The legendary, high-speed, two-seater Chair 6 to Southback is the gateway to the resort's deepest powder and most technical terrain. More steep terrain and powder lie off Northway Peak, while the blue trails from the summit better serve intermediates. There are a few more options than Brighton in terms of mountain-based accommodation, with three hotels at the mountain's base. However, with Seattle less than a two-hour drive away, it's a scenic and manageable day trip from there.

Nearest town // Seattle

BACKCOUNTRY FOR BEGINNERS

Bluebird resort in Colorado is the first of its kind 'backcountry' ski resort. There are no lifts, but it offers full-service education, gear and epic avalanche-controlled and patrolled terrain.

The first thing I noticed when I pulled into Bluebird Backcountry's parking lot? The very nice lady walking around in the snow handing out fresh-baked cookies from a Tupperware box. Getting welcomed with a chocolate-chip cookie set the tone for me at Bluebird Backcountry, a one-of-a-kind ski area located halfway between the tiny town of Kremmling and Steamboat Springs.

I was there to ski backcountry lines, which traditionally is an intimidating endeavour. Instead of riding lifts and skiing groomed runs at a resort, I would be exploring the wild, ungroomed slopes on public lands, far from the safety net. To climb the mountains, skiers attach 'skins' – sticky strips that provide traction on the uphill climbs – to the bottom of their skis and use special boots and bindings that free the skier's back heel to provide a greater range of motion than traditional binding systems. Backcountry skiing can be a revelation. 'Earning your turns' by climbing the mountains under your own power can be gruelling, but the benefits are obvious: solitude and fresh powder at every turn.

But there are dangers – avalanches being the most obvious – and backcountry skiers should always be up on their avalanche risk assessment and rescue skills. Still, interest has boomed in recent years. Typically, skiers new to the backcountry will either hire guides or learn from mentors over the course of years. But guides are an expensive temporary solution, and mentors are hard to find. Bluebird was designed to fill that void by offering backcountry skiers on-site expertise, terrain that's been assessed by professionals for avalanches, plus warming huts and even ski patrol – oh, and chocolate-chip cookies. Imagine the climbing-gym model and apply it to backcountry skiing.

'It's hard for people to learn to backcountry ski,' says Bluebird's co-founder, Jeff Woodward. 'Taking an avy course is a big leap. Bluebird is the top of the funnel – the first place you go for a backcountry education, and the place you keep coming to continue learning. We wanted to create a super welcoming vibe.' Hence the chocolate-chip cookies.

Bluebird is the first of its kind: a human-powered ski resort with 1200 acres (486 hectares) of inbounds terrain, but no lifts, no helicopters, no cats, not even a T-bar or tow rope. Instead, skiers follow designated skin tracks that climb the vast terrain behind the lodge, delivering them to fresh powder, steep chutes

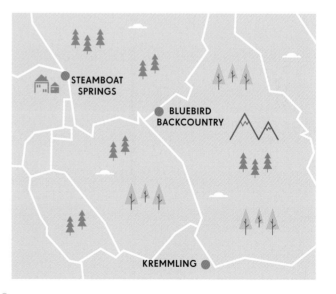

SOLITUDE

A large part of the appeal of backcountry skiing is the solitude. More skiers are venturing into the backcountry to avoid the ever-growing crowds at resorts. While Bluebird will inevitably be more crowded than a typical backcountry zone that has no facilities, it's still possible to find quiet thanks to the 4000 acres (1620 hectares) of skiable terrain. More importantly, Bluebird caps the number of skiers allowed on the hill at 200 per day, ensuring you'll never have to wait in line for bacon.

From top: fresh tracks are guaranteed; the unique Bluebird setup is perfect for backcountry beginners. Previous page: learning with a heavy focus on fun

and mellow glades. The resort opened in the winter of 2020 after a series of test events and a raucous Kickstarter campaign that netted $100,000 worth of enthusiasm, billing itself as the first human-powered backcountry ski resort in the country.

Bluebird operates on a privately owned 50,000 acre (20,200 hectare) cattle ranch in a quiet corner of Northern Colorado, roughly two hours northeast of Denver. Everything about the operation is low-impact and meant to be removed at the end of the season, so the base lodge has an Everest Base Camp vibe. There's a large, temporary building that looks like a giant white wagon top, adorned with prayer flags. Beside that white 'lodge', picnic tables and sitting areas with chairs and fire pits have been carved out of deep snow. Inside, there's green turf on the floor, plastic Adirondack chairs scattered throughout, and card tables where guests can fill out surveys, rent equipment and sign up for guides or lessons. If you're skiing alone and looking for a partner? Just drape a Hawaiian lei over your head and look for other skiers with similar leis.

I myself was relatively new to backcountry skiing when I first visited Bluebird, so I signed up for a guided adventure (another

"Interest in backcountry skiing has boomed in recent years"

3000 acres/1200 hectares is up for grabs if you have a guide). After a beacon and gear check, I started climbing the skin track, which followed a wide road that rose steadily through rolling meadows. I was with a small group of skiers following two guides deep into the white expanse above the base lodge.

Maybe 30 minutes from the base lodge we hit the Perch, a mid-mountain warming hut where a dozen skiers were resting in the sun, while a volunteer cooked bacon and chilli on a grill. Bacon is an integral part of Bluebird's business plan. Skiers have options from the Perch. Climb in one direction and there are wide-open bowls, climb another and you'll find steeper trees. Our guide led us to a stash of powder that had gathered from a recent storm between a line of firs and a barbed-wire fence. The group took turns dropping into the powder stash, then we attached our skins to seek out another. There are plenty of steep lines to ski at Bluebird, but the terrain we hit was mostly low-angled slopes, void of the usual avalanche danger of backcountry skiing. That's part of the appeal of Bluebird – it's backcountry 'lite'.

A third of all guests show up without their own backcountry skis, renting them from Bluebird. 'Education is first,'

Woodward says. 'Adventure is second.' But the adventure is pretty damn good too.

I skied Bluebird during its first winter, in 2020. It has since moved to a different location on the same ranch, but the vibe is still the same. There is still a Tupperware box of cookies, and you can eat fresh bacon, then ski in the backcountry. The only thing that's changed is the terrain – there's more of it for all levels of skiers, especially for those unsure of their backcountry chops. From the Perch, skiers can hit Meat Hill, a mellow meadow with 200ft (61m) of vertical drop that stacks powder during storms. Or they can climb the Lost In The Woodwards Skin Track and hit the Hundred Acres Woods, which has a bevy of low-angle glade skiing through a stand of skinny birch trees. 'All of our skin tracks and downhill runs are marked', explains Woodward. 'So it's easy to find your way around.'

Experienced skiers can skin up Bear Mountain – the 9845ft (3000m) peak that serves as the high point for the new ski area – and drop incredibly steep treelines off the north face of the summit. In total, there are 28 marked runs that are graded just like at your favourite resort. **GA**

DIRECTIONS

Best time to go // Some advanced runs don't open until storms stack up, so late February and early March often deliver the most diverse terrain.

Gear required // Ski touring kit, with Alpine Touring boots, bindings and skins, is the preferred gear for the terrain. Bluebird offers backcountry equipment rentals, including the requisite safety gear: beacon, shovel and probe.

Nearest town // Tiny Kremmling is the closest town with facilities.

Getting there // Denver is the nearest large airport. From Denver, it's about a 2.5-hour drive.

Where to stay // Bluebird offers a campsite and yurts. The Grizzly Hostel has budget accommodation. If you're looking for fancier lodging, Steamboat Springs is 45 minutes away.

Things to know // Backcountry safety equipment (an avalanche beacon, shovel and probe) are mandatory to ski Bluebird. It is also only open from Thursday to Monday.

Opposite, from top: midwinter in Rocky Mountain National Park; heading upwards in the White Mountains of New Hampshire

MORE LIKE THIS
BEGINNER BACKCOUNTRY

WHITEGRASS SKI TOURING CENTER, WEST VIRGINIA

Much like Bluebird, Whitegrass operates on a working ranch. Unlike Bluebird, Whitegrass isn't in the Rocky Mountains, it's in the Southern Appalachians of West Virginia. But this ski area sits in a particularly snowy piece of the South, picking up more than 160in (406cm) of lake-effect snow every winter. Technically, Whitegrass is a cross-country ski centre. There's even a groomed skate-ski track near the base lodge. But Whitegrass actually occupies a historic ski area that, at one time, featured a lift and downhill runs. So, the terrain can be steep and skiers can skin to the 4460ft (1360m) peak of Cabin Mountain if they have the legs, and choose from a variety of downhill lines, from tight trees to open meadows and more mellow roads. Or just do laps on the slope that used to sport the ski lift right behind the base lodge.

Nearest town // Davis

JOHN SHERBURNE SKI TRAIL, NEW HAMPSHIRE

This is a historic ski trail built on the east side of Mt Washington in the 1930s by the Civilian Conservation Corps. The trail runs for 2.4 miles (3.9km) from the bottom of Tuckerman Ravine to the parking lot of Appalachian Mountain Club's Pinkham Notch Visitor Center. It drops 2400ft (732m) in elevation with slopes typically under 25 degrees, so avalanche risk is very low. It is the classic intro to backcountry skiing experience in New England, and it's one of the many backcountry trails that are overseen by Granite Backcountry Alliance, which maintains backcountry glades throughout the region for the public. You can find info, bathrooms and hot food at the Pinkham Notch Visitor Center at the base of the trail, and many guide services offer rentals and trips.

Nearest town // Gorham

HIDDEN VALLEY SKI AREA, COLORADO

Hidden Valley Ski Area opened in the 1950s and boasted a couple of lifts servicing 2000ft (610m) of vertical drop with terrain for all types of skiers. Sadly, the resort closed in 1991. Today, the infrastructure of the resort is gone, but the runs are still there, and the 'ghost resort' is now part of Rocky Mountain National Park. Hidden Valley has become a hotspot of winter fun inside the park, from families sledding the lower slopes to backcountry skiers exploring the upper reaches of the former resort. Many of the former ski runs are low angle powder stashes, and have become a mainstay for would-be backcountry skiers looking to learn the nuances of the sport. The area's proximity to Estes Park makes it easy to rent gear or hire guides.

Nearest town // Estes Park

DREAM LINES IN ALASKA

*You have to be pretty brave to ride the extreme spines in the great state of Alaska.
It also costs an arm and a leg – unless you go DIY.*

'I don't really know what the weather is doing tomorrow, but my iPhone has just one snowflake on it, so maybe it'll be clear?' said Joe Schuster, owner of Sportsman's Air Service in Anchorage, Alaska. We were standing inside his one-room office on the tarmac, wearing our snow pants and packed for a two-week winter camping and ski expedition. Being that he was an experienced bush pilot in remote wilderness areas, we expected Schuster to have more sophisticated weather forecasting technologies, or at least some kind of radar map. Once we realised he wasn't kidding, we made another shop run for last-minute supplies and waited by the phone for a green light.

Weather windows can take weeks to materialise in Alaska, but clear skies blessed us early the next morning, so our team of four loaded all our gear into the single-engined, propeller-driven DHC-3 Otter aircraft, equipped with skis for snow landings, and took off for the Tordrillo Mountain range, scouting a landing for spot on a glacier in a steep-walled cirque 100 miles (161km) from civilisation. Three long-time Pacific Northwest ski adventure buddies and I had been scheming up a trip in search of the steep Alaska spine lines – the ones that you typically see top pros boosting big, long tracks down in ski movie segments. More often than not, those clips are shot from a gyro-stabilised camera mounted to the front of the same

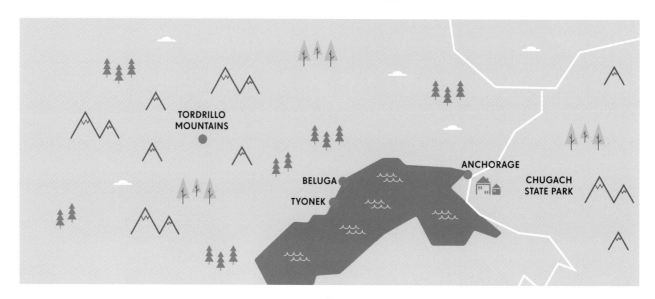

*"It was all-time steep powder-skiing with
almost an entire mountain range to ourselves"*

helicopter that dropped them on the peak. The thing is, we didn't have Red Bull or Teton Gravity Research picking up the bill, nor a film crew to procure weeks of helicopter time for many tens of thousands of dollars.

Consider us, big mountain ski bums – 'dirtbags' with the chops to shred big lines – without the resources to stay in, or have any interest in, a luxury one-percent heli-lodge (like the very lodge that typically accesses this area) for two weeks in bathrobes and slippers. Instead, we endeavoured to have Joe drop us off in a well-positioned base camp in a cirque of trophy lines and we'd access them by skinning and climbing under our own human power, making exclusively fresh turns in untouched snow on slopes between 40 and 55 degrees.

There's an eerie feeling when you're standing on a glacier next to a pile of food and equipment, watching your plane and last connection with the outside world take off – you're completely on your own, far away from any kind of help, until the sky stops dumping snow long enough for the pilot to come back and pick you up. The feeling quickly subsided when we looked around at the amphitheatre of 2000ft (610m) snow curtains hanging from the jagged peaks in every direction we could see.

Weather is always the biggest variable to just about anything in Alaska, and flying in is only part of the game. After we'd done a day of warm-up laps just above camp, the infinite blue sky faded into a low fog and we hunkered down in our tents for two full storm days, periodically surfacing to stare out from inside the ping-pong ball, or hit a few laps on the binding-less powder surfer.

Then the weather broke and the crystal-clear skies sparkled warm April daylight on several new feet of fresh maritime snow glued to the walls, leaving the steepest, north-facing cirques refrigerated in the shade. These wet, coastal storms come in heavy before below-

zero overnight temperatures cement the snow in place, providing relative stability from avalanches as early as two days after they fall.

Every day, we'd rope up in teams of two with our crevasse rescue gear on our harnesses, meander around depressions in the glaciated terrain and push out a little further, skinning to the base of our scouted lines and switching over to crampons and ascent plates (like snowshoes for steep, loose snow that's too deep for just boots). Then we'd climb the snow ladders several thousand feet in a few hours to the top of whatever wide-open face looked tastiest. From the top, we'd each paint our own pristine, untracked line down the spines with snow sloughing to either side of us, then boost off cliff drops and straight-line the snowy aprons over mostly covered bergschrunds (crevasses) to the valley floor.

Despite the reliability of Alaska snow in spring, avalanches are always a consideration, but so is cold and frostbite, crevasse fall, rockfall released from warming snow, and any injury big or small that might not receive medical attention for days. But beyond those back-of-mind concerns, it was all-time steep powder-skiing with almost an entire mountain range to ourselves – except on day nine when we woke up to the sound of a helicopter in the early morning.

The bird circled our camp twice and proceeded to drop a load of skiers off on a saddle between the peaks above us. We were miffed that they'd chosen to drop right on top of our remote, human-powered camp rather than fly their aircraft somewhere else, but then had a laugh as we watched them ski our mellowest warm-up run, which we'd already tracked up days before. We mooned the chopper as it flew the guests home for brunch at the nearby Tordrillo Mountain Lodge. They'd just paid $17,500 per person for a week of luxurious warm beds and second tracks on our run, not including gratuity. Our willingness to walk and climb and sleep in -30°C sleeping bags put us right in the honeypot of the top 0.1 percent of ski terrain on the planet for less than $1,000 each.

We'd gotten exactly what we came for. But after 10 days of staring at one particular pronounced spine cutting across the face of a down-glacier cirque in the northerly shade, we decided to go for it. The Alaska Factor – where everything looks much closer and smaller than in reality – was real, and our approach took the whole morning of skinning, climbing and billy-goating into position at the top of the 45-plus-degree line.

It skied like an eternal dream – every turn scream-inducing and it never seemed to end, until it did, with our entire crew party-shredding down the apron and into the sunshine, our hands raised to the sky and our adrenaline portals flung wide open as feelings of stoke and accomplishment coursed through our toes and fingertips.

When the plane came to pick us up, we admired our work from the sky. Later, we looked into the last line we had ridden. 'The once ridden, never climbed, 3000ft face,' the internet called it. Then we watched a video of Red Bull athlete Travis Rice rip the same line top to bottom – after being dropped off by his helicopter flight from the Tordrillo Mountain Lodge. **SY**

LUX AK

The infamous alternative to the DIY version of this trip is a stay at the legendary Todrillo Mountain Lodge, a base camp for the wealthy, with a helicopter on standby, salmon fishing guides at the ready during down days, and top-shelf liquor. The Tordrillo Mountain Range is home to 11,070ft (3370m) Mt Spurr, the highest volcano of the Aleutian Arc.

Left: human-powered ascents. Previous page: gravity-powered descents

DIRECTIONS

Best time to go // Early April is really the only month when weather and snow-stability line up.

Gear required // A full winter camping and expedition setup: four-season tent, -30°C sleeping bag, cook tent, Camp Chef Mountaineer aluminium cooking system, several days worth of fuel, lots of cheese.

Nearest town // Talkeetna is a three-hour drive from Anchorage.

Getting there // Fly to Anchorage, then drive to Talkeetna and hire a bush plane, often through a hunting outfitter.

Where to stay // In Talkeetna, the Denali Fireside Cabins are great; in the backcountry, your tent.

Things to know // This is an expedition for very experienced winter campers and skiers and riders, with avalanche and basic first-aid training. Also, cucumbers don't last long in subzero temperatures.

MORE LIKE THIS
REMOTE ALASKA BASE CAMPS

PIKA GLACIER

Located in Denali National Park in the Alaska Range, this popular summer rock-climbing destination is known as Little Switzerland for its scenery, with a clear view of Mt Foraker 17 miles (27km) to the northwest. Denali is about 30 miles (48km) to the northeast, but hidden behind the spires that enclose the Pika. Fly in from Talkeetna using Sheldon Air Service and make camp below the steep skiing lines of the Trolls and the Crown Jewel spires. Rope up to ski down the glacier and get on runs like Hobbit Hop and the northwest-facing couloir off the Hobbit that's 1500ft (460m) and over 42 degrees. Ski down the Pika to Italy's Boot for laps on the toe of the steep northeast-facing couloir. To get a view of Denali, head over to towards Munchkin and look down the Crown Glacier with a few laps on Milk Run. Watch out for Ravens eating your food, rubbish and waste.

Nearest town // Talkeetna

WRANGELL-ST ELIAS NATIONAL PARK & PRESERVE

With 13.2 million acres (5.3 million hectares) encompassing three entire mountain ranges and one partial, the largest US national park – the size of six Yellowstones – has endless possibilities for some of the biggest and most remote skiing terrain in the world. Among nine of the 16 highest peaks in the United States, this is an entire world of its own and requires local skiing and pilot knowledge to get you into the right zones for skiable lines. Some fix their gaze upon 16,421ft (5005m) Mt Bona with a summit reaching more than two vertical miles (3.2km) up from the glaciers below. Like every big peak in Alaska, conditions can be finicky depending on weather and crevasse openings, so consider a lower elevation option like the Granite Range, 60 miles (97km) to the south, with fewer tall peaks and more snowy couloirs. Look out for willow ptarmigan making appearances around camp.

Nearest town // McCarthy

CHUGACH MOUNTAINS

Terrain, snowpack and accessibility have made Valdez and Thompson Pass a mecca of Alaska heli-skiing, but if you don't want to spend $10,000 to sit in a lodge and watch it rain, plane camp options abound. Tok Air Service offers flights into legendary and well-known areas like The Tusk and The Books as well as to the remote and relatively unexplored Dora Keens. Pick from a full menu of mellow glacier runs, 'trainer spines' with lower consequence exposure and clean runouts, to big league peaks and long, steep couloirs. The advantage of a Chugach mission is being able to wait comfortably in Valdez until it's time to fly, with the added bonus of flying into a camp from which you can ski out and back into town, regardless of weather issues that might delay your pickup. This option lowers your flight costs even further with a one-way ticket.

Nearest town // Valdez

Clockwise from top: Alaska backcountry feels as big as it looks; sunshine and blue sky at base camp on the Pika Glacier; aerial view of a glacier in Wrangell-St Elias National Park

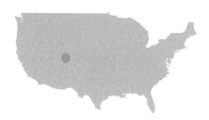

ICE CLIMB IN OURAY

The world's first ever 'ice-climbing park' was opened back in 1994. It remains the oldest and best place for newbies to learn – and for pros to train – on the planet.

'I have never, in all my life, seen someone fight the ice like you,' said my patient instructor, Jimmy Flynn. 'Don't fight the ice. Trust the ice.' Now, this was not the type of constructive criticism I needed, given that I was hanging from a straight wall of ice roughly 40ft (12m) from the ground, and 7780ft (2371m) above sea level. At least I wasn't alone. Up and down the mile length of Uncompahgre Gorge, a mix of climbers ranging from novices like me to world-class athletes were pressing their bodies up against the ice at the Ouray Ice Park. Located just outside Ouray – the San Juan Mountain town in southwestern Colorado, often called 'the Switzerland of America' – this was in fact the world's first man-made ice-climbing park.

Ice-climbing is essentially the act of ascending ice formations. Those formations can be natural features such as frozen waterfalls, or cliffs and rock slabs covered with ice that's been refrozen from flows of water. Climbers use rigid 'step-in' crampons, with 14 spikes on each, that kick and grip the ice. Specialised scaled-down ice axes that look like foot-long fish hooks are used as the arm leverage points. Ice screws are also embedded by the lead climbers to protect the climber in case of a fall, and also help in belay construction.

The Ouray Ice Park is remarkable. Here, the ice has been manufactured by a mostly volunteer team of 'ice farmers', who carefully groom its 150-plus climbing routes using excess town water fed through a system of 300 sprinklers and spouts. It's part engineering feat, part natural sculpture garden, and part extreme adventure wonderland.

'Relax and use your legs,' advised Jimmy. 'Most climbing is all about your legs, as they are much stronger than your arms. Try to keep moving in an easy motion, using your ice axes and arms as leverage points and not to physically pull you up.' Apart from looking like Freddy Krueger, I discovered your placements are uncertain compared with rock climbing, your feet are more slippery, and the surface is a whole lot more uneven. But the movement is simple. You simply kick, kick, stand up, swing – and repeat until you arrive at the top of the route. Or fall, trying.

A 30-minute hike from the entrance of the park to the bottom of the gorge led us to an area called the School Room. Here, Jimmy had demonstrated how to kick our crampons into the ice, then swiftly swing one ice axe at a time overhead. Our grip had to stay

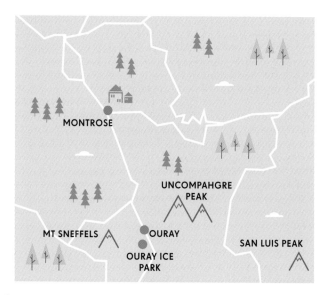

© Danita Delimont / Shutterstock

relaxed to avoid cutting off blood flow to the fingers. One of my fellow students and friend, Kirk, graciously offered to belaye me by staying on the ground to hold tension in my safety rope while I climbed. We both did a few climbs, enjoying the exertion, both physical and mental, as well as the exhilaration.

We then moved on to the beginner climbs in the park itself. You could see why Ouray has become the epicentre of ice-climbing in the States, and how the sport had saved the town. Founded in 1876, Ouray was sustained by gold and then silver mining for a century. When the metals ran out in the 1970s, the community relied on summer tourists, hikers and off-roaders to keep businesses afloat. However, in winter, with the closest ski resort of Telluride a good hour's drive away, it became a ghost town.

The Uncompahgre Gorge had a few natural climbs used by locals, but suddenly had more when leaks from a large pipe that delivered water to the hydroelectric plant in Ouray froze in the subzero gorge walls. The terrain, and the consistent source of ice, attracted interest from climbers further afield. Eric Jacobsen, the owner of Ouray Hydroelectric and the gorge, saw the potential and agreed to lease the land for recreational purposes to Ouray County for $1 a year. Not long after, in 1993, local climber Jeff Lowe organised the first Ouray Ice Festival to showcase the sport

> "To this day, the park
> is run by community volunteers
> and remains free to the public"

THE MILLION DOLLAR HIGHWAY

The 'Million Dollar Highway' is the name commonly used for the stretch of Highway 550 from Ouray to Silverton. The highway originated as the Otto Mears toll road that was built in 1883 to link Ouray with the Red Mountain Mining District. The name 'Million Dollar Highway' came from the high cost of construction of the road in the 1920s, given the tough terrain it cut through. It has also been labelled 'America's most beautiful drive'.

Clockwise from top: Colorado's ubiquitous aspen trees; getting a feel for ice axes and crampons at the Ouray Ice Park; ice-climbing claws are called crampons. Previous page: steeper ice raises the challenge

of ice-climbing. The next year, the Ouray Ice Park was formed. It provided formal organisation to what previously had been a loosely organised grassroots effort. To this day, the park is run by community volunteers and remains free to the public.

The effect on the town was transformative, as the carefully planned climbs allowed all levels of climbers to enjoy some of the most reliable ice-climbing in the world. The Ouray Ice Festival now attracts athletes and visitors from all over, every January. Shop windows carry the sign: 'Please remove crampons before entering.' The unofficial town slogan is, 'Have an ice day.'

After a first day climbing, we spent the early evening on Ouray's Main Street. It was packed with tourists marvelling at its preserved-film-set-like Queen Anne and Victorian buildings. Many have recently been converted into boutique properties, including the six-room Imogene Hotel. We also couldn't argue with The Ouray Brewery's claim that it had the finest rooftop dining in the Rockies. Though that could have been the locally brewed Box Canyon Brown beer talking.

On day two, halfway up the Pic O' Vic, a near-vertical 130ft (40m) ice wall, and my most challenging climb, I was thinking another afternoon with the beer may have been preferable. Yet, I knew I had to simply stop fighting the ice. I swung my ice axe overhead, remembering to initiate a sharp downward movement from my elbow and add a flick of the wrist to nail a secure hold. When it caught purchase with a lovely solid clang, I knew I was back in business.

Taking a deep breath, I swiftly kicked my right boot up and into the wall, followed by the left, sinking the razor-sharp blades of my crampons into the ice-like fangs. Suddenly, I had the feeling of gaining momentum; a leg, leg, axe, axe movement that had me eating up the ice, or at least ascending at a rate faster than my previous glacial pace. It was somehow both meditative and adrenaline-fuelled. Fifteen minutes later, I managed to make it to the top. Lacking a flag to plant at the summit, I settled for a well-earned breather and took in the sights of the beautiful San Juan Mountains. **BM**

DIRECTIONS

Best time to go // The Ouray Ice Park is open from mid-December through mid-March and the Ouray Ice Festival is held each January.

Gear required // There are guide and gear shops in the centre that will kit you out. Otherwise, you need warm ski-like clothing. Swimwear for the hot springs.

Nearest town // Ouray.

Getting there // It's a 1.5-hour drive from Montrose or Telluride Airports; a six-hour drive from Denver, Salt Lake City, Albuquerque or Colorado Springs.

Where to stay // Box Canyon Lodge provides great log cabin accommodation and use of its hot springs. Imogene Hotel is a boutique hotel in the centre of town.

Things to know // The century-long mining history of the town is preserved at the Bachelor Syracuse Mine. Take a tour and go into Gold Mountain, then pan for real gold yourself. A traditional miner's breakfast is served on site.

*Opposite: the man-made ice tower
at Champagny, France*

MORE LIKE THIS
OUTDOOR ICE-CLIMBING GYMS

CANMORE, BRITISH COLUMBIA

The Canadian Rockies have some of the best ice-climbing in the world, with the epicentre in the valleys surrounding Banff, Canmore and Lake Louise. Most involve waterfall ice-climbing, one of the most exhilarating of the ice-climbing disciplines. The natural waterfalls reliably freeze for much of the winter, offering long and challenging multi-pitch routes for experts and fantastic crags and climbing areas for beginners. Most climbs are easily accessible and beginners should head to places like Junkyards and Grotto Falls, King Creek, Johnston's Canyon and Haffner Creek. The crown jewel of the area is Ghost River, which is about 37 miles (60km) from Canmore. And the drive is spectacular.
Nearest town // Canmore

CHAMPAGNY LE HAUT, FRANCE

A wood and steel structure sits in the valley of Champagny le Haut at an elevation of 4760ft (1450m) near the French Alps resort of La Plagne. The 72ft (22m) tower is sprayed with water which turns to ice in the valley's polar temperatures. Legendary French ice-climber Damien Souvy designed the tower to make the discipline accessible to beginners through to elite climbers. There are on-site guides helping you to improve and climb higher. The tower's design means you can make progress quite safely, with a gradual incline. Once at the top, the views of the stunning Vanois National Park add even more frisson to the occasion.
Nearest town // Turin, Italy

SANDSTONE ICE PARK, MINNESOTA

This man-made ice park uses a system of water pipes, pex tubes, misting nozzles and low-flow showerheads to create ice flows on the quarried sandstone walls in Robinson Park. It even has lights to let you climb at night and, like at Ouray, the Sandstone Ice Festival is held every year in January. There is one big low-angle area known as Land of the Lorax, which is quite a good place to start for newcomers. The Stage Wall, the highest wall in the park, has much longer and more challenging routes up vertical ice. The ice-farming is done by dedicated volunteers and has climbable ice from late December to early March. The Ice Park is free and open to the public.
Nearest town // Minneapolis

EAST COAST CLASSIC

Vermont's Jay Peak is hard to get to, a little obscure, and subject to brutal Canada-USA border weather. But it also has soul, and defines skiing on the East Coast.

I cried when I left Montana for Vermont. I'd just spent four winters dragging out grad school in Missoula so I could ski the Northern Rockies where the sport was still wild, grimy and working class – the way I like it. The thought of fighting for fresh snow in between extended bouts of hardpack with my fellow native New Englanders again was soul crushing. Jay Peak cured me of my bias.

'Jay' is Vermont's northernmost ski area. For the first four decades after it opened in 1956 it was more well-known with French Canadians than the skiing masses from southern New England and New York. It was both international and a local's hill. Jay has a second parking lot and base area called 'Stateside', where the skiers from Burlington, the surrounding 'Northeast Kingdom', and northern New Hampshire would boot up. And those core locals were pretty much the extent of the US crowd. To get to Jay, an urban and suburban skier would have to drive past a bevy of bigger and more famous resorts like Killington, Sugarbush and Stowe. It just didn't happen all that much.

But then the larger sport of skiing changed, which set Jay up for its present-day status as perhaps the most relevant ski area in the east. The change was for the worse. In the 1980s, liability lawyers cast a chill on ski area operators. Anyone over 45 probably remembers when every jump on the hill was roped off. Ski patrol would also pull your pass for the crime of skiing fast – no matter how skilled you were. During these dark days, the east also nearly lost tree-skiing. Some resorts went so far as to permanently rope the woods off. The sport of skiing, which was rooted in escapism from the confines of the industrial revolution, was industrialised. Not just with lifts and time-share condos and hamburgers, but with antithetical restrictions bent on taking the free out of freeskiing.

And then there was Jay Peak, isolated in the borderlands and often veiled by storm clouds dumping more snow than any other New England ski area. In the late 1990s, aged 31, I showed up to manage the mountain's retail operations until I could figure out magazine writing. I arrived from 'do what you want' Montana, not knowing anything about this liberal renaissance. Driving in for my interview I passed through half a dozen Vermont hamlets that ranged from rural depression – the freshly gutted hog hanging from a maple in the front yard, a toddler's toys splattered in pig-blood – to pastoral quaint, the idyllic postcard stuff people think about when they envision the 'green mountain state'.

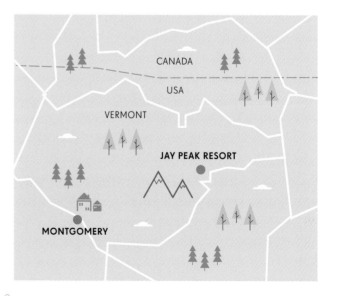

JAY CLOUD

Jay boasts 360in to 400in (914cm to 1016cm) of snowfall a season, which dwarfs a lot of western snowfalls. The mountain is shrouded so often that a legend called the Jay Cloud has proliferated. It's not wrong. Jay stands above this part of the world and it catches storms out of Canada before the rest of New England's ski areas. This combination of orographic lift and geography sets up strong storm cycles.

At the time, Jay was owned by a Canadian who simply wasn't going to let the lawyers run the place. This was glaringly obvious to a serious skier. Jay offered legit alpine terrain that's still among the steepest in the region. It continued to run a citizen's downhill race right through the height of the litigation era and beyond.

But what really set Jay apart, and still does today, is its tree-skiing. Glading – thinning the forest to allow for skiable alleyways in the forest – is part of the Jay tradition. Not that tree-skiing was for the masses back then. It was only members of the tree-skiing cult who would take it upon themselves to clear the underbrush in the off-season.

But then skiing changed again and a newfound sense of adventure pushed back on the lawyers. By the late 1990s, wider skis – which allowed for more floatation in powder – were reinvigorating a sport that had lived in snowboarding's shadow, at least as far as the national media was concerned. (It's apropos of this story that the new skis were inspired by snowboards – a Vermont invention.) The skis changed everything. Floating in powder in the trees was previously only for those with tendons like cables. Now, anybody could do it. And by the late 1990s they did.

New England skiers flocked to Jay for its steeper and deeper terrain and snowpack. And when the powder was cut up on the designated runs, the new skiers naturally took to the trees like the locals did. (Helmet use also became widespread at this time.) Recognising they had a good thing going, Jay's management decided to embrace the trend. Glading accelerated. The ski school started to promote tree-skiing lessons – which would have been completely unheard of previously. And the mountain even tacitly endorsed the glading of a backcountry zone that allowed skiers to descend off-area to a pass on the highway and then catch a ride back to the hill.

Pulling into the base area back in the late 1990s, I assumed the tram – a lift typically found at marquee resorts like Jackson, Snowbird and Palisades – was a monument to wishful thinking. From the base, Jay isn't particularly impressive. Still, Jay was the closest ski hill to my wife's teaching job, so I took the work, crestfallen though I was. And then it dumped. And it kept on dumping. Not wet snow followed by rain like you get in southern New England, but blower, cold smoke, aerosolised anthrax – powder so light it spilled over the shoulders on big days.

That first Jay powder day was one of the best days of skiing of my life, and I'm writing this 25 years later, after having skied in Europe, Iceland, Chile, Alaska and all over British Columbia. We were plummeting our way through perfectly spaced trees with

"That first Jay powder day was one of the best days of skiing of my life"

From left: Jay Peak has a middle-of-nowhere feel; snow-covered spruce trees after a storm; fresh tracks from top to bottom. Previous page: Jay Peak is tree-skiing at its best

powder billowing at our hips. Jay's glades were cut by skiers and snowboarders with an emphasis on flow, so you never had to shut it down and begin again.

Now, I'm not saying Jay Peak is Valhalla – although there is a gladed run there of the same name. Nightlife is limited. It's cold and remote. I once started my wife's car at 43 below zero (no wind chill) and exploded the plastic housing around the shifter when I went to idle down the screaming engine. I watched as wind blew a chunk of ice as big as a lunch tray and five inches thick off the roof of the shop and hit a guy in the helmet – another upside to head protection. And like all of New England, then and now, Jay wasn't immune to rain on snow events. But jaded as I was from the west, I had a great winter.

When the snow was good, I'd ski in the woods. When powder was scarce, I'd poke around the lift-served backcountry. When conditions went to hardpack, I'd ski fast on the downhill boards. I ate poutine, the French-Canadian staple of French fries in an insulating coat of cheese. And no matter how much of the world I skied or powder I chased as an editor and writer in the decades that followed, I never forgot how vital, culturally rich and routinely excellent East Coast skiing can be. And I've never forgotten. I have a Ski the East sticker on my ski tuning bench right now. **MP**

DIRECTIONS

Best time to go // Winter is changing everywhere, which makes it hard to predict great conditions. Watch the weather for persistent cold temperatures and forecasts of an Alberta Clipper weather pattern in January and February.

Gear required // Skis between 95mm and 105mm at the waist or a loose and surfy powder snowboard. Bring a swimsuit for Jay's indoor waterpark.

Nearest town // Montgomery is a Vermont mountain town with deep snow banks and a ton of charm.

Getting there // From Burlington, make your way to Route 242 north. If you cross into Canada, you went too far.

Where to stay // For the best experience, stay at a B&B or VRBO in Montgomery. But if you have kids, the resort is the call. The waterpark and ice-skating will keep them moving.

Things to know // Hardwoods are hard. You need to be able to make quick turns on ungroomed snow to stay safe. Unsure? Take an intro to tree-skiing lesson with the school.

Opposite, from top: Stowe Mountain
Resort is easier to get to from East
Coast metro areas; Sugarbush Ski
Area, Vermont, is another delightfully
rough-around-the-edges icon

MORE LIKE THIS
EAST COAST CLASSICS

STOWE, VERMONT

Yeah, yeah, Stowe is owned by the biggest resort operator in the world and you will certainly fight weekend and holiday crowds, all using the 'Epic Season Pass', but Stowe is still one of the best ski areas in New England and its terrain is hard to match. As with Jay, off-trail and off-area skiing never really died here – it abuts the Mt Mansfield backcountry complete with frozen waterfall drops and naturally gladed terrain. But if you go to Stowe, you need to ski the cut trails too. The best ones – the Front Four iconic black runs of National, Goat, Starr and Liftline – are bucket-list shots that are emblematic of how runs were cut before ski area industrialisation's dull boulevards. They twist and turn and rise and fall like well-cut mountain bike trails.

Nearest town // Stowe

SUGARBUSH, VERMONT

I'm not saying Sugarbush took its cues from Jay Peak, but today Sugarbush is Jay's biggest competitor when it comes to rowdy off-trail skiing. It advertises 'nearly 30' skiable wooded areas (what we call glades), but Sugarbush's marquee zone is the 2000-acre (809-hectare) Slide Brook Basin, which once was off limits and too thick to ski. It's technically labelled 'off-area' or backcountry, but you can sign up with a ski school for a tour. If you go solo, you need to know that the area isn't patrolled, and when you get to the bottom, you'll need to catch a local bus back to the base area.

Nearest town // Waitsfield or Warren

KILLINGTON, VERMONT

It's derided as 'K-Mart' by weirdly territorial New England skiers, but it doesn't make sense to avoid some of the best skiing in New England just because Killington is huge. This is where I learned to love tree-skiing, not for the whoop-de-do trails of my childhood skiing in New Hampshire, but for untracked snow in tight forests. In high school, a buddy and I got an informal lesson in bushwhacking from some thickset older guys with torn jackets. We were ducking ropes way up on Killington Peak back then. Today there are glades all over 'The Beast's' 1500 skiable acres (607 hectares), including open double-black-diamond-rated fare. Killington Peak's upper reaches feature double-black glades – home to some of The Beast's most-coveted powder stashes. From the K-1 Lodge, there's easy access to freshies in the Big Dipper, Anarchy and Julio glades.

Nearest town // Woodstock or Rutland

YELLOWSTONE IN WINTER

America's National Parks are impressive natural wonders – some are even more impressive after the crowds have gone and they become blanketed with snow.

A few years ago, my father died of melanoma, the day after Thanksgiving. In the following months I needed space to grieve my loss. I longed to go somewhere big and solitary – a landscape that wasn't intimately associated with my father, yet one he would have gravitated towards. Of Swedish descent, Dad grew up in northern Minnesota and was a winter guy. Skis were his favourite mode of transport and recreation.

One place that felt large enough to absorb his absence was Yellowstone National Park. Of all the lower 48 parks in the United States, 3472 sq mile (8992 sq km) Yellowstone feels the most ruggedly expansive in an iconic Wild West kind of way. It's a diverse ecosystem of peaks that rise as high as 11,350ft (3460m) and canyons that drop 1200ft (366m) straight into the Yellowstone River. Surrounding the rivers are wide valleys where elk and bison roam. There are also more than 600 lakes and ponds, the largest being 136 sq mile (352 sq km) Lake Yellowstone, which is overshadowed by Old Faithful, the iconic geyser that gives visitors a clue to the supervolcano below that last erupted 640,000 years ago. Within this vast expanse live more than 200 species of animals, from apex predators like grizzly bear to calliope hummingbirds, the smallest bird native to the United States.

Dad and I never had the opportunity to see Yellowstone together, but I had visited the park on a solo road trip the previous summer, marvelling at hulking bison, hiking 10,219ft (3115m) Mt Washburn, and waiting, along with a few thousand others, for Old Faithful to blow. I had merely ticked the highlights, which made the urge to experience this singular place in winter even stronger.

Between 15 December and 15 March, the park is open, but most of its roads are closed. In January, Yellowstone receives less than one tenth of the million-plus visitors it has in an average July or August. That's because the park averages 150in (381cm) of snowfall per year and visitors have only three ways to see it. The first is to travel the only road accessible by private wheeled vehicles. Although it's beautiful, I had driven this route before and didn't want to be limited to seeing the park through my car window. Option two is to sign on with a guided snowmobile or snow coach tour, both of which traverse the same 185 miles (298km) of groomed park roads that are also open to skiers and fat-tyre cyclists. The park is perennially rated one of the best places in the world for snowmobilers, but, still, I preferred to see

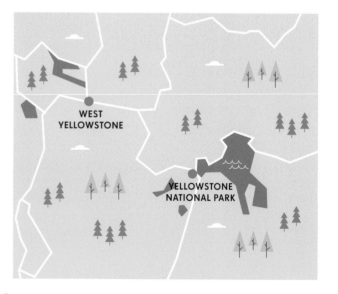

WEST YELLOWSTONE

YELLOWSTONE NATIONAL PARK

the beauty self-propelled and in silence. The final – and, to me – most appealing option is to venture out on skis or snowshoes on the miles of tracked and untracked trails in the park.

Unable to secure a last-minute lodging reservation within the park, my partner Brian and I were staying at Lone Mountain Ranch, a historic property established in 1915 outside the northwestern park boundary. I'm a lifelong Nordic and alpine skier, but I am not comfortable with my avalanche skills and neither is Brian. For safety reasons, we hired a backcountry guide, Martha Crocker, through the ranch, who was willing to take us to one of her favourite low-angle trails in Yellowstone, Specimen Creek. In the northwest corner of Yellowstone and easily accessible off Highway 191, the Specimen Creek trail is eight miles (13km) long (one-way) in the winter and follows a beautiful meandering little river surrounded by dense forest ridges on either side.

The snow was deep, but the tracks were nicely skied in. Deep white snow drifts were backed by a brilliant blue sky. Enormous pines lined our well-tracked riverside trail as we glided slowly along, uphill for a few hours, until the trail opened into a portion of forest that was badly burned in a recent fire. The charred yet still standing lodgepole pines were a stark and surreal reminder of the brutality of a forest fire, but the denuded trees offered views to the mountains beyond that wouldn't have otherwise been possible. That's when the immensity of the park, and the abundance of life living within it, hit me.

Yellowstone contains several species at the top of the food chain that are active in winter, like wolf, cougar, coyote and even bear, all of which hunt large game like elk and bison. The evidence of their existence is everywhere, like the pine we glided past that was marked by the claw of a grizzly bear. Lower, back down by the creek, the snowbanks were imprinted with fresh otter tracks that the wily mammals recently used as slides to plunge into the water.

This solitary day-long meander through the park only piqued my desire to see more of it – especially icons like Old Faithful – without being surrounded by thousands of other humans. Unable to ski the 60 miles (97km) round trip from West Yellowstone to Old Faithful in one day, Brian and I signed up for another day tour, this time in a Bombardier aircraft. Built between the 1930s and 1960s, these Canadian 'bombs' have a retro chic appeal, with skis on the front and a rubber track system in the back, and robust engines strong enough to navigate snowy terrain without sinking. They are like a slow-motion snowmobile for up to 10 people – albeit much warmer because everyone sits in an enclosed space around a u-shaped, wrap-around seat surrounded by windows. The coolest part: the roof can open to the sky, like a safari jeep, which is ideal for watching big wildlife.

We joined a party of seven other guests from all over the country. In the Bomb, on our way to Old Faithful, we passed snow-covered bison along the Firehole River, stopping multiple times in our tracks for safe photo opps (always staying at least 100 yards away, the park's mandatory distance requirement). The big

WINTER WILDLIFE

Winter is the easiest time of year to spot wolves, who are generally more sluggish and elusive during the warm, crowded summer months. Their thick black or grey fur is easy to spot against the snow in a wide valley, especially if a pack – the average size of which in Yellowstone is 11.8 animals – has gathered to feed around a bison or elk kill.

From top: about 500 grey wolves live in and around Yellowstone; a low-angle landscape makes for great cross-country ski tours. Previous page: bisons – the beautiful beasts of Yellowstone National Park

"The immensity of the park, and the abundance of life living within it, hit me"

beasts didn't move much, but they were magnificent, with necks so powerful that they have the mechanical strength of a snowplough.

When we arrived at Old Faithful, Brian and I retrieved our backcountry skis from the rack on the back of the bomb. With limited daylight and a precise return time to West Yellowstone, our goal was to ski the short and easy four-mile round-trip route on the Black Sand Basin Ski Trail to Daisy Geyser. But first, we threaded our way over the snow- and ice-covered boardwalk to get a front-row seat to the park's world-famous show, a luxury that would have been impossible in summer. Erupting between 17 and 20 times per day, Old Faithful goes off roughly once every 72 to 84 minutes.

Luckily, we hit the timing right: within minutes, water and steam shot up through the gunmetal-grey winter sky like a rocket launching into space. I watched silently and in awe, understanding that some forces – namely the sun that killed my dad and the supervolcano that lives under Yellowstone National Park – are far too powerful to comprehend. **SP**

DIRECTIONS

Best time to go // 15 December to 15 March
Gear required // Freeheel and Wheel bike and ski shop
near West Yellowstone park entrance rents skate, classic
and backcountry skis and snowshoes.
Nearest town // West Yellowstone is the wintertime hub for
skiers, snowshoers and fat-tyre cyclists.
Getting there // Bozeman Yellowstone International Airport
is 90 miles (145km) north of West Yellowstone. Shuttles and
taxis run from the airport year-round, and car rentals are
also available at the airport.
Where to stay // There is currently only one winter lodging
option in the park, Old Faithful Snow Lodge & Cabins. Fifty-
two miles (84km) north of the park is Lone Mountain Ranch,
a luxurious property with private modern cabins.
Things to know // There is actually a greater wildlife density
in Yellowstone in winter, upping your chances of seeing
animals such as wolves.

MORE LIKE THIS
NATIONAL PARKS
THAT BLOOM IN WINTER

BANFF NATIONAL PARK, BRITISH COLUMBIA

Canada's first national park is a postcard-perfect landscape of razor-sharp snowcapped peaks in the Canadian Rockies, established in 1885, two years after three Canadian Pacific Railway workers stumbled upon a series of hot springs on the flank of 8041ft (2450m) Sulphur Mountain. To accommodate visitors in this wild new western park, Canadian Pacific Railway built the magnificent Banff Springs Hotel on the outskirts of town of Banff, overlooking 9672ft (2948m) Mt Rundle. Thirty-eight miles (62km) away on a beautiful alpine lake, they built Lake Louise chalet. These two glamorous hotels have been book-ending winter adventures like backcountry skiing, dogsledding and ice-skating on Lake Louise ever since. Unlike in Yellowstone National Park, the hot springs are temperate enough for humans: the mineral-rich water at Banff Upper Hot Springs, nestled high on the slopes of Sulphur Mountain, is a soothing 47°C (116°F) in winter.

Nearest town // Alberta

ACADIA NATIONAL PARK, MAINE

Only 65 sq miles (168 sq km), Acadia is so beloved that it has more than four million annual visitors, most of whom arrive in the summer. One of the park's many charms is its 45-mile-long (72km) network of carriage roads funded by philanthropist John D Rockefeller, Jr, which were built between 1913 and 1940. Designed to be motor-free byways that horse and carriages could use to enjoy the park, the paths are beautifully constructed, with stone-faced bridges, granite coping stones used as guardrails, and beautiful views of the rolling peaks and the Atlantic Ocean beyond. In the winter, 32 miles (51km) of the carriage roads are groomed, making them a perfect venue for skiers and snowshoers. Depending on the snowpack, experienced snowshoers and winter hikers can explore the park's numerous hiking trails. Birders will thrill at the harlequin ducks and snowy owls that winter over Acadia.

Nearest town // Bar Harbor

ROCKY MOUNTAIN NATIONAL PARK, COLORADO

With 77 peaks over 12,000ft (3600m) in the heart of Colorado's Rocky Mountains, this 415 sq mile (1074 sq km) national park is a realm of powder snow and big pines under brilliant blue skies. It can also be a dangerous morass of winter storms, a place where the snowpack, avalanche risk, and trail and road conditions are constantly changing, so come prepared. Hidden Valley, a former ski area 7 miles (11km) from the Beaver Meadows and Fall River Entrances on the east side of the park, is a good spot to start with winter exploration. With ski runs no longer serviced by lifts or tows, the old resort offers excellent sledding and relatively safe places to practice backcountry skills. Experienced backcountry skiers with avalanche training have a few dozen ways to get deeper into the park. Those without would be wise to stay on low-angle slopes or hire a guide.

Nearest town // Boulder

Clockwise from top: Gorham Mountain in Acadia National Park; a soak at Banff Upper Hot Springs; early spring hiking in Rocky Mountain National Park

BODE MILLER ON CANNON MOUNTAIN

The most successful male ski racer in North American history is a contrarian with an independent streak a mile wide. Cannon Mountain in New Hampshire is a big reason why.

The first time I ever skied with lifts was at Cannon. Because I was homeschooled until third grade, I skied an enormous amount. From kindergarten through second grade, I skied every single day of the season. Eventually, I had these enormous wads of Cannon Mountain lift tickets on my parka. At first, my grandmother would drive me up in the mornings. When she wasn't able to drive me any more, I started walking – I got to the hill at two in the afternoon. Then, I started hitchhiking to the mountain – as a five year old. I knew everyone in that little town and they knew me. At the end of the day, I'd get dropped off at 7pm and my grandmother would ask, 'How was your day?' I didn't know it at the time, but I was developing a completely unique level of risk assessment and independence. Those traits would later guide me through my race career.

My roots are deep here. My grandfather, who served in the Pacific Fleet in World War II, and my grandmother, who was a Lake Tahoe skier, decided to start a ski lodge in remote northern New Hampshire. They named the lodge Tamarack and opened it in 1956. They had perhaps two or three customers all winter. They knew they had to do something else to make it work, so my grandfather ended up building 11 clay tennis courts. He also built rope tows on the property in winter. The ski lodge continued to be unsuccessful, but the tennis courts proved to be more popular. They turned Tamarack into a tennis camp in 1960. And my mother and father met at Tamarack.

Everyone who has any background and family history in northern New Hampshire is a skier or has skiers in the family. My uncles were ski racers who were successful on the US pro tour. So, when my mom and dad split up when I was six, I lived in the lodge and

homeschooled and, really, I just kept skiing. I didn't require a whole lot from the family. I took care of myself on the mountain. When my uncle Peter 'Bubba' Kenney died though, the family decided there wasn't enough supervision and I was put into school.

Suddenly, I was confronted with the reality that I couldn't ski every day. And then as I made my way through grade school, money got tight and the ski passes that my grandmother had bought for me were out of reach. I'd been entering ski races at that time, but I didn't really care about winning or losing. I just tried to do the best I could. But this time the prize was a season pass. For the first time in my life I tried to win.

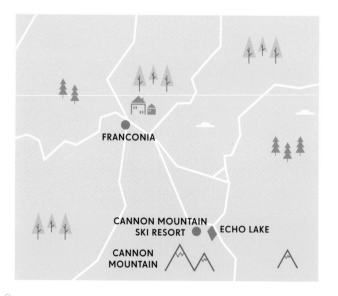

*"The beauty of small but vital ski areas like
Cannon is that they offer kids freedom, but
also the ability to ski a lot of laps"*

I'd skied hundreds of days at Cannon, self-correcting the entire time. I knew how to crash. I won that race three years in a row from grades four to six against much older and bigger skiers. I won my season pass, which was hugely important to me. It was then that I realised ski-racing could get me things I needed without having to do manual labour on the tennis courts – although I did plenty of that too.

The beauty of small but vital ski areas like Cannon is that they offer kids freedom, but also the ability to ski a lot of laps. And repetition is one of the most important elements of ski racing. It's why downhill is so challenging: you can't ski a downhill course every day. But for all other aspects of racing, an intimate mountain like Cannon is all you need. New Hampshire can be as cold and as inhospitable as any place in the USA. Cannon was gnarly. Back then it was always icy. They didn't groom much. You had to learn to tune your skis.

There was a coin-operated NASTAR course on Cannon. I would pay a dollar and then the guys in the shack – race kids from the college, typically – would let me run it all day. I would ski that course over and over. I had it in my mind that if I could make the perfect turn I could eventually turn a series of perfect turns into

the perfect run. That goal is what drove me my entire Olympic and World Cup career.

At seven or eight years old I did my first USSA (United States Ski and Snowboard Association) races. By eighth grade I was the fastest kid in New Hampshire. But even so I had coaches who refused to admit that my self-styled training programme was working. I had to overcome that resistance. It wouldn't be for the only time. I'd outgrown the Cannon race programme, so my mother called a friend and got me into a race academy at Sugarloaf in Maine called Carrabassett Valley Academy. I was a freshman. But we couldn't afford the tuition. So I lived 26 miles (42km) away in a cabin with another family. Each morning I would do chores and then snowmobile eight miles (13km) to the road before hitchhiking 18 miles (29km) to school. Again, this did not seem foreign to me.

Eastern ski areas like Cannon and Sugarloaf grow great skiers. These mountains matter. They're also a ton of fun. When we weren't training, we were freeskiing. And when you're freeskiing you're thinking tactically. Cannon predates modern trail design. The trails meander, but with purpose, as if the builders were thinking about where they would make their next turn. At 2180ft (664m), Cannon has the biggest vertical drop in New Hampshire,

WELCOME TO
CANNON
JUST AHEAD

SKI VETERANS

Because it's state run and adjacent to big swathes of dramatic public lands, Cannon gives off more outdoor-adventure vibes than a posh luxury resort. It feels like you're skiing in a national park, and the living history is only bolstered by the retirees that ski 100-plus days a year and know their skiing history. Chat them up on the aerial tram.

From left: Cannon Mountain is a family ski area with an edge; surrounded by small towns it has a community feel. Previous page: Bode Miller competes at Whistler Creekside during the Vancouver 2010 Winter Olympics

DIRECTIONS

Best time to go // March is the call. As winter ends you'll either get a late storm, or warm weather and an early corn cycle. To do Cannon right, bring a grill and a cooler full of Boston Lagers for après tailgating.

Gear required // If you're skiing Bode's home hill, you should ski on Bode's skis. The Peak 88 is capable of transitioning from carved turns on the groomed snow to off-piste skiing on Tucker Brooke – a backcountry line that leaves from the Mittersill side of Cannon and requires a car shuttle.

Nearest town // Franconia is a New Hampshire outdoor town with a strong community of outdoor athletes.

Getting there // From Boston, drive north on I-93 until you enter the Notch. When you pass Echo Lake you're there.

Where to stay // To get a feel for New Hampshire's living ski history, stay at a B&B or VRBO in Franconia.

Things to know // If you aren't super confident about holding an edge on true hardpack, back off the gas a little.

but that's nothing compared to European skiing. It doesn't matter. Skiing is about more than vertical feet. Later, when I was in the World Cup, we kept freeskiing. The generation just after mine – Ted Ligety and Travis Ganong – were into it even more than mine.

At the end of my race career, my wife (Morgan Miller) and I settled in Southern California. Suffice to say that Southern California is a bit different from where I grew up. I recognised that times had changed and I couldn't offer my children the same childhood I'd had. I also didn't want that for them. But I did want them to experience more freedom and self-reliance. By being in nature and managing themselves, children learn things that can't be taught. So, we resettled in Spanish Peaks, Montana, on Big Sky resort in 2020. All the kids have taken to the place. They aren't quite yet at the age where they can walk out the door on their own, but that day is coming.

I look at skiing and life holistically. The question is always how do you have fun and stay safe? That applies whether you're travelling through Europe or Canada, or making your way to your local ski area in New Hampshire. It's what I've been doing since I was a five-year-old figuring out how to stay warm on the mountain and get back before dinner. **MP**

Opposite, from top: Boyne Mountain in Michigan is small but mighty; Bridger Bowl near Bozeman, Montana has a local vibe and epic terrain

MORE LIKE THIS
OLD-SCHOOL INDIE SKI AREAS

BRIDGER BOWL, MONTANA

If there's another template for the local's ski area turned incubator, it has to be Bridger Bowl, which sits just 16 miles (26km) from Bozeman, Montana. The mountain is locally owned and run as a not-for-profit. To ensure that it never goes into debt, it buys new chairlifts and snowmaking guns with saved cash. The savings allow for egalitarianism. If you're a Bozeman kid, you'll get to ski there. If you're a student at Michigan State University (MSU), you'll probably buy a Bridger season pass as opposed to the pricier Big Sky. Add in some of the steepest lift-serviced skiing in the Northern Rockies and a self-reliant ethos, and naturally a skiing culture followed. For the past 40 years, Bridger has been spitting out top-level athletes across disciplines, but it's steep skiing that the place is famous for. The extreme terrain off The Ridge churned out skiing legends like Tom Jungst, Scot Schmidt and Doug Coombs, and ski mountaineers like Conrad Anker and Kristoffer Erickson.

Nearest town // Bozeman

SUGAR BOWL, CALIFORNIA

Sugar Bowl is one of California's last independently owned skis areas – and it shows. Where else could a skier like the Olympian and Hahnenkamm winner Daron Rahlves start a race series that's part mass-start skier cross and part big mountain freeskiing competition? It's called the Silver Belt Banzai, and it descends pretty much all of Sugar Bowl's 1500 vertical miles (2414km). The high speed, damn-the-torpedoes mindset dominates at Sugar Bowl – which consistently churns out top-level skiers from the race academy based here – and the terrain, which is rollicking and sustained and covered in 500in (1270cm) of snow each winter. It's untamed skiing, even though Sugar Bowl was the first ski area in California with a chairlift. If you want to get a feel for Tahoe skiing away from the mega resorts and bro-brah attitude, make your way to Rahlves' adopted home hill.

Nearest town // Norden

BOYNE MOUNTAIN, MICHIGAN

Midwest skiing is often ridiculed because of a lack of vertical. But ski areas like Boyne Mountain in Michigan and Buck Hill in Minnesota punch way above their weight classes when it comes to developing top skiers. There are a few reasons for this. You simply don't need massive vertical to improve as a skier. All you really need is time on the hill. And because the Midwest is an easy flight and a manageable drive from the Rockies, local skiers hone their skills at Boyne and then head out West on vacation to tear it up. So would you book a destination visit to a ski area like Boyne Mountain, with its 500 vertical feet (152m) and 415 skiable acres (168 hectares)? Probably not, but if you're driving through that part of the country you should bring your skis and burn 30 laps. Or raise a family of skiers. Boyne may be challenged on vertical, but it oozes passion.

Nearest town // Boyne Falls

SKATE-SKIING SOLITUDE

The Boundary Waters Canoe Area Wilderness on the US-Canada border is full of vast lakes that, when conditions are just right, provide the perfect skate-skiing flight path.

Skiing on a lake – especially skate-skiing, that awkward-looking v-formation technique brought to the world's attention by Bill Koch in 1982, when he skate-skied his way to the World Cup Nordic title – is rare. Lakes can be windswept and full of dangerous hazards like open water or pressure ridges, where two plates of ice meet and create a treacherous peak that's often hard to see in flat light. But, here in the *Great Lakes*, once in a great while there comes a short window when the ice has frozen so smoothly and the snow has fallen just right – enough to cover the lake, but not so much that it makes it too deep to traverse – that the conditions are perfect for a skate-skiing adventure and an exhilarating rush akin to human flight.

For more than 20 years, my parents lived year-round in a cabin on an island in the middle of Lake Vermilion, a rugged, meandering 62 sq mile (161 sq km) body of water in northern Minnesota lined with white pine that impossibly grew out of behemoth slabs of granite. To the north and east, Vermilion borders the iconic Boundary Water Canoe Area Wilderness (BWCAW), a million-acre playground of interconnected lakes and rivers. In the summertime it is traversed by a quarter-million canoeists and kayakers.

Come winter, this region bordering Canada becomes nearly empty of people, namely because it's very, very cold. On 2 February, 1996, my father's cousin, Kathleen Hoppa, once an official National Weather Service observer, recorded the state record-low temperature of -51°C (-60°F) in the nearby town of Tower. That kind of cold can flash-freeze your eyeballs.

But, as many people who live in northern climates understand, winter is the most sublime season of all. The air feels sharp and pure, the landscape is a mind-clearing monochromatic blanket

of white, and life is so solitary that even the faintest movement in the far distance – like a human cross-country skiing or a lone wolf skulking across the ice – can easily be detected (it's likely more common to see a lone wolf cross Lake Vermilion than a lone skate-skier – it's not for lack of skiers).

Minnesota is known for producing Nordic champions, including Olympic gold medallist Jessie Diggins, who grew up skiing the hundreds of kilometres of beautifully groomed, wooded trails. These trails wind through sheltering pine and birch forests, so there's no need to brave the fierce and frigid wind and variable ice and snow conditions that can make lake-skiing dangerous.

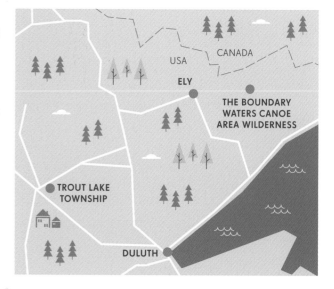

*"The air feels sharp and pure,
the landscape is a mind-clearing
monochromatic blanket"*

One year, however, perfect lake-skiing conditions – thick ice with a consistent layer of well-packed snow topped by 3in (8cm) of lighter, new-fallen snow, very little wind, and air temperatures below 0°C – coincided with my family's Christmas celebration at my parents' cabin. Eyeing this opportunity, my sister, a competitive Nordic ski racer at the time, decided it was time for us to ski into the Boundary Waters, a round-trip one-day expedition of at least 20 miles (32km) that would take us across three massive bays, over a quarter-mile-long wooded portage, and finally into 7600-acre (3076 hectare) Trout Lake, one of the nearly 100 entry points to the 2000 lakes, ranging in size from 10 to 10,000 acres, that comprise the Boundary Waters. To see this wild, beautiful country in the silence of winter would be to enter an alternate universe.

Many people ski the Boundary Waters in the winter. But most are camping, which means they are pulling a sled and using backcountry skis that have metal edges and fish scales (grooves in the bottom of the ski that act like skins). These are heavy, stable skis that are meant to go slow and plough through all kinds of conditions like banks of drifting snow and pressure ridges. We, on the other hand, would be using our lightweight

skate-skis that are designed to go fast on a freshly groomed track of meticulous corduroy. Hence, they have no traction on the bottom. Learning how to skate-ski requires patience and practice. But when the technique is executed correctly, which often takes years to accomplish, it feels like your body is moving together in perfect synchronicity.

In warmer months, my sister and I had paddled our canoe from the cabin and into the Boundary Waters almost a dozen times. But this one-day winter expedition would be a first. Our party also included Ellie, my 12-year-old niece and a committed high school ski racer who wanted to log some training miles. We started out mid-morning, two days after Christmas. It was an overcast day hovering around a surprisingly high 20 degrees. The expected daytime high temperature was 3°C (37°F) – too warm, we worried, because the snow would begin to melt. But we took our chances and set out, following the shoreline closely to avoid harrowing narrows where currents might be strong, and ice might be thin.

There was barely a puff of wind, which made the final wide-open crossing of Lake Vermilion and onto the Trout Lake portage, a carefree, consistent, joyful glide.

OPEN SPACE

It is estimated
that only 3 percent
of the Boundary
Waters Canoe
Area Wilderness'
250,000 annual
visitors go in winter.
That's 7,500 visitors
in one million acres
of wilderness.
It also means
that multi-day
adventures require
a deep knowledge
of serious winter
camping and
survival skills.

*From left: winter in the Boundary
Waters Canoe Area of northern
Minnesota; the BWCA is comprised
of a million acres. Previous page:
walking on water in the wilderness
around Ely, Minnesota*

DIRECTIONS

The quarter-mile-long portage into Trout Lake, which sits higher than Lake Vermilion, parallels a stream with a frozen waterfall. With skate-skis, it was impossible to climb, so we took them off and slipped and slid in our stiff skate boots through shin-deep snow until we finally reached the other side: the promised land of Trout Lake and the entry point to the Boundary Waters.

We hit the ice and glided across the silent wilderness, admiring the pillows of snow that had fallen on the white pines. The only other sign of life on the lake was a solitary set of wolf tracks. Already 10 miles (16km) into our journey, we stopped to fuel up on real food: holiday cheese and crackers, nuts and Christmas cookies eaten in meditative silence. From south to north, Trout Lake is nearly 10 miles (16km) long, with seemingly endless bays to explore. With the snow fast and light, we skied deeper into the wilderness, racing the daylight to reach the end of the lake. But it was only six days after the winter solstice and darkness arrives shortly after 4pm in northern Minnesota at this time of year. To be safe, we turned towards home, soaking in the beauty and silence of the wilderness, eagerly anticipating the hot sauna and a festive meal with family waiting for us at home. **SP**

Best time to go // Late December through early March.
Gear required // Skate or backcountry skis, depending on snow conditions. Piragis Northwoods Company in Ely, in conjunction with Cast Outdoor Adventures, offers fully guided custom trips and a unique 'Quick Start' programme, which includes a five-hour lesson on winter survival skills.
Nearest town // Ely, Minnesota.
Getting there // Fly to Duluth, rent a car, drive 100 miles (60km) north to Ely via Scenic Highways 61 and 1. There are numerous entry points to the BWCAW near Ely, many of which are much easier to access than Trout Lake.
Where to stay // Stay Inn Ely is a five-room boutique hotel in downtown Ely. Guests share a fully equipped kitchen, dining room and living room with a fireplace. The coffee shop, Northern Grounds, is a few steps away.
Things to know // A free, self-issued permit, obtainable at any entry point into the BWCAW, is required in the winter.

*Opposite: Engadin Ski Marathon near
Maloja, Switzerland is the second
largest in the world*

MORE LIKE THIS
SKATE-SKIING EVENTS

CITY OF LAKES LOPPET WINTER FESTIVAL, MINNESOTA

This two-day celebration of winter is the antithesis of a solitary wilderness skiing experience. Every year at the beginning of February, hundreds of skiers gather to race a classic or skate-ski 23-mile (37km) marathon. The course traverses parkways, woods and four lakes in south Minneapolis. Saturday is the classic ski race and Sunday is the skate race on the same course. In between is the celebratory Luminary Loppet, a candlelit night-time walk, snowshoe or ski around Lake of the Isles, a beautiful urban body of water lined by stately homes, where participants view fantastical ice sculptures, sip hot chocolate, and end the evening at the Luminary Party, an outdoor gathering with local musicians, food trucks and beer. If straight-up skiing isn't your thing, the Loppet Festival also includes fat bike, ski-orienteering, skijouring and snowshoe races.
Nearest town // Minneapolis

ENGADIN SKI MARATHON, SWITZERLAND

The second-largest cross-country skiing event in the world, the 26 mile (42km) Engadin Marathon brings more than 14,000 participants from 60 countries to the Upper Engadin Valley in early March, where racers start in the idyllic village of Maloja and ski over frozen lakes under the shadow of the majestic and craggy Swiss Alps to the finish line at S-chanf. For those uninterested in competing in a full marathon, there are shorter events, including a half-marathon, a women's 11 mile (17km) race, and a co-ed night race over the same distance, where the moonlight shows the way. Don't worry, while the skiing may leave you breathless, this event is not entirely painful. There are several luxury hotels and inns in the area, like Maloja Palace, a neo-renaissance luxury hotel built in 1884 by the Belgian Count, Camille Maximilien Frédéric.
Nearest town // Maloja

THE SLUMBERLAND AMERICAN BIRKEBEINER, WISCONSIN

Participants fall so much in love with this 31 mile (50km) skate marathon through the woods of northern Wisconsin that many of them have competed in it upwards of 30 times. The only Worldloppet global ski event based in the United States, the beloved Birkebeiner takes place every year at the end of February. The challenging, hilly course starts in Cable and travels through dense woods on exceptionally groomed trails before the final sprint across Lake Hayward. It is on this 191 acre (77 hectare) lake, where the wind can be fierce and deadly to exhausted skiers, where the race is often lost or won. But it's not over until they cross the International Bridge to the finish line on Main Street. Expect to feel a wave of emotions throughout this race – from the silent wonder of the northern woods to the excruciating pain of the steepest hill in the race, to the joyous electricity of the cowbell clanging crowds lining Main Street.
Nearest town // Cable/Hayward

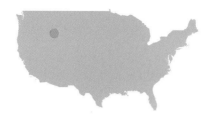

BRYAN IGUCHI
ON JACKSON HOLE

Legendary snowboarder Bryan Iguchi traded in boardsport glory for soul riding when he moved from California to Jackson Hole at 21. It was the best decision he ever made.

I n the early 1990s, I had a realisation: I was a professional snowboarder and I didn't really know a lot about the mountains. Or snow. I decided Jackson Hole was the place to learn.

I grew up in Southern California and ended up living in Big Bear for a while, riding the park every day. But in high school, I got this one amazing opportunity: I was sponsored by a ski bus tour company called LA Ski and Sun Tour, which got me to Utah and to other resorts in the Rockies like Aspen and Jackson Hole. It was the first time I had ever ridden powder. I remember pulling up to Jackson, looking at it, and just the scale and the seriousness of it gave me this impression of wilderness and a sense of freedom to grow as a rider – it's a unique resort, to say the least.

Surfing was my first love. My mom used to take us to the beach. We'd swim all day then grab some burgers, then sit and watch people surfing. Then I started surfing myself. I grew up about 30 minutes from the ocean – in an agricultural town in Ventura County called Moorpark – but I wanted to be a surfer and I tried to go surfing as often as I could. It was obviously a lot easier to skateboard more often and so I actually got sponsored as a skater first. When I was 12, I was surfing and skating pretty regularly and I started reading all the magazines, cover to cover. It was so inspiring. At 13, I got sponsored by Epic Skateboards and I started doing competitions, mostly in California. My friends and I would skate street and jump ramps, empty backyard pools; we'd hang out in Venice on weekends to watch and skate with pros – Venice was pretty intimidating back then. There was a heavy gang influence in Los Angeles skate culture – it was kind of a change of the guard from the Dogtown-era skaters to modern street skating. And then I watched my first snowboard film and everything changed.

When I was 15, a high-school friend of mine showed me a snowboard video after school one day. It completely blew my mind. I never imagined that you could ride a board in snow. It looked like surfing, like doing endless bottom turns on a wave, but then you could also do a method, or whatever trick you wanted, off rock features. Being a skater and surfer, I had all these tricks in my head and I could just see exactly how that would translate on snow. Transitions were everywhere and it really sparked my imagination. We also ended up having a historic winter in California, and so my buddies and I started snowboarding all the time. I fell in love with it.

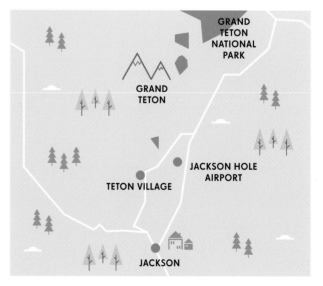

NATURAL SELECTION

Jackson Hole Mountain Resort is where snowboard legend – and Jackson Hole native – Travis Rice first launched his game-changing Natural Selection competition in 2008, with the feel of a Big Wave surf contest. Contestants get the green light when conditions are right and then the best freeriders in the world drop a ridiculously steep face, riddled with hand-built features that require serious skills and creativity. Most creative and technical run wins.

Naturally, I became a park rider. Eventually, I was sponsored by Vans and Volcom – both still sponsor me to this day, along with Arbor snowboards – and I was doing tons of snowboard competitions. I moved up to Big Bear and met Rob DaFoe, we started building snowboard park features and jumps for the resort, so we had unlimited access to the parks and half-pipe and that really accelerated my riding ability.

I remember during one road trip when we were filming, we were travelling between Mammoth and Tahoe and we decided to stop at Virginia Lakes. I was looking at the mountains and I was thinking: 'Why don't we just turn here and see if there's something we can ride?' So we started hiking towards one of the mountain passes. We found these jumps and I think we ended up filming most of the movie in the southern Sierras, just off the mountain passes. But we had zero avalanche training, no beacons, no shovels, no business being in the backcountry. I was a park kid at the time – I came from park riding and trick competitions and I didn't really understand the mountains at all. I started camping out more, treating it a little more like surfing: sitting, waiting, being patient with conditions, and

> *"Being in this more natural, undeveloped place, with more opportunities for solitude, I found peace in it"*

trying to understand the elements I was dealing with before I got into something. I was also really inspired by Craig Kelly, who was known for his skill in the backcountry. I was definitely searching for what I felt was a more soulful approach.

I moved to Jackson Hole in 1995 – I was 21 years old. It was a complete 180-degree change and a completely different style of riding. I really connected to Jackson, this small town with a small core scene. It just felt real. And, yeah, it did put the brakes on the sponsorship momentum and all that, but I set out to be a snowboard bum – I never had any intentions of being professional snowboarder. Sure, I dreamed about it, but I didn't need it. Being in this more natural, undeveloped place, with more opportunities for solitude, I found peace in it. What's cool is that snowboarding is nearly 40 years old, but it's still an evolving sport. Look at splitboarding – moving through the mountains, the same way people have for generations – it makes me feel connected to a bigger part of mountain culture.

I was still young, but I had got most of the partying out of my system in California – I was here to ride. I met my wife, Lily, here in Jackson soon after. She and her best friend – now sister-in-

law – opened Teton Thai, which is still like this super popular little family restaurant near the resort. I was even working there myself at one point, along with a bunch of other family and friends. Lily and I got married in 2005 and we had our sons in 2009 and 2012. And that's probably been the most amazing thing about this place – watching my boys discover these mountains for themselves has been incredible.

Jackson Hole Mountain Resort can be pretty intimidating. It's a serious mountain, it attracts some pretty hardcore skiers and snowboarders. But I remember just being so excited to explore the place. It's this big gnarly mountain and it takes a while to find the flow. The mountain has a lot of moods. But that tram line – there's nothing like it anywhere in the world. Whatever vision they had, where to put it, it's just kind of a ridiculously good top-to-bottom run. It's a perfect mix of steep riding with big cliff drops and freestyle-friendly kickers. Whatever way you choose to ride it – if you want to hit Corbetts or S&S, or go down the bowl and head over to the Expert Chutes – it's all so awesome. And then you're in Dick's Ditch, a big natural half-pipe that takes you all the way to the bottom. Tram-line runs are truly incredible. **WC**

Clockwise from top: powder days at Jackson Hole Mountain Resort are special; but so are storm days; the legendary ski town is 40 minutes from the resort. Previous page: Bryan Iguchi feeling at home in the Jackson Hole area

DIRECTIONS

Best time to go // Jackson Hole has pretty reliable winters. December through April is a safe bet; Jackson's stormiest month is typically February.

Gear required // A reliable all-terrain board or pair of skis, and kit ready for steep technical terrain, but also deep powder when accessing Jackson Hole's famous sidecountry.

Nearest town // Jackson Hole Mountain Resort is a 40-minute drive from the ski area.

Getting there // Jackson Hole has its own airport and is accessed via 13 major US cities.

Where to stay // Stay at the slopes – where there are fantastic options – or in town, an iconic western outpost that oozes atmosphere.

Things to know // A rite of passage is to hike out to Cody Peak and drop into either Once is Enough or Twice is Nice, both long, deep runs that begin with a few spicy jump turns and then open up into pure bliss bowl-skiing.

MORE LIKE THIS
WIDE OPEN, WILD WEST

BIG SKY, MONTANA

Big ski resort, big open spaces, this is Big Sky. About an hour south of Bozeman, Big Sky is another ski resort where the sheer remoteness and scale of the landscape adds an element of adrenaline. Skiing in Montana, in general, feels a lot like skiing in Wyoming, where inaccessibility thins crowds and invites a very particular type of skier or rider. But the mountain itself is impressive too, with terrain, steeps, features and hike-to runs to match any in the US. Big Sky actually held the title of biggest ski area in America a few years back (the crown seems to change hands every couple of years now), with 6000 skiable acres (2428 hectares). More impressive, though, is the vertical span: 4350ft (1326m) from top to bottom, largely thanks to Lone Peak tram hitting the top of the 11,167ft (3404m) peak. One Big Sky run, 50-degree Big Couloir, is only skiable if you check in with ski patrol first and bring a buddy and avalanche gear with you. Take the edge off afterwards with a bloody mary at Headwaters Grille.

Nearest town // Bozeman

TELLURIDE, COLORADO

Telluride has its own airport, and often the landing here is scarier than the skiing. And, given the terrain, that's saying quite a bit. The charming Victorian western town – with its equally stunning ski area – ticks all the boxes except one: it's not the easiest to get to. And this is a good thing. Telluride sits in the drier southwestern part of the state, which diverts many Colorado locals to the more accessible Summit County ski areas. It also breeds diehards. There are many skiers and riders – from in- and out-of-state – who return here year after year just for the special terrain. The town itself is in a sort of box canyon, surrounded by impossibly steep, alpine 14,000ft (4267m) peaks; mountains in which the ski resort is nestled. There are a little over 2000 skiable acres (809 hectares) – 40 percent of which is expert-only – spread out over the ski area's 4425 vertical feet (1349m). Hike-to terrain like Palmyra and Black Iron Bowl is some of the best sidecountry in the world.

Nearest town // Telluride

SNOWBIRD, UTAH

Snowbird ski resort, which sits in Big Cottonwood Canyon, about 40 minutes from Salt Lake City, is not hard to get to at all (in fact, its proximity to a major airport means plenty more time skiing). But it does feel out-of-the-way and has terrain that makes the mountain feel very big indeed. Founded by Dick Bass – the first person to complete the Seven Summits – back in 1971, Snowbird has always let its terrain and snow conditions speak for itself. 'Steep and deep' gets thrown around a lot, but the phrase was probably invented here. Five hundred inches of annual snowfall and 2500 skiable acres (1012 hectares) means it's the type of place that will keep you busy for days after a storm. For one of the purest powder skiing or riding experiences at any ski resort, anywhere, hit Mineral Basin. Or, for a Bryan Iguchi-approved run, hit Snowbird's tram line, his second favourite in the Rockies.

Nearest town // Salt Lake City

Clockwise from top: the rustic western charm of Telluride, Colorado; Snowbird's tram line is the best run on the mountain; inbounds terrain feels out-of-bounds at Big Sky Resort, Montana

CANADA

AN ARCTIC SAFARI

Polar bears may be fearsome apex predators, but seeing these majestic animals up close, near the Arctic outpost of Churchill, has a way of changing that perception.

My skin prickles into goosebumps, but it's not from the chill in the air. I've just locked eyes with a 1,200lb (550kg) polar bear as it proudly prances toward me. I take comfort in knowing that I'm protected as I stand in silence on the towering outdoor platform of a Tundra Buggy – a tank-like, all-terrain snow vehicle with a viewing deck that's elevated about 10ft (3m) off the ground. But I'm also highly aware that this is his territory, not mine.

I'm taking a trek through the vast tundra of Churchill, Manitoba, on a polar bear excursion with Frontiers North Adventures, along with a small group of fellow travellers. Polar bear viewings can be enjoyed here by boat, helicopter or tundra vehicle, but unpredictable weather and wildlife mean that sightings are never guaranteed. Our tour guide, Markus Petak, has 14 years of experience navigating this bear-inhabited terrain, so I'm feeling lucky.

There are no signs of civilisation in sight when we finally spot a bear – we've ventured nearly two hours from town – and while

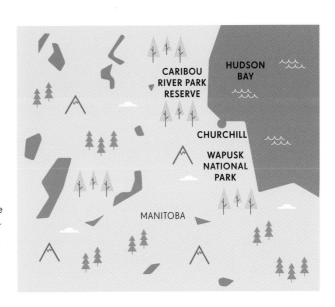

CARIBOU
RIVER PARK
RESERVE

HUDSON
BAY

CHURCHILL

WAPUSK
NATIONAL
PARK

MANITOBA

this special encounter is spellbinding, it's also slightly intimidating. The blanched beast stops in his tracks only steps from where we stand, tilting his nose upwards and wiggling his nostrils to sniff out his surroundings. I stand frozen, holding my breath so I don't startle him. After a pause, he turns and trots off towards a new target, uninterested in our presence. Our group exhales in unison as the bear walks away – and then the adrenaline kicks in. After several moments spent standing in silence, we're now engaging in supercharged chatter, recounting every detail of the moment we've just shared.

It's a warm October afternoon and the beautiful balmy weather makes it easy to stand on the buggy's platform for an extended period of time, although the crisp air hints at the cooler conditions to come. I've visited at the right time of year – the months of October and November are when the polar bear population is at its highest here, because the animals gather in the area to wait for the big freeze. Soon, thick sheets of ice will form along the coast of Hudson Bay, enabling the hungry bears to travel on the ice surface to hunt for ringed seals (unlike other bears, the polar variety don't hibernate).

These polar bears have been waiting for their much-needed high-fat feasts since the big ice-melt in June, and after several months spent roaming around inland, they're ready to return to the frozen ocean in order to fuel up. Unfortunately, the number of days between meals continues to grow. Global climate change is slowly shortening the sea-ice season in Hudson Bay, narrowing the window when polar bears are able hunt seals and thus increasing the length of time they'll need to store fat. This makes them vulnerable to extinction.

Frontiers North Adventures works closely with Polar Bears International, a non-profit conservation organisation composed of a passionate team of conservationists, scientists, researchers and volunteers. Its work focuses on ensuring the long-term survival of polar bears, striving to save the sea ice through science, advocacy and media, while hoping to inspire people to care about the Arctic, the threats to its future and its connection to our global climate.

As an element of this partnership, Frontiers North Adventures has invited Polar Bears International's Brooke Biddlecombe – an Arctic ecologist and researcher – to join our group for the day on our Tundra Buggy excursion. As we roll through the tundra, she shares her research findings with us, making our experience all the more richer. After a brief talk from Biddlecombe, we know that the four-legged brute we spotted is a male, because it is uncommon to spot female polar bears by the shore at this time of year.

Whereas male polar bears migrate to the water's edge earlier in the year in anticipation of hunting season, females tend to stay inland, caring for their cubs in maternity dens. They keep out of sight of the males, which be a threat and often cannibalise the cubs. Biddlecombe also explains that polar bears are a sexually dimorphic species, meaning adult males tend to be much larger

Clockwise from top: Arctic fox near Churchill; bear with cubs on snow-covered coast in Canada. Previous page: polar bear on the Hudson Bay coast at sunset

than their female counterparts – sometimes double the size – and this bear was big.

As we disembark from our Tundra Buggy at the end of the day and drive into downtown Churchill, our opportunities to spot polar bears continue. We even see one on the side of the road, napping among a pile of beachfront boulders, reminding us of their presence around the people who call the town home. Churchill is a small, isolated town with a population of just over 800 year-round residents. The town is known as the 'polar bear capital of the world' because nearly 1,000 polar bears migrate to the area between July and November every year. This high polar bear density is a result of the town's proximity to Hudson Bay and the way ice forms at the mouth of the river that feeds into it – it's the last place the ice melts, and the first place it forms, so bears race to the area to maximise their feeding time.

With more polar bears than people roaming inland during peak months, the town of Churchill has procedures in place to protect

THIN ICE

A human adult can easily fall through when trying to walk across a layer of thin ice, but polar bears – despite being five times heavier – can navigate their way across without breaking the surface. This is because their wide, flat paws (which can be up to 12in/30cm wide) help them disperse their weight evenly. They spread their legs and flatten their bodies as they cross the ice to avoid breaking it.

"Our group exhales in unison as the bear walks away – and then the adrenaline kicks in"

DIRECTIONS

both the locals and their four-legged neighbours. Car doors are left unlocked to provide rapid sanctuary from the prowling predators, while, if a polar bear poses an ongoing threat and can't be shooed away from town, it's tranquilised and taken to the Polar Bear Holding Facility (or 'polar bear jail'), where it's isolated for up to a month in an air-conditional cell before being relocated up north by helicopter. A Polar Bear Alert team patrols the perimeter of town regularly, and a phone-in warning line keeps locals up-to-date on sightings.

As I tuck in for the night after an adventurous day on the tundra, an alarm sounds outside my window. It's the 10pm warning for residents, indicating the start of a loose curfew, encouraging people to remain indoors after dark. All is quiet outside now, and as I slowly fall asleep, I imagine what it must be like to share the streets with the largest land predators in the world, in a remote town that sits on the edge of the Arctic, accessible only by train or air. The locals I've met seem happy to call Churchill home, and although I'm only a passing visitor, I can see why. **BB**

Best time to go // Peak polar bear viewing season is from mid-October to mid-November.

Gear required // Dress in layers as the Tundra Buggy is heated, but it can be chilly on the viewing platforms. You'll also want to bring a camera, sunglasses, extra camera batteries and a reusable water bottle or travel mug.

Nearest town // Churchill, Manitoba.

Getting there // Churchill is a 2.5-hour flight from Winnipeg or a 48-hour train ride from Winnipeg by Via Rail. There are no roads in and out of town.

Things to know // Most tour packages include transfers from the airport or rail station, accommodation, activities and excursions. As this is polar bear country, it is important to be 'bear aware' at all times.

MORE LIKE THIS
CHURCHILL'S ARCTIC SAFARIS

DOGSLEDDING

Get whisked away on a wild ride through the boreal forest of Churchill on a dogsledding adventure with Wapusk Adventures, an indigenous-owned and operated tour company based in the Manitoba town. Métis owner and founder Dave 'Big Dog' Daley has lived in the region for over 60 years, and his family-run, award-winning dogsledding tours go beyond the riveting ride. The experience begins with a cultural talk in a heated log cabin, where Daley shares his family's famed history of dogsledding, the meaning of the sport to his Métis heritage, and his long journey as a record-breaking dogsledder and founder of the Hudson Bay Quest dogsled race – a 220-mile (354km) world-renowned romp born out of a desire to revive dogsledding as a sport and tradition of the north. Daley also reveals how he successfully runs a long-distance racing kennel and properly trains numerous sled dogs while providing them with the best care possible.

Nearest town // Churchill

BELUGAS

Churchill is also known as the 'beluga whale capital of the world', as the wild waters of Hudson Bay and the Churchill River estuary are prime sites for spotting the singing marine mammals. More than 50,000 beluga whales migrate to the area in July and August to feed, give birth and shed their outer layer of skin. Watching them swim along the shoreline can be a truly spectacular sight. They are often referred to as the 'canaries of the sea' due to their wide range of sing-song vocalisations. Frontiers North Adventures offers a Belugas, Bears & Blooms tour during the summer months, which includes water, land and rail adventures. It's a great opportunity to connect with the culture and wildlife of Churchill during peak beluga-whale-spotting season. Frontiers also hosts a Churchill Belugas and Bears Explorer tour, which allows you to see both magnificent creatures by Zodiac and Tundra Buggy.

Nearest town // Churchill

NORTHERN LIGHTS

Churchill is one of the best places on Earth to see the northern lights (aurora borealis), because auroral activity occurs for around 300 days a year in the region. The town lies directly beneath the Auroral Oval in the Northern Hemisphere, and its remote location makes for prime dark-sky conditions. Peak viewing season falls between late November and early March, and tours such as Northern Lights and Winter Nights, offered by Frontiers North Adventures, provide the perfect way to witness the magical subarctic skies. Take your northern lights adventure to the next level with a stay at the Tundra Buggy Lodge – a pop-up hotel located on the Churchill Wildlife Management Area out on the tundra and away from city lights – where you can sleep, sup and stargaze in the heart of polar bear country during the months of October and November.

Nearest town // Churchill

Clockwise from top: soft northern lights dance over sparse spruce trees and wind-blown snow drift; letting the dogs do the work with Manitoba Sleds; beluga whales in Hudson Bay

THE CANADIAN ROCKIES BY FAT BIKE

Balloon-tyre bikes are an ingenious way of covering a lot of ground in the wildest national parks during the winter.

As soon as Clare McCann arrives outside my Banff motel with two 'fat bikes', two helmets and a hearty 'good morning', I immediately have some questions. The owner and self-appointed 'director of stoke' at Bikescape, an adventure tour company based in the Canadian Rockies, McCann is going to take me out for my first snow-biking experience, made possible by the vehicles' knobbly or studded balloon tyres. I'm perfectly comfortable on a regular bicycle – I'm not into mountain biking, but I tool around town on my ancient cruiser fairly regularly – but this looks pretty different from any type of biking I've tried. In winter, when my bike gets hung up, fat bikes get tuned up.

On this crisp, sunny March day, snow is lingering across the trails, forests and mountains of Banff National Park, but it has been a few days since fresh flakes have fallen in town. An avid cyclist, McCann tells me that her mission is to get more people riding bicycles, whether that's by teaching basic bike skills to local kids at her cycling camps, or leading experienced mountain bikers across Banff's gnarliest terrain, or even gently guiding newcomers like me through the art of winter riding.

Seeing how nervous I am, McCann tells me to start slowly. The bike I'm on is an electric model, outfitted with the trademark thick, studded tyres. First, I just try pedalling around the motel car park.

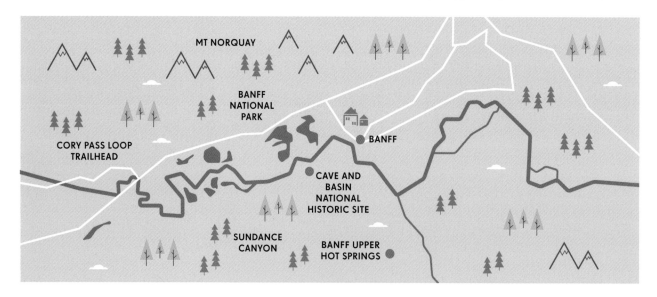

Although the bike feels much heavier than my old city cruiser, its tyres, which are much wider than those on a typical mountain bike, offer more stability. The metal studs grip the snow and engender confidence. One thing's for sure, if I were on my regular bike, I would be lying in the ditch next to the car park.

Eventually, McCann and I set off down the street, where the pavement is a mix of packed snow and bare asphalt. Even with the power dialled down to the lowest level, I feel like the e-bike wants to race. I decide I'd prefer to pedal through town at a more leisurely pace so I turn the power off. McCann points out that I can turn it back on when the going gets steeper.

McCann tells me she started her business after being laid off early on during the Covid pandemic. She explains that fat-tyre bikes – which were actually developed some time in the 1980s for riding around Alaska and tackling sandy terrain in New Mexico – are the newest way to explore Canada's oldest national park. Whereas snowmobiles and other motorised vehicles are prohibited from travelling trails within the park boundaries, fat bikes, which include electric snow bikes, recently got the green light from the park administration. McCann is quick to point out that you can cover far more terrain by fat bike than you could on snowshoes.

Eventually, McCann asks what is perhaps the most important question on a fat-biking tour: am I warm enough. And, although I'm wearing long underwear, a wool sweater, insulated snow pants and boots, a down jacket, a hat under my helmet and my warmest

"The bike seems to float across the top of the snow, rather than sink into it"

mittens, the answer is no. My hands, especially, are feeling chilly. On e-bikes, you typically generate less body heat than in sports such as cross-country skiing, so hand- or toe-warmers are a common fat-biking accessory. I need to keep my hands and fingers warm and flexible, since I need them to shift gear and steer.

When we ride past Banff railway station, cross a busy main road and head into the woods, I feel myself getting nervous again, although the nervousness is now mixed with excitement. The trail is gentle as we turn down towards the creek, but I'm finally riding on nothing but snow. The crunch of the studded tyres quiets as we pedal on the wooden path. The bike seems to float across the top of the snow, rather than sink into it, while gripping the ground at the same time. We're cycling through the trees on the packed snow when McCann motions for us to stop near the water. As I hop off my bike to look around, I see reflections of the evergreens shimmering in the partially frozen creek, while the snow-covered peak ahead catches the morning sun.

After continuing through the forest a little further, we turn back towards town. Banff is busy this week with skiers and snowboarders, who've come for the trails at Banff Sunshine, Lake Louise and Mt Norquay, the three nearby ski resorts. Yet the ski crowds are tiny

⛷ WATER BORN

Banff, Canada's first national park, was established in 1885 thanks to its underground hot springs. In 1883, three railroad workers tried to stake a claim to a spring deep in a cave, hoping to develop it for tourism. Canada's government intervened, protecting the area that eventually became Banff National Park. Today, you can visit the Cave and Basin National Historic Site to learn more about these origins. To soak in Banff's steamy waters, head for Banff Upper Hot Springs.

Clockwise from top: Banff Upper Hot Springs; Columbia Icefield Skywalk in Jasper National Park, north of Banff; snowshoes allow for long snowy hikes. Previous page: midwinter fat biking in Banff National Park, Alberta, Canada

compared with the summer-season visitors that Banff National Park draws, yet, for me, the scenery is equally dramatic in winter. As we follow a mix of trails and secondary roads, McCann guides me towards the Banff pedestrian bridge, a curved span that arcs across the Bow River. Halfway across the wooden-planked bridge, she instructs me to stop again and turn around. Snow-topped Mount Rundle towers above.

When the ride is over, I realise that I've covered more ground on a fat bike, even at my unhurried pace, than I ever could have on foot. Although my initial focus was on handling the bike, I'd begun to relax enough to take in the beauty of this national park I'd visited so many times in summer and winter.

If a hardcore biking experience is more your speed, McCann will happily guide you to the steeper and twistier trails throughout Banff National Park. But if you simply want a quietly epic morning on Banff's gentle snow-covered pathways, beneath its mountains and along its rivers, it's best to slow your roll. **CH**

DIRECTIONS

Best time to go // Snow typically starts to fall in the Canadian Rockies by October, but December through March is the peak season for snow sports.

Gear required // Rent a fat-tyre bike with a helmet from Bikescape or other outdoor gear shops in Banff. Wear a windproof jacket and trousers with layers underneath. Keep your hands and feet warm with gloves, socks and boots.

Nearest town // Banff, Alberta.

Getting there // Calgary Airport is a 90-minute drive to the east. Shuttle buses run between the airport and Banff.

Where to stay // Of Banff's many options, The Dorothy and The Juniper are cute, updated motels, while the historic Fairmont Banff Springs hotel has an elaborate pool and spa.

Things to know // Visitors need to purchase a national park pass for each day they're within the park boundaries. Buy the passes online at www.pc.gc.ca, www.banfflakelouise. com or at park entrances and visitor centres.

MORE LIKE THIS
FAT-BIKE FUN IN CANADA

OTTAWA, ONTARIO

Canada's national capital ranks among the world's coldest capital cities, but that just makes its urban outdoor-adventure season last longer. Ottawa is known for the Rideau Canal Skateway – the world's largest ice-skating rink – but the region also has numerous trails for fat-tyre biking. The multi-use Capital Pathway crosses the Ottawa region with more than 125 miles (200km) of trails for walkers, runners, snowshoers and cyclists, including snow bikers. Massive Gatineau Park on the Québec side of the Ottawa River is often considered the city's backyard; in winter, around 30 miles (50km) of trails are available to fat-tyre cyclists. Another multi-use route, the Kichi Sibi Winter Trail, which runs along the Ottawa River, was formerly known as the Sir John A Macdonald Winter Trail, named after Canada's first prime minister. It was given a new name in 2021, after revelations about Macdonald's role in establishing the residential school system, which forcibly removed generations of indigenous children from their families and required them to attend church-run boarding schools. It's a grim history to ponder as you traverse the snowy route.
Nearest town // Ottawa

FERNIE, BRITISH COLUMBIA

On the British Columbia side of the Canadian Rockies, a three-hour drive southwest of Calgary, the town of Fernie is a year-round mountain biker's haven. In winter, many of the trails that draw summer-season shredders morph into snow-covered fat-biking routes. You can ride on trails in nearby Mt Fernie Provincial Park, as well as Fernie Alpine Resort, the downhill ski mountain. When you come off the trails, get cosy in a tiny home at Snow Valley Lodging, or bunk in a private pod at Raging Elk Adventure Lodging. Bonus: if you wander through Fernie's back alleys, you can check out its dumpster art – colourful murals painted on the town's rubbish bins.
Nearest town // Fernie

QUÉBEC'S NATIONAL PARKS

Québec's network of provincially managed parks (known as 'national parks') includes many trails that welcome fat-tyre bikers, and most offer convenient bike rentals as well as winter-season accommodation. In the Eastern Townships, close to the US border, winter cyclists can explore a range of routes in Parc national du Mont-Orford, while west of Montréal, there are trails to tackle in Parc national d'Oka. Fat-tyre cyclists who venture north of Québec City can find plenty of snow in the hills and valleys of Parc national de la Jacques-Cartier or Parc national des Hautes-Gorges-de-la-Rivière-Malbaie. There are more winter biking routes overlooking the St Lawrence River in Parc national du Bic, gateway to the Gaspé Peninsula. If you'd rather challenge trails that are even more remote, consider a trip into the deep snows and beneath the frozen waterfalls of Parc national d'Aiguebelle, in the Abitibi-Témiscamingue region of western Quebec, 30 miles (50km) northeast of Rouyn-Noranda and more than 370 miles (600km) northwest of Montréal. You can combine fat-tyre biking with other snow sports – including snowshoeing, Nordic skiing, ski-shoeing and ice-climbing – for an epic winter adventure.
Nearest town // Montréal, Québec City or Rouyn-Noranda

Clockwise from top: bike or hike in Parc national de la Jacques-Cartier, Québec; Fernie is a gateway to the vast Canadian Rockies; Ottawa's urban fat-bike trails add adventure to a quick trip.

FAR OUT ICE FISHING

*In the northernmost, coldest part of Canada, the local Inuit have long established a way
of life in which living off the land in subzero temperatures is an art form.*

I'm bouncing across the frozen Cumberland Sound, bundled into a *qamutik*, a traditional Inuit sled that looks like an elongated wooden bathtub attached to wooden runners. A fisher from the community of Pangnirtung, on Nunavut's Baffin Island, races ahead on his snowmobile, pulling my sled across the ice. I'm struggling to stay warm under a ragged olive-green camouflage tarpaulin that keeps billowing in the wind. It's a tarp that wouldn't camouflage anything against the stark white and blue expanses of ice and snow, and the cloud-free April sky.

Riding two to a *qamutik*, our small group of adventurers is travelling to the winter fishing grounds where our lead guide, Peter Kilabuk, normally fishes for turbot beneath the ice-covered bay. We're venturing out in the -10°C (14°F) temperatures to learn something about ice fishing, but also, I hope, for a window into Inuit culture. Approximately 85 percent of Nunavut's 40,000 residents are Inuit, scattered across a vast region that stretches from the North Atlantic and Hudson Bay to the Arctic Ocean. Nunavut's closest neighbour, across the narrow Nares Strait, is Greenland. The territory is also Canada's newest, having only become part of the country in 1999. Three-hour flights to Iqaluit, the territorial capital, bring travellers from Ottawa or, seasonally, from Montreal, but no roads link the territory to the rest of the country or connect the 25 communities of Nunavut, an Inuktitut word meaning 'our land'.

Once our caravan of snowmobiles and sleds is loaded with coolers, fishing gear, and tools, we set out across the snow-dusted frozen water. Leaving from Pangnirtung, we travel more than 20 miles (30km) – about an hour's ride. We pull up outside the wood and tar-paper warming hut that Kilabuk and his adult son had

towed to this spot several months earlier, claiming their fishing area for the season. Kilabuk explains that every fishing family stakes out their winter territory simply by bringing their hut to a spot that they choose. 'Do people ever argue about where they can fish?' I ask. Kilabuk shakes his head and gestures across the vast expanse of ice. There are plenty of fish for everyone.

A former member of Nunavut's legislative assembly, Kilabuk represented Pangnirtung in the territorial government from the territory's creation until 2008. Although he now runs an outfitting company, Peter's Expediting & Outfitting Services, fishing has long been part of his life too.

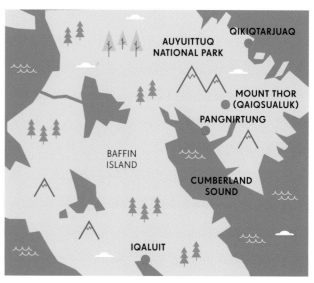

ARCTIC TURNS

Thirty-one miles (50km) south of the Arctic Circle, Pangnirtung is the closest community to Auyuittuq National Park. Winter activities in Auyuittuq ('the land that never melts') include tours to the Arctic Circle by snowmobile and *qamutik*, backcountry skiing and snowshoeing. Adventurers can explore the Akshayuk Pass, a 60-mile (97km) natural corridor between glaciers, and Mt Thor (Qaiqsualuk), the world's tallest cliff face, a 5495ft (1675m) vertical peak.

Kilabuk and his son had previously bored a fishing hole through the ice outside their hut. With help from the three other fishers, who, like Kilabuk, are all of Inuit heritage, he lays a fishing line along the snow so they can bait the hooks set at intervals with scraps of salmon. Kilabuk ties one end of the line to a 'kite' – a piece of metal resembling a silver cookie sheet, bent in the middle to form a wide V. Aiming the kite into the fishing hole, he and his partners guide the line into the water, slowly letting it sink to the bottom of the Sound. Turbot are bottom feeders, Kilabuk explains, so he needs to send the line as deep as possible.

'First, I have my coffee. Then we'll fish,' he announces, once he has set the fishing line. He tells us we'll need to wait about two hours before enough fish will be drawn to the bait. We squeeze our parka-clad bodies onto the benches inside the hut, as Kilabuk heats water on a camping stove, offering instant coffee. I had assumed that the Inuit had fished this way for many generations, but Kilabuk explains that a group of Greenlanders came to Pangnirtung in the 1980s to share their knowledge of ice fishing for turbot, and it has become the Inuit's preferred way to fish for the past four decades.

Like many indigenous peoples, the Inuit have a complicated history with the rest of Canada. From the late 1800s until the 1990s, the Canadian government removed indigenous children – including Inuit youth – from their families and sent them to church-run residential schools, with the goal of erasing their traditional culture. It's not surprising that many Inuit are ambivalent about their territory's connection to the rest of Canada.

As we continue waiting for the fish to bite, it is warm enough for us to take a short, slippery walk across the ice. Only a small snow-covered ridge breaks up the views across the ice in all directions. Eventually, Kilabuk puts on bright orange gloves and begins pulling the line up through the ice, asking each of us to guess how many fish we've caught. The pessimist in the group says 'three';

> ## "The crew count the fish and find that they've hauled in 47 turbot"

the optimist says '34'. Wrenching each flat, silver fish off the hook, Kilabuk throws it into a pile. Pull, toss, pull, toss. He drops a few undersized ones back under the water – the 'keepers' were each more than 18in (45cm) long. The crew hauls in 47 turbot, which Kilabuk estimates at 200lb to 300lb (90kg to 135kg).

Now that the fishing is done, the fishers pick up the pace, rapidly loading the sleds for the trip back to town. After keeping a small amount for their families, they will sell the turbot to the local processing plant, which will ship most of the catch to buyers in Japan. Bundled back into the *qamutik* as we race across the ice, I muse over how the fish from this isolated Inuit community will find their way to tables across the world. **CH**

Clockwise from top: curious polar bears prowl Baffin Bay; locals stake out fishing holes. Previous page: wildlife photographers on Bylot Island near Pond Inlet, Nunavut

DIRECTIONS

Best time to go // March and April are the best months for ice-fishing and other adventures, as the days begin to lengthen while plenty of snow and ice remains. Be prepared to consider alternative activities if conditions aren't suitable.
Gear required // A heavy parka, snow pants, wool or fleece sweater, long underwear, thick mittens, hat, scarf, warm socks and insulated boots are crucial. A face mask or balaclava will protect you from the wind; bring ski goggles or sunglasses too.
Nearest town // Pangnirtung, Nunavut.
Getting there // The only way to travel here is by air. You can fly to Iqaluit from Ottawa or Montréal. From Iqaluit, there are regular flights to Pangnirtung.
Where to stay // There's a basic lodge and a couple of B&Bs in Pangnirtung, including the friendly Fiordview B&B.
Things to know // Outfitters that can organise ice-fishing and other winter adventures include Peter's Expediting & Outfitting Services and Iqaluit-based Inukpak Outfitting.

MORE LIKE THIS
ICE-FISHING TRADITIONS

HOKKAIDŌ, JAPAN

Although fish caught under the ice in Nunavut often end up in markets across Japan, the country has its own ice-fishing traditions. Located in Japan's far north, the island of Hokkaidō is known for its winter adventures, including skiing and snowboarding, and for the annual Sapporo Snow Festival, with its intricately crafted, large-scale snow sculptures. But you can also go ice-fishing for *wakasagi*, a small fish known in English as pond smelt. One destination for winter *wakasagi* fishing is on Lake Abashiri in northeast Hokkaidō, which typically freezes solid enough for fishing between mid-January and mid-March. Guides take you onto the frozen lake where they set up colourful tents to shelter fishers from the cold. You'll learn how to set your line and pull in the smelt. And while not all ice-fishing experiences allow you to sample your catch, in this case, you can. Your guide will fry up your fish to snack on, tempura-style.

Nearest town // Abashiri

UUMMANNAQ, GREENLAND

Consider another ice-fishing adventure in Nunavut's nearest neighbour – Greenland. Ice-fishing has long been part of the culture on this North Atlantic island that draws its heritage from both Inuit and Danish traditions. While you can catch different fish in different parts of the country, halibut are among the most plentiful species. From Uummannaq in western Greenland you can travel by snowmobile onto the frozen fjord to fish for halibut, and you might catch catfish or redfish as well. Ice-fishing season here typically runs from February to April. And while you're out on the ice, raise a glass of whatever hot drink you have and toast your ice-fishing counterparts across the strait in Nunavut.

Nearest town // Uummannaq

LAKE TAHOE, CALIFORNIA, USA

If you think California is all beaches and palm trees, think again. Although the largest state in the western US is known for its sun and surf, head inland to its mountains and you'll find plenty of winter adventures. Skiers and snowboarders travel to the Lake Tahoe region in the Sierra Nevada Mountains – where northern California meets Nevada – which receives both heavy snow and abundant sunshine. To add an ice-fishing adventure to your mountain sojourn, head south of Lake Tahoe itself and along the Carson Pass Highway (State Route 88), where several smaller lakes typically freeze solid enough for ice-fishing between December and March. At Silver Lake, you can fish beneath the ice for several species of trout, including rainbow, brown, brook and Lahontan cutthroat. Another trout-fishing destination is nearby Caples Lake – it's convenient to Kirkwood Mountain Resort, where you can ski or snowboard between your fishing days. Several shops in the Tahoe area will rent you an ice auger, the drill you need to cut your hole. Bring sunglasses, too, because even in the mountains on a cold winter day, you're still in sunny California.

Nearest town // South Lake Tahoe

*Clockwise from top: ice-fishing on a lake in Hokkaido,
Japan; fishery near Uummannaq in Greenland;
roadside ice-fishing at Caples Lake near South
Lake Tahoe*

THE BC BEHEMOTH

Whistler Blackcomb is North America's largest ski resort — by some distance. But its main allure lies in taking its hidden corners and unexpected turns one ski at a time.

On a snowy weekday morning at Whistler Blackcomb, after following a stranger into a stand of trees, I found myself billy-goating (hopping across exposed terrain) along the edge of a narrow cliff band. 'You're fine!' yelled Sam, the local who I'd just met on the lift. 'Send it! There's at least a metre of snow below you.'

'Wait, how much is a metre again?' I wondered. And my new friend Sam definitely had no idea whether I was fine or not. But peer pressure is a potent drug. I pointed my tips over the edge and popped down into the powder, hoping for the best. I came up giggling, lacing through trees below, ready to repeat the run.

By hitching my trailer to Sam the friendly local, instead of manically trying to cover as much ground as possible, I unlocked something that had previously eluded me about Whistler. To ski it right, you have to focus. You don't need *everything*; you just need *something*. And narrowing your range is the secret to skiing the mountain right.

You can hit Whistler Blackcomb so wrong or hit it so right. That's both the allure and the downfall of North America's largest ski resort, which has 8171 acres (3306 hectares) of skiable terrain over two interconnected mountains, 16 bowls and three massive glaciers, and averages 46oin (1160cm) of snow per year. It is

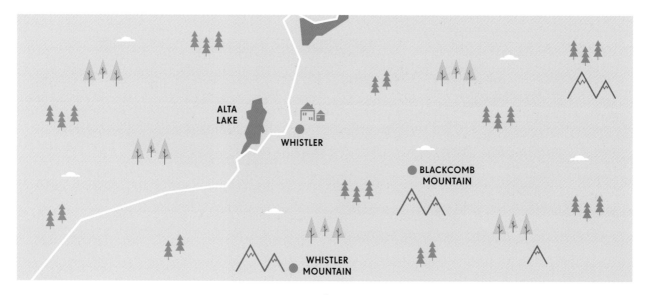

⚔ PISTE TO FEAST

British Columbia has a large East Asian community, and that shows up in the province's food. When you're in Whistler, try to get a seat at uber-popular Sushi Village, especially if you can get a seat in one of the tatami rooms. The restaurant and it's house rolls have been a Whistler staple since the mid-1980s. If you can't get in (or you're on a really cheap budget), hit the deli at Fuji Market for more affordable fresh sushi, along with a dense variety of Asian snacks and grocery items.

"Whistler has secrets and it has soul"

so damn big, and there is so much terrain you could cover, it's simultaneously exciting and overwhelming.

I'd long studied iconic photos of people hitting the massive Air Jordan cliff, or making a pristine pow (powder) turn with the Black Tusk mountain in the background. There was never any doubt I'd ski Whistler, it just took a while to take the plunge. Photos can be deceiving, for example, and bigger isn't necessarily better. In fact, it can easily be worse. The steep, metamorphic mountains of the Pacific Coast Ranges are fickle, weather ravaged and susceptible to storm swings. Even the bifurcated peaks of Whistler Blackcomb can be intimidating: the trail map; the fog; the after-dark scene at the village; and the way the weather changes as you move down the slope, from crystalline powder at the top of the Peak Chair to water-laden slop at Creekside. If you're not careful, the wide swathe of forests between bowls can quickly swallow you up, or you could find yourself on the edge of a cliff in a low-visibility whiteout, with a local egging you on.

And in that respect, I have failed here many times before. For instance, on my first trip to Whistler, I spent the whole time traversing the middle of Whistler Mountain, trying to find pockets of decent snow. I was constantly stuck in foggy slop down low; agitated, sweaty, never sure where I was going. I kept finding myself on meandering groomers like Franz's, heading in the opposite direction to where I wanted to be. Eventually, I got so soggy from the just-above-freezing snow that a well-meaning older gentleman on the lift offered me the squeegee attached to his glove so that I could clear my water-drenched goggles (a local secret, he told me). It helped, but it didn't do anything about the fact that I was soaked down to my underwear, miles away from where I started.

But that edge of intensity is what keeps Whistler interesting. It's what keeps a quorum of core skiers in the valley and exactly what makes the mountain a bucket-list place to ski. Whistler Mountain has been one of the biggest resorts in North America since it opened in the 1960s. When it merged with its neighbouring friendly rival, Blackcomb, in 1997, it became massive. But there's a reason it hasn't become a hokey, overrun Disneyland like other resorts of its scale–despite a massive base area build-up for the 2010 Vancouver Olympics, and despite being owned by Vail Resorts since 2016. Whistler has secrets and it has soul.

I've spent an unhealthy number of years trying to figure out why mountains like Whistler Blackcomb pull people in. I'm fascinated by the appeal of ski hills, to the point that I even wrote a book, *Powder Days*, about why people, myself included, get obsessed with something as frivolous as skiing. A big part of it is our innate need for exploration. Whistler has what the best ski areas of any scale have, from tiny Bolton Valley to spacious Big Sky: secret stashes (areas of untracked snow), including a plethora of just-off-the-map hidden gems; and the kind of terrain that takes decades to explore and understand. And, because it's so huge, it has them in spades. That's the soul skier appeal of Whistler. It's not that the mountain is so massive; it's not that you can shop at an enormous

winter-sports apparel store and then pop around the corner to see a world class DJ (although sure, there's that too). It's because, on a random stormy Tuesday, you can disappear into a stand of mossy, ancient pines and spend the rest of your day neck-deep in bottomless snow. And then do it again the next day.

Although it is supremely satisfying to unlock those stashes, it does require some strategy. Whistler isn't a mountain that's going to give it up easily, and not all locals are as accommodating as Sam. But, for a start, he and his fellow Whistler skiers know to keep eyes on the snowline and the forecasts; to be strategic and patient; and to pay attention so they can jump when patrol drops a rope. And with size to spread the crowds, not all hardcores will necessarily be near enough to that rope to benefit. It's hard to go wrong if you head to Whistler Mountain's Peak Express, which holds the puckering steeps of the West Cirque. You can also ski Peak to Creek, a long groomer, if chutes aren't your thing. On Blackcomb, spend the entire day in the trees of the Crystal Zone, which makes for great storm skiing, or point yourself to the Glacier Express if it's clear and you want to get up high on the Horstman Glacier.

Whistler nightlife requires a strategy too. Settle into one section of the village and don't get overwhelmed by the number of options. Befriend a local at Merlin's and park yourself there for the evening. Remember, you can't do it all in one day – or night. **HH**

Opposite from top: fog covers the lower mountain while the alpine is bathed in sunshine in Whistler, BC; Canadian flag flying near the Rendezvous lodge on top of Whistler Mountain. Previous page: Whistler's size often means solitude

DIRECTIONS

Best time to go // January historically has the most snow, but March is close behind, and comes with longer days. It's hard to go wrong in the winter.

Gear required // Weather conditions trend towards wet and variable, so you'll want gear that's waterproof and breathable. Powder skis will probably serve you well.

Nearest town // Whistler itself.

Getting there // Whistler is roughly a two-hour drive from Vancouver Airport, and shuttles run frequently

Where to stay // There's a wide range of hotel options in Whistler Village.

Things to know // Keep your eye on the freezing level and the temperature. The base area can be rainy when it's dumping powder on the peaks.

Opposite, from top: powder-skiing in the Kicking Horse sidecountry; touring for fresh tracks at Revelstoke

MORE LIKE THIS
BC'S BIGGEST TERRAIN

REVELSTOKE

Whistler might claim the most terrain in North America, but Revelstoke, on the edge of the Selkirk Mountains has the most vert. The mountain's 5620 vertical feet (1713m) of drop holds high alpine bowls, pillowy tree skiing, leg-burning long groomers and some of the most full-on extreme terrain on the continent, including Mackenzie Peak's Mac Daddy Face. When the sky opens up, you get gorgeous views of the Monashees and the Columbia River, but honestly, it's dumping more often than not. The resort was developed relatively recently – it opened in 2008 – so the base village feels modern and cool, and the town itself has stayed charming and low-key.
Nearest town // Revelstoke

KICKING HORSE

Like Whistler, the terrain at Kicking Horse spreads up and out, encompassing four mountain peaks, and five notable alpine bowls, including the new Rudi's Bowl, which opened up a range of more extreme terrain. Not that it was needed. The laid-back resort is full of high-impact terrain, including nearly 90 steep, in-bounds chutes. To get a feel for the expanse of the mountain, take the Golden Eagle Express Gondola, which shoots you up some 4000 vertical feet (1200m) to the top of reassuringly named CPR Ridge. From there you can drop into Crystal Bowl. Or, if you just want to take in the scenery, you can meander down a winding green run called It's a Ten, all the way to the base.
Nearest town // Calgary

RED MOUNTAIN

For a lot of skiers and snowboarders, the ideal ski area looks something like this: steep deep trees, enough rocky chutes to keep me on my toes, long sunny bump runs, a plethora of hike-to terrain. Crowds should be minimal, there should be a classic double chair for when my legs need a break, and a cosy, chatty bar for when they're totally cooked. It looks a lot like Red Mountain, the under-the-radar resort in tiny Rossland, BC. Red Mountain somehow holds incredible terrain, has a classic bar, Rafters, and a gorgeous hotel, The Josie, as well as friendly locals—and is, somehow, rarely busy or skied out.
Nearest town // Kelowna

SOUTHERN
HEMISPHERE

POWDER IN PORTILLO

Chile's most famed ski resort draws an international crowd for its terrain and South American flair. But, most of all, it provides a midsummer snow fix for Northern Hemisphere snowbirds.

For your average ski bum, most ski resorts are relatively simple to figure out. We can pretty much roll up to any ski town, anywhere in the world, take a look at the trail map or ask some locals, sort our way around the slopes and find the best bar for après-ski drinks. But skiing in Chile is different. The country's rich culture and rhythms make its ski scene one of a kind – and it's never what you'd expect.

Instead of the beer and nachos found at cafes in just about every US ski resort, empanadas and pisco cocktails are what Chilean skiers eat and drink. Unlike in North America or Europe, no one wakes up early to get fresh groomers, or even fresh powder. Sleeping in and slowly sipping a café con leche is a mandatory start to the day in Chile. Dinner is served around 9pm or 10pm, when, elsewhere, I'd usually be fast asleep dreaming of the first chair.

When I first headed to the Chilean resort of Portillo, the journey from Santiago to the mountains was perhaps just as memorable as the skiing. We drove the historic Trans-Andean Highway, higher and

LOS ANDES

PORTILLO

LAGUNA
DEL INCA

RÍO BLANCO
NATIONAL
RESERVE

© Liam Doran / Ski Portillo

higher, towards the Chile-Argentina border. The twisty roadway has 29 switchbacks – which, on the way home, I was calling *curvas*.

At the base of the Portillo ski area, deep in the Andes mountains, is the Hotel Portillo, a lemon-yellow box-shaped hotel that sits at an elevation of 9450ft (2880m). Also here as a backdrop is Laguna del Inca, a stunning alpine lake that shimmers cobalt blue. The snowy mountain peaks of the Andes surround the lake, and the hotel sits perched on the edge of the water, overlooking it all. A lovable saint bernard, usually asleep at the hotel's entrance, is the official mascot of Portillo and welcomes arriving guests.

Without much fanfare, I was handed a room key, a lift pass for the week and an 'adios'. I was already disoriented, but in the good way that comes when visiting other countries. I spent my first few days of a week-long stay at Portillo just trying to figure everything out – when to eat, how to ride the wild poma lifts that catapult you up the mountain and even what to wear to dinner (apparently not GoreTex). It wasn't really until day three that I finally developed something of a routine. Particularly, what to order at the bar: '*Un pisco sour, por favor.*'

Portillo attracts all sorts, including North American ski bums looking to get their powder fix in the summer, Europeans on holiday, and Brazilian and Chilean ski families who return year after year. Like many others, I flew all the way from the US, where it was summer, to the Southern Hemisphere for winter skiing. For an American, the novelty of a powder day in August, of getting on the plane in flip-flops and swapping them for ski boots upon landing, never gets old.

If there was one tradition that I took to most quickly, it was slowing down, taking it easy and savouring a new place. Instead of rushing for the first tracks, like I was used to back home, I submitted to Portillo time. There is no town nearby – it's just the Hotel Portillo and a few surrounding structures.

One of the first ski areas in South America, Portillo was originally built by the Chilean government; it opened in 1949 with two single chairlifts and a surface lift. Runs were groomed by the Chilean army and ski instructors were brought in from Europe. At first, the only way to get there was by railway. Eventually, a road was built and the resort was purchased at auction in the 1960s by two North American investors, Bob Purcell and Dick Aldrich. Bob hired his nephew, Henry Purcell, to run the hotel, and by 1980, Henry and his brother, David, became the owners of Portillo. These days, Henry's son, Miguel, is the general manager and the place still retains the vibe of a family-owned institution run by expats. The hallways of the hotel are dotted with framed black-and-white photographs of the Purcell family and all the storied national ski racers from other countries who've come to train here over the decades, drawn to summer snow during the Northern Hemisphere's off-season.

On the slopes, you can rip groomers alongside Austrian or Swiss ski racers who are training on a high-speed downhill course, or just snowplough your way down Portillo's beginner terrain, of which there is a lot. Most of the slopes at Portillo sit above the treeline, so I spent most of my time slashing wide turns in vast open bowls with

⛷ COME AND GO

It takes practice to load and ride the unique surface lifts here, called *va y vient* ('come and go') rope tows, which were specifically designed by French engineers to pull skiers up steep avalanche-prone chutes, where it was impossible to build lifts. Ask for help if you need it, but, in short: stick the frisbee-like disc between your legs, hold both poles in one hand, and when you're ready to go, shout '*Listo*' to the lift operator. Then hold on with all your might.

Clockwise from top: heading up at Portillo; alfresco lunch at Tio Bob's; après pisco sours. Previous page: Hotel Portillo is as iconic as its surrounding peaks

"Instead of rushing for the first tracks, like I was used to back home, I submitted to Portillo time"

nothing in the way. The snow felt similar to what I was used to in the Rockies: deep, cold powder. However, plenty of people come here for the sunshine, not the storms, as it's sunny 80 percent of the time. Portillo's lift-served terrain offers about 2500ft (760m) of sustained vertical drop, which is roughly the same as Alta in Utah. For experienced backcountry skiers there's a well-known couloir called the Super C that drops 5000 vertical feet (1500m) back into the ski area (beware, this chute is no joke, and requires avalanche safety gear and backcountry knowledge).

Towards the end of my visit, I felt like I finally had the place wired. I, too, was starting my day with café con leche and fried eggs with toast; I moseyed to the lifts at the crack of 10am; I would head to the Plateau lift only once the sun hit the rest of the mountain, then eventually tire myself out carving groomers or tackling a few steep chutes. And I would actually take my ski boots off for a white-tablecloth lunch at the classic mid-mountain restaurant, Tio Bob's – named after former resort owner Bob Purcell – and refuel with grilled steak and papas fritas. Chile is known for its fabulous wines; waiters are keen to announce this. All-inclusive here means four meals a day, including a 'tea-time' in the late afternoon.

Thankfully, Portillo's lifts keep on spinning until 5pm, perhaps accommodating for those long, three-course lunches and wine in the early afternoon. At dinner, everyone dresses up, as is custom, and the maître d' will escort you to an assigned table. The bar, it seems, never closes. **MM**

DIRECTIONS

Best time to go // Portillo is open from June to October, but the best snow conditions are typically from mid-August to mid-September. Most people stay for the full seven-day package, though the resort also offers a three-night stay.

Gear required // Rent ski and snowboard gear on site if you don't want to lug your own on an international flight.

Nearest town // Los Andes, 38 miles (61km) to the west.

Getting there // Fly into Santiago, then take a Portillo shuttle bus or private transfer for the 100-mile (160km) journey to reach the ski area, near the Argentine border.

Where to stay // Hotel Portillo has 123 rooms and is the main lodging. The resort also operates two smaller, adjacent lodges and eight private chalets.

Things to know // Portillo is great for kids, with daily activities, a cinema and a games room. Parents will appreciate the on-site daycare for infants to age seven.

Opposite, from top: a trip to Valle
Nevado is an easy add-on to a Portillo
itinerary; hit La Parva on the same
trip for the Chilean hat trick

MORE LIKE THIS
CHILE'S BEST SKI RESORTS

SKI ARPA

This isn't actually a ski resort, it's a backcountry operation that uses 22-person snowcats to deliver skiers and riders to the top of snow-laden slopes in the shadow of 22,837ft (6961m) Aconcagua, the tallest peak in the Western hemisphere. Ski Arpa, Chile's only snowcat outfitter, is situated in a high-elevation bowl, topping out at 12,500ft (3740m) and with more than 4000 acres (1600 hectares) of skiable terrain. Located above the town of Los Andes, Ski Arpa is a 2.5-hour journey from Portillo, making it a good add-on option after a week at the resort. You can rent backcountry skis and an avalanche beacon, shovel and probe, if you don't own those essential items. Come for the day, or opt for overnight packages that include nearby lodging and meals. There's no groomed terrain and no snow-making here. That means there's no easy way down, so this experience is only suitable for expert skiers and riders. If you want to find powder in Chile, this place is a safe bet.

Nearest town // Los Andes

VALLE NEVADO

Portillo is the best spot for that all-inclusive ski-and-lodging Chilean experience, but Valle Nevado, one of the largest ski resorts in South America, is a great one-day add-on before or after a Portillo visit. At Valle Nevado, skiers get access to some 23,000 acres (9300 hectares) of terrain and reliably good snow, just 40 miles (64km) east of Santiago. Unlike many throwback-style resorts in South America, this one feels surprisingly modern, with high-speed detachable lifts, the country's only superpipe, and renovated hotels – some of which have ski-in, ski-out access – offering room-and-board packages for a range of budgets. Have an Ikon Pass? You get up to seven days of skiing here. If you manage to ski the entire resort and want even more, there's a heli-ski outfitter that takes off from the base area and whisks skiers to 5000ft (1500m) Alaskan-style backcountry lines. The ski resorts of La Parva and El Colorado are also nearby, if you want to string together a ski trip to multiple destinations.

Nearest town // Farellones

LA PARVA

Round out your Chilean ski trip with a day or overnight stopover at La Parva, known for its expert-only, north-facing, treeless steeps and deep powder. This welcoming resort also has plenty of intermediate and beginner terrain, too. It's not far from Santiago – about 35 miles (60km) from the city – and in the same three-valley region as Valle Nevado and El Colorado, making it convenient to link a visit to all three. The site of the first Chilean ski club, La Parva, home to freeskiing contests, is steeped in ski lore and culture, and is a pilgrimage place for skiers from the world over. With no hotels on site, you'll either stay in a hotel in the quaint mountain village of Farellones, a few miles down the road, or you can book a condo near the base of La Parva, though those don't come cheap. There's a rowdy hike-to line above the ski area called La Chimenea that attracts the bravest of skiers and riders to test themselves in a 50-degree, stone-walled chute that drops 1000 vertical ft (3000m).

Nearest town // Farellones

HIKING OZ'S HIGHEST IN WINTER

Mt Kosciuszko might be the least dramatic of the world's famed Seven Summits, but tackling it in winter – via a rarely visited route – is a more than worthwhile adventure.

Wan winter sunlight danced lightly across the frost-fringed tussock of the old airstrip as 'roos grazed silently, indifferent to the raucous dawn chorus of sparring kookaburras. Nearby, platypus foraged in the frigid Swampy Plains River as dense eucalyptus forest tumbled impenetrably down the mist-tinged western ribs of the Australian Alps' Main Range. The chill air hastened me across the road from the Geehi Flats campground towards the hidden bulk of Hannels Spur, a rarely travelled winter route to the top of Australia's highest peak, Mt Kosciuszko.

Known as the 'Roof of Australia', the Main Range of the Australian Alps is the highest section of the Great Dividing Range, the continent's 2200-mile/3500km-long backbone and main watershed. Australia's longest river, the Murray, rises nearby, forming the border between New South Wales and Victoria. In 1985, US climber Dick Bass was the first person to successfully climb all Seven Summits, the highest mountain on each continent. His list specified the Australian mainland and thus 7310ft (2228m) Mt Kosciuszko, although its place is now generally taken by New Guinea's 16,024ft (4884m) Puncak Jaya as the highest in Oceania – and a more interesting climb. However, whereas Mt Kosciuszko's normal tourist approach from the southeast (Dick Bass's original route) is hardly a test – a straightforward 3.5-mile (6km) stroll along a mostly raised boardwalk from the top of the Thredbo chairlift – there are far more challenging routes to the highest summit of the sixth largest country on Earth.

Roughly half of Kosciuszko National Park's 2664 sq miles (6900 sq km) are designated wilderness areas. More snow falls on the Australian Alps than on Switzerland, and while Kosi might be modest in altitude, there is nothing between its summit and Antarctica to dilute brutal Southern Hemisphere squalls. Once off the tourist track, the sheer scale and remoteness of the park – with its million-plus acres of backcountry – becomes apparent. The rarely visited Western Fall side of the Main Range is one example of this wilderness area, containing steep, heavily forested ridges; hellish bottomless gullies; pristine Alpine meadows; remote boulder-strewn tors; and zero infrastructure. And the historic Hannels Spur route, first described by Polish explorer Pawel Strzelecki in 1840, is a serious and committed undertaking. With its 5900ft (1800m) altitude gain, it's the highest and arguably hardest of any track on the mainland.

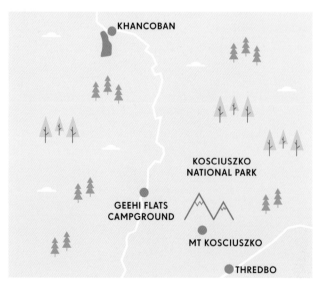

This is wild, remote country, with only one switchbacked access road, no settlements and notoriously fickle weather.

I chose to snowshoe the demanding 14-mile (22.5km) route over two days, although cross-country skies are also a popular mode of transport in winter. Wandering across the large paddock at the base of the spur, I took a short detour to Doctor Forbes Hut – one of the dozens of stone and tin shelters scattered throughout the High Country – which has provided basic refuge to backcountry venturers for over 80 years. Once domiciles of graziers, miners, surveyors and early skiers, these remote huts utilised whatever materials were available for their construction.

The long paddock ended and a single sign pointed into the forest where the Hannels Spur route immediately began climbing at an alarming angle. Heavily overgrown and neglected for years, this scarcely walked track, once regarded as a huge hassle for hikers, is now slowly regaining popularity after some recent love from the National Parks & Wildlife Service (NPWS).

The next few hours were spent viewless as the route wound tortuously uphill through thick scrub, until it finally reached the open clearing of Moiras Flat just above the snow line. The tall Alpine ashes gave way to gnarled snowgums, and the snow, unsurprisingly, deepened the higher I climbed until I relented and strapped on my Evos. Eventually, I breached the treeline at around 5900ft (1800m) and reached the snowy hanging bowl of Byatts Camp, nestled under rocky Abbott Peak. I was fairly exhausted by that stage and decided to camp by the creek, which I'd heard bubbling somewhere below the snow-covered boulders on the southern edge of the bowl.

I had only been asleep a few hours when a storm started blasting down the valley, hurling snow and sleet; the demon wind was screaming and tearing, bowing my tent poles to breaking point. Sleep was no longer an option as I spent the rest of the night holding my trekking poles to reinforce my shelter.

The tent held and the next morning was still – the air clear as crystal, with a cobalt sky over a new layer of deep, soft snow. I packed quickly then climbed out of the bowl, following cairns across the open cirque of Wilkinsons Valley. In whiteout conditions it would be easy to get lost in Wilkinsons Valley and last night's storm was still fresh in my mind, so I didn't linger. There are enough memorials to the inexperienced in these mountains. So I headed straight for Mueller's Pass and the well-trodden Main Range (Lakes Walk) Track.

And here, I did dally. Mt Townsend, Australia's second-highest peak, at 7247ft (2209m), beckoned off to the north. Some historians suggest that this was the actual mountain that Strzelecki climbed, rather than Kosi. It is certainly a more prominent-looking, adventure-worthy peak, though being off the paved track it's also off the radars of most tourists and only has a fraction of the visitors of its more famous sibling. But I couldn't resist. I dumped my pack, skirted below Mueller's Peak and made a beeline for the summit about 1.5 miles away. I made good time until I encountered the stiff scramble up snow-covered boulders on Townsend's summit pyramid. My reward was the sensational views west back into Geehi, the Western Fall

⛷ HIGH HONOURS

Mt Kosciuszko was named by Polish explorer Paul Strzelecki after he was struck by its resemblance to a mound in Krakow commemorating Tadeusz Kościuszko. The Polish freedom fighter was a hero not only in Poland, but also in the US where he fought in the War of Independence with the Continental Army. Strzelecki wrote: '...though in a foreign country, on foreign ground, but among a free people, who appreciate freedom... I could not refrain from giving it the name of Mt Kosciuszko.'

Clockwise from top: variable snow cover requires the right gear; the roof of Australia; Oz's famous gum trees and kookaburra. Previous page: dawn over Kosciuszkco National Park

Wilderness, the Murray River valley, and perhaps the best view of Mt Kosciuszko from any direction, rising truly impressively above the far side of Wilkinsons Valley.

Retracing my steps, I made my way toward Kosciuszko and the final summit spiral. Constructed by NPWS to limit the erosion of the surrounding fragile Alpine heath, the corkscrew footpath seemed a good idea considering the amount of puffer-jacket-clad tourists taking selfies – the same tourists I'd shared the summit with when I hit my high point.

But judging the view inferior to Townsend's, I congratulated myself on my route-less-travelled and joined the day trippers heading back to Thredbo. Just before Thredbo's top chairlift station, I veered right onto the imaginatively named Dead Horse Gap track, which is where my journey diverged from the masses. I snowshoed all the way down to the car park, in relative solitude, to just below the Gap where I'd left my car the day before. When I rolled back into the campground at sunset, the 'roos were still grazing and the kookaburras traded insults over the sun's dying rays. **SW**

'I couldn't resist. I dumped my pack, skirted below Mueller's Peak and made a beeline for the summit'

DIRECTIONS

Best time to go // June to September.

Gear required // Snowshoes (or cross-country skies with skins), a four-season tent and good sleeping bag.

Nearest town // Thredbo or Khancoban.

Getting there // Geehi Flats campground is a 20-mile (32km) drive from Khancoban, or 28 miles (45km) from Thredbo. You'll need to leave your car at Dead Horse Gap, 3 miles (6km) west of Thredbo, for recovery. There is no public transport. Khancoban is a 5-hour drive from Melbourne Airport; Thredbo 5.5 hours from Sydney Airport.

Where to stay // Geehi Flats campground offers simple bush campsites by the Swampy Plains River.

Things to know // Weather on the mountain is notoriously fickle with high winds and temperatures at least 10°C lower than at Geehi. A sunny day can change into a whiteout or blizzard in an instant.

Opposite, from top: the summit of
Mt Ossa; sunset over Mt Feathertop

MORE LIKE THIS
CLASSIC WINTER ASCENTS IN AUSTRALIA

MT BOGONG, VICTORIA

Winter transforms Victoria's highest peak – which is more of an enormous, flat-topped hill in summer – into a magnificent snowsports wilderness. A three- to four-day circuit explores all four of the peak's major ridges. Climb Eskdale Spur above the verdant tree fern and mountain ash forest lining Mountain Creek. The snowline appears before Michell Hut and snowshoes or XC skis will manage you through twisted snowgums. Above the treeline, snow poles head up a steep, scary-looking snow slope to the large, flat summit. An easy traverse leads to picturesque Cleve Cole Hut and camp-worthy snow meadows. The hut is a good base for skiers and snowboarders exploring Bogong's southern gullies. Descend T-Spur to Big River, climbing onto the Bogong High Plains where Roper Hut offers rustic shelter. Timms fire trail descends to Big River again before a long climb up Quartz Ridge leads back to Bogong's summit at 6516ft (1986m). The Staircase spur will take you home.
Nearest city // Melbourne

MT OSSA, TASMANIA

Not many people are crazy enough to tackle Tasmania's famous Overland Track in winter, but those who undertake the six-day, 40-mile (65km) through-hike are rewarded with a magical snow-covered landscape of dolerite-capped crags, frozen tarns, lonely buttongrass moors, myrtle beech forests and Dr Seuss-like pandani. But that's only if the notoriously atrocious weather lets up, otherwise it will all be atmospheric mist. No permits apply in winter and the trail can be walked in either direction, with backcountry huts spaced at regular intervals. Snowshoes (or at least microspikes) will be needed for the higher northern sections, icy boardwalks and any attempt on Mt Ossa, Tasmania's highest peak at 5305ft (1617m). Located roughly halfway between the Pelion and Kia Ora huts, Ossa is formidable at any time of the year, especially so in winter when a 45-degree snow slope must be traversed to gain the summit access gully. Don't expect a view.
Nearest city // Hobart

MT FEATHERTOP, VICTORIA

Often regarded as the only true peak of alpine countenance on the Australian mainland, the iconic snow-covered pyramid of Mt Feathertop (6306ft/1922m) is a magnet for budding mountaineers, novice XC skiers or anyone wanting to share their love of the mountains with the less experienced. There are several routes of varying difficulty, but the most popular is also the most spectacular – a family-friendly traverse along the fabled Razorback, a high, narrow ridge linking Victoria's second-highest peak with the Great Alpine Road near the resort village of Hotham. The views, especially west to Mt Buffalo, are incredible, the route relatively easy and the altitude gains minimal due to the already high elevation. Doable with snowshoes or XC skies, this is a great introductory ramble for anyone wishing to dabble in snow adventures. Although it's possible as a day outing, most elect to camp overnight. Sunrise over the High Plains is a thing of wild beauty.
Nearest city // Melbourne

SUB-SAHARAN SKIING

Little-known Lesotho is a mountainous, landlocked country encircled by South Africa and rich with tradition. It also happens to have one of the continent's few ski resorts.

At a little-known ski resort in a little-known country in the middle of South Africa, guests are so cut off from the rest of the world that the staff go to great lengths to ensure overnighters are well watered, well fed and well entertained. There is 'bumboarding', for example – the art of sitting on a butt-shaped piece of plastic and sliding down the slopes, gripping onto the board's handle and hoping for the best. My own run was so disorienting that I had no idea I'd actually won the race until we got back into the bar and the winners were announced. My prize, if you can call it that, was to hang upside down, hooked into the bindings of a snowboard, clamped to the ceiling, while taking a shot of something sweet and apple-flavoured, to a chorus of cheers from those lucky enough not to have won anything.

On close inspection of a map of South Africa, you might notice that the country resembles a jigsaw puzzle with a piece missing. That off-centre hole within its borders is, in fact, the nation of Lesotho, a mountainous land dubbed the 'Kingdom in the Sky'. Lesotho is completely surrounded by South Africa and, one would assume, not much different than one of the latter's provinces. Yet, crossing the border seemed a gateway into another world. In the upper reaches of the 11,700 sq mile (30,300 sq km) mountain kingdom – which has the highest lowest point of any country on Earth, at 4593ft (1400m) – is the Afriski Mountain Resort.

The ski resort sits in one of the coldest and snowiest areas of the country. Indeed, people had been downhill skiing in these parts for a couple of decades before Afriski was established in 2002. Today, curious skiers and snowboarders travel from as far away as Cape Town and Johannesburg to indulge in the truly unusual experience of downhill skiing in sub-Saharan Africa.

In Lesotho, things feel a little less polished and a lot more laid-back than they do in South Africa. Even the immigration officials took time for a friendly chat as we arrived at the border following a four-hour drive from Johannesburg. After we'd crossed, we passed through Butha-Buthe, a sleepy place where donkeys wander the streets and thatched *rondavels* (round houses) dot the gentle hills surrounding the town. It was warm and sunny, and was hard to believe that in a couple of hours we would be donning skis and hitting the slopes. Lesotho's economy largely revolves around agriculture, and we saw shepherds clad in traditional woollen blankets, gum boots and the distinctive national headgear,

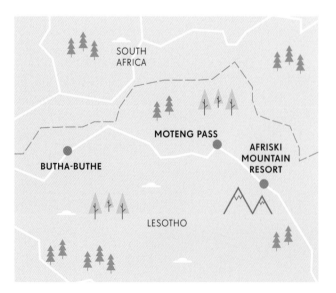

© Edwin Remsberg / Getty Images

⛷ INSPIRED BY MOUNTAINS

You won't be in Lesotho long before you notice the importance of the national hat. The straw *mokorotlo* appears on the national flag, as well as on car licence plates, and it is worn throughout the country, whether with the traditional herder's dress or the more formal attire of the city dweller. The hat's emblematic design is said to have been inspired by Mt Qiloane, a petite peak outside the town of Thaba Bosiu, topped with a 100ft (30m) sandstone pillar.

Clockwise from top: a typical village of roundhouses; a rare sign in Africa; rope tow to the top. Previous page: local shepherds near the ski slopes

"I was the first person waiting to enjoy the freshly made snow. In fact, I was the only person, at least for a while"

a woven, conical hat. And with the entire country sitting above an elevation of 3281ft (1400m), we also saw mountains. Lots of them. Winter temperatures often plummet below -15°C (5°F) and snow is pretty reliable up high from May to September.

The first 30 miles (50km) of driving up towards Afriski Mountain Resort was straightforward enough and fairly flat. But, suddenly, the road that connects the remote villages of eastern Lesotho began to climb and, as it did, the wide, sand-edged road became a narrow potholed pass, with back-to-back hairpin bends that tested the transmission of our bottom-of-the-range rental car. Finally, we reached the peak of Moteng Pass, where we stopped and surveyed what felt like the whole of Lesotho. At a little over 9000ft (2800m), we had our first taste of the winter weather in the Lesotho Highlands, quickly realising that we hadn't packed well for this trip. I used to ski as a teen growing up in the UK, where the slopes of Europe are a short flight away, but when you live in Cape Town, snowsuits and ski goggles tend not to come in handy. For this trip, we'd cobbled together a comical cold-weather wardrobe involving yoga leggings under cargo trousers and woollen jackets covered by cheap raincoats bought at the border.

Half an hour later, we pulled over again as Afriski's main slope came into view, a smooth stretch of powder just discernible on the snowy mountainside. Sometimes the resort operates without the help of snow machines, but although there was a picturesque dusting of snow in the Maluti Mountains as we approached, the snow cannons were blasting when we reached the resort, ready for the next day's skiers.

The following morning, I was the first person waiting to enjoy that freshly made snow. In fact, I was the *only* person, at least for a while. Afriski has six small slopes, the main one being an intermediate, half-mile long run with a couple of sections that offer

a minor challenge to the more advanced skier or snowboarder. I took the button lift up and skied down close to a dozen times before anyone else arrived, my only companions being the trio of Basotho shepherds watching my rusty moves from the comfort of their traditional blankets.

Afriski's lack of crowds is one of its biggest draws. The ski season generally starts a week or two before the South African school holidays in early June, and carries on for about a month after the schools have returned. Visiting at the start or end of the season, outside the peak weeks, is a sure-fire way of having the place to yourself, as I did. By mid-morning, a few day trippers had arrived and a small queue formed for the button lift. Here, I met an expat French family, now based in Cape Town, who were so thrilled with the empty slopes that they vowed to come here again for their powder fix rather than making their annual trip back to the Alps. Of course, Afriski's runs are less challenging: there are only 1.1 miles (1.8km) of slopes to tackle, no double-diamond runs and no off-piste action. There is, however, the Kapoko Snow Park, with its jumps and ramps aimed at more experienced snowboarders.

Haunted by the thought of how sore I would soon be, I de-booted and joined a few others in the Gondola bar for a much-needed bottle of Lesotho's national beer, Maluti. Soon after, the bumboarding shenanigans began and I was taking a shot upside down, strapped to a snowboard in sub-Saharan Africa. **LC**

DIRECTIONS

Best time to go // The Afriski season runs from early June to late August or early September. If possible, get there at the start or end of season and avoid weekends. The resort is open year-round, but outside these times snow-based sports give way to activities including hiking, biking and fishing.

Gear required // You can rent boots, skis, snowboards and poles on site. You will need proper cold-weather gear.

Nearest town // The closest town of any size is Butha-Buthe, 45 miles (75km) west, near the South African border.

Getting there // Johannesburg is about a six-hour drive. The mountain roads are a bit rutted but you won't need a 4WD.

Where to stay // The resort has a range of accommodation from backpacker dorms and basic rooms to self-catering chalets and fancier lodges. If Afriski is full, there's also accommodation at Oxbow Lodge, 10 miles (17km) away.

Things to know // Public transport services to this part of Lesotho are rare, so rent a car to reach Afriski.

Opposite, clockwise from top:
the highest ski lift in Africa at
Oukaïmeden, Morocco; namesake
tree at Cedars Ski Resort, Lebanon;
South Africa's Matroosberg Private
Nature Reserve

MORE LIKE THIS
UNLIKELY SKI SLOPES

MATROOSBERG PRIVATE NATURE RESERVE, SOUTH AFRICA

The season at Matroosberg is short and entirely weather dependent, but if you're in the area at the right time, then spending a few hours on the slopes here makes for a good story. The rustic resort is little more than a two-hour drive from Cape Town, and provided the region has had enough winter snow, there's a window of a week or three when you can join a gleeful pack of South Africans for the only opportunity to snowboard in the Western Cape. You'll need to bring all your own gear and join the Ski Club of South Africa should you want to use the lifts. You can also do ice-climbing here, again assuming you have your own equipment. Accommodation on site includes simple cottages and a dorm-style ski hut. You'll need to follow Matroosberg's Facebook page for the snow reports, but your best bet is to be ready for powder from mid-July to mid-August. Be aware that Capetonians don't see much snow, so the reserve gets very popular after a good squall.

Nearest town // Cape Town

OUKAÏMEDEN, MOROCCO

When you picture a trip to Marrakesh, fresh powder probably doesn't figure in the mind's eye. But only 50 miles (80km) south of the city is the long-established winter resort of Oukaïmeden. Much larger than Afriski, it offers 6 miles (10km) of slopes for both skiers and snowboarders. Sitting at around 10,000ft (3000m) in the High Atlas Mountains, the resort caters for first-timers, intermediate skiers and has a few sections that will appeal to the more advanced winter sports enthusiast. Oukaïmeden pretty much operates at the whims of Mother Nature, so the runs can lack the well-groomed finesse of a European resort, with bumps and occasional ice giving the slopes an off-piste feel. Oukaïmeden does have plenty going for it though, not least the fact that it's much easier on the wallet and far less crowded than Alpine slopes. The season usually kicks off in December, but the snow is at its best in January and February.

Nearest town // Marrakesh

CEDARS SKI RESORT, LEBANON

Skiing in the Middle East might initially seem an unlikely concept, but Lebanon counts half a dozen resorts within its borders. The oldest of these is Cedars, two hours northeast of Beirut. Lebanon's first ski lift was erected here in 1953, but people were skiing in northern Lebanon's Bsharri Mountains for a good few decades before that. It's a modest but well-loved resort with 5.6 miles (9km) of runs evenly split to cater for beginners, intermediate skiers and those seeking a bit more adrenaline. One of the country's highest resorts – its altitude reaches 9350ft (2850m) – Cedars' season tends to last longer than most, kicking off in late November and often continuing well into April. When you're ready to swap ski boots for hiking boots, head out to see the nearby Cedars of God, a swatch of forest featuring the Lebanon cedar – the increasingly rare tree that is immortalised on the country's flag.

Nearest town // Beirut

MUSHING THROUGH THE ANDES

Dogsledding is a rich tradition that has spread throughout the world, including the snowiest southern regions of South America.

As Konrad's 4WD makes its slow, ponderous way up the deeply rutted snow-covered track and through dense coigüe forest, we are greeted by a chorus of howls and barking. The woods open up and a cabin comes into view, surrounded by kennels, with their canine occupants on their feet outside, jumping and straining at their leashes. Konrad assures me that the dogs are not in distress. 'They are very sociable animals, very talkative,' he explains. 'They're just happy to see us.'

Konrad – a tall, athletic, chisel-jawed man in his forties, originally from Germany – shows me around. We're near the top of a low mountain. I can see a plateau opening up a little way beyond, fringed by araucaria (monkey puzzle) trees, native to this part of Chile. Konrad will be my guide throughout a week-long dog mushing expedition in the Andes. The idea of husky sledding here, in the Chilean Lake District near the border with Argentina, seems rather surreal, especially because it's summer back home in the UK.

I ask Konrad how he found himself in this part of the world. He tells me that after 15 years as a German fighter pilot, he wanted a complete change of scenery and a more rewarding lifestyle. 'I love it here in Chile,' he says. 'It's an amazing country, full of untouched nature and endless possibilities for exploration.'

Konrad then introduces me to his several-dozen huskies. Blue-eyed, brown-eyed, brown-and-blue eyed, they jump all over me, with some putting their paws on my shoulders. 'So, how many dogs will pull me?' I ask. Konrad eyes my short stature critically. 'Depends on height and weight. Five to seven dogs normally. For you, five will be plenty,' he says.

'Nebula and Mystique will be your lead dogs, and these four will make up the rest of your team,' Konrad continues. 'When I start training the dogs as they get old enough to work, you can quickly see which ones are more dominant and better at leading. But during the trip, it will be your responsibility to drive the sled and look after the dogs when they're not working.'

Konrad begins to teach me how to mush correctly. He shows me how to put the harness on. The dogs are strong, but luckily they are also very co-operative and know to keep still while I clip them to the sled. Standing at the back of my sled, I acquaint myself with the 'emergency brake', which is a spiky metal anchor that can slow or stop the sled. Just like a boat anchor, you throw it behind the vessel and it drags in the snow.

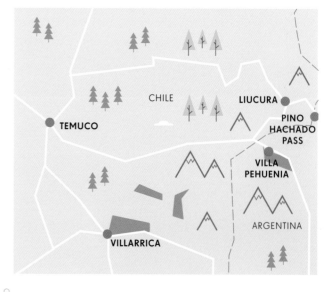

Then Konrad teaches me a bit of husky dialect. 'Dogs are not like horses, so there's no pulling at the reins,' he tells me. 'You direct them using sounds. "Gee" means "right"; "ha" means "left"; "hike" means "run"; and "whoa" gets them to stop.' During a practice ride, I notice more vividly how different the dogs look from each other, despite them all being essentially the same breed. 'I've got Siberian and Alaskan huskies, plus cross-breeds, since I do dog racing in my spare time,' Konrad explains. 'Siberian are the ones originally domesticated in Arctic Russia from wolves, whereas Alaskan ones tend to be crossbreeds.' My own dog team begins emitting small whines, clearly keen to get going again. You can see the excitement in their demeanour. 'Yes, they really enjoy running and pulling the sled,' says Konrad. 'A husky will never do anything that it doesn't want to do.'

Looking back, the three days of prep, of bonding with the dogs and feeling the mounting excitement about my forthcoming adventure, live in my memory particularly vividly – more so than parts of the Andes crossing itself.

On the morning of our departure, I meet my companions for the Andes crossing trip (done in groups of four, minimum). We load into the 4WD with our gear for the week; the dogs and sledding equipment are securely stowed in the trailer behind us. It's a three-hour drive from the husky farm to the hamlet of Liucura, near the border with Argentina, where we leave the road and climb as high into the mountains as possible, up to the snow line, where we unload the sleds and strap our gear into them.

"A husky will never do anything that it doesn't want to do"

From here on in, we are breaking virgin trails through the snow as the dogs pull at their harnesses and lead us uphill, towards the Pino Hachado Pass, which brings us over into Argentina. Crossing between the two countries is surreal. There is little to mark the national boundaries here, apart from some lonely border posts, half-buried in snowdrifts. As I look back behind me, towards Chile, I see the snow-covered, conical shapes of volcanoes rising out of dense forest.

I quickly settle into the rhythm of our adventure. On this first day we break for lunch after only two hours, feeding and watering our dogs, then ride for another couple of hours before daylight begins to fade and we find a sheltered spot in the araucaria forest to pitch our tents and unroll our four-season sleeping bags.

I feel like an early explorer, breaking new trails across virgin snow every day and not seeing a single soul during the course of our mushing. Wind drifts impact the snowfall on the mountains, meaning that no Andes crossing is ever the same. The surrounding beauty never gets tiring; it's just one jaw-dropping landscape after another.

DOG DAYS

Dogsledding is interwoven with human history in the Arctic. Carbon-dated remnants of sled runners suggest that domesticated huskies pulled sleds in far-eastern Russia as early as 6000 years BCE. In North America, dogsledding has been a part of Inuit culture for millennia, though it's thought they used a dog or two to pull minimal cargo, rather than teams of multiple dogs – a practice developed in Russia in the 18th century. The first formal sled race was held in Nome, Alaska, in 1908.

Clockwise from top: overnighters will require winter camping; bonding with the dogs is part of the adventure; five to 10 dogs pull a single person. Previous page: day tours enable mushers to test kit and conditions

Soon, I'm used to sleeping in a tent in the forest, wearing several layers of thermals and a hat, but that only makes me appreciate it all the more when we're invited to stay in a warm cabin in Villa Pehuenia and soak in the hot tub beneath the Southern Cross, sipping bitter but energising maté through a *bombilla* (metal straw).

There are challenging moments: the crossing of frozen rivers with the sled runners skidding on the ice, and the strenuous up-hills, where we have to dismount to actually help the dogs. There are some frightening times, too, such as being caught out in the open somewhere on the Argentinian side between the Pino Hachado Pass and Villa Pehuenia in a whiteout (or '*viento blanco*'). We were completely blind.

One night, clustered around the wood-burning stove, warm and safe, we share how frightened we felt at the time. We weren't in any danger, Konrad assures us. 'Since it's impossible to navigate during a whiteout, we have to trust in our huskies to find the best way through,' he says. **KC**

DIRECTIONS

Best time to go // Although it's sometimes possible to do husky sledding in Chile's Lake District as early as May and as late as October, the peak months are June to August, when snow conditions are excellent.

Gear required // Konrad's company, Aurora Austral (https://auroraaustral.com), provides all the necessary gear for husky sledding, as well as tents and cooking equipment. You have to bring layers (an essential equipment list is provided), as well as a sleeping bag. Extra winter gear is available for rent.

Nearest town // Villarrica.

Getting there // From the international airport in Santiago, you can fly south to Temuco, from where the Aurora Austral husky farm is less than a two-hour drive. Pick-up is available.

Where to stay // One of the cosy cabins at the husky farm.

Things to know // Hand and foot warmers are a boon when you're driving sleds.

Opposite, from top: Valle de los Lobos
near Argentina's southernmost town,
Ushuaia; huskies need to keep cool,
even in winter

MORE LIKE THIS
SOUTH AMERICAN DOGSLEDDING ADVENTURES

CAVIAHUE, ARGENTINA

In the little town of Caviahue in the Neuquén province of the Argentinian Lake District, Javier and Josefina Álvarez run a Siberian husky kennel, breeding sled dogs and offering day excursions to visitors. You don't get to drive your own sled; instead, you sit on cushions, warmly wrapped up, while the sled driver stands behind you and utters commands to the dogs. Unlike many other husky sledding operators, which have an even number of dogs pulling the sleds, Javier tends to work with teams of seven, with one lead dog, and the two strongest members of the team harnessed closest to the sled. On half-day outings to the waterfall on the Río Agrio, you speed past the frozen Caviahue lake with views of the surrounding mountains and the Copahue volcano, before entering sparse araucaria woodlands.
Nearest town // Zapala

CHAPELCO, ARGENTINA

Pioneering dog musher and breeder Pablo Germann, originally from Ushuaia, has raised more than 60 huskies near the Chapelco ski resort some 12 miles (20km) away from the nearest town of San Martín de los Andes. Taking the gondola up to 5250ft (1600m), you are met by your guides and acquainted with your team of six to eight dogs and the Canadian sled on which you'll be seated during the adventure, while the driver commands the dogs from the back. During the two-hour outings, the dogs race through a mix of lenga and araucaria forest, as well as the wide-open spaces of the pampas, allowing you to fully appreciate the beauty and diversity of the mountain landscapes.
Nearest town // Chapelco

USHUAIA, ARGENTINA

Some five miles (18km) northeast of Ushuaia, Argentina's southernmost town at the bottom of the world, the Valle de los Lobos (Valley of the Wolves) is home to dozens of Siberian huskies and Alaskan malamutes, as well as their human owner, Gato Curuchet, a cat among dogs (*gato* means 'cat' in Spanish). Originally from the province of Buenos Aires, Gato dreamed of Alaska as a kid – having been brought up on a literary diet of Jack London stories – but ended up living with his canine friends at the opposite end of the world. Apart from the bragging rights that come from completing half-day excursions in the Valle de los Lobos (the world's southernmost spot for dogsled adventures), you can take part in longer dogsled trips, plus other wintry adventures, such as a sledding and snowshoeing combined day out.
Nearest town // Ushuaia

TRAVERSING BALL PASS

This classic New Zealand mountain crossing in the Southern Alps is one of the best overnight adventures in a country known for its wild side.

The sun is dropping behind the peaks of New Zealand's Southern Alps. The Hooker Glacier is far below and a single set of footsteps lead away, across virgin snow. All is still. Our little orange tent is perched nearby on a small rocky outcrop. Across the valley, Mt Sefton reigns majestic, while much closer, sheer Aoraki/Mt Cook looms majestically above everything else.

Unlike their European namesakes, the peaks of this mountain chain stretching some 310 miles (500km) along the spine of Te Waipounamu – New Zealand's South Island – are wild, jagged, heavily glaciated and battered by a relentless maritime climate, not to mention frequent seismic activity. Infrastructure is minimal, with not much more than a scattering of rustic backcountry huts and the odd chopper dropping off random adventure freaks into the middle of a white nowhere. These are the mountains on which Sir Edmund Hillary cut his teeth before conquering Mt Everest. They're reminiscent of Canada's Rockies or Alaska's Brooks Range – but without the bears.

Although Queenstown is New Zealand's glitzy, self-styled adventure capital, attracting its fair share of powderhounds escaping the northern summer, it is Mount Cook Village, some 150 miles (240km) north, where serious mountaineers come to twirl their ice axes. Many come for a crack at Ball Pass, a classic Alpine crossing, connecting the Hooker and Tasman valleys, via a high col, under the lofty gaze of Aoraki's Caroline Face. In spring, once the winter avalanche threat has receded, the route can normally be completed in good weather in two or three days using ice axe and crampons (ropes are not normally required). By midsummer, the snow has mostly melted, the approaches have turned into scree gullies, water is harder to find and crevasses are opening on the retreating Ball Glacier.

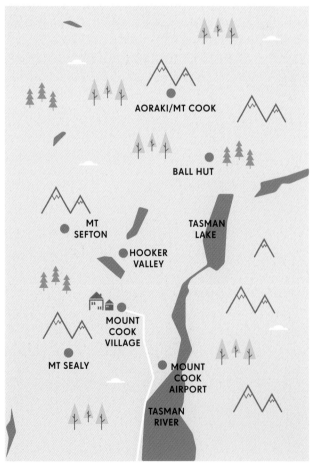

© Steve Waters

HILLARY'S ALPS

Mountaineering in the Southern Alps was well-established by the time Edmund Hillary climbed his first peak, Mt Ollivier in the Sealy Range above Mt Cook Village. The raw 20-year-old was immediately hooked and in subsequent trips bagged neighbouring summits of Kitchener, Annette and Sealy itself. Soon the wilder massifs beckoned and he moved on to Malte Brun before topping Aoraki/Mt Cook twice, blazing a new route up the South Ridge. The rest is history.

"Mt Sefton pokes lance-like through the clouds like some wild, jagged eyrie in a Tolkien fantasy"

Our friends dropped us off earlier in the morning at the White Horse Hill car park, where we took the well-travelled tourist track towards Hooker Lake. Before the shoreline, the unmarked Ball Pass route veered right, across the outlet stream and up the convoluted, untracked, treeless eastern side of the valley. In an area that was devastated by a ferocious storm in 2019, our route wound tortuously in and out of crumbling gully erosion and jumbled moraine for several strenuous hours. But the hard work was more than compensated for by stellar views of the remnants of winter icebergs still lingering on the lake's southern waters below.

Eventually we reached the wide alluvial fan at the bottom of a steep snow gully, just past the end of the lake. We were in luck, as in summer the gully is a tiring, loose scree slope. We put on our crampons, untethered our axes and clipped on our helmets. After a quick refresher in the downhill French Technique and the self-arrest method of stopping, we were on our way up. The snow was firm and delightful to climb, the views back down to the Hooker mindblowing.

It was a textbook ascent to our atmospheric campsite on this sublime plateau where we're blown away by the magnificent surroundings.

And now our perfect first day is rapidly drawing to a close as the temperature plummets with the sinking sun, so we dive into our toasty sleeping bags inside our humble dome – the tent is a necessity, with no useful huts on the Hooker side of the pass.

We wake early to beautiful clear-blue skies and the sun caressing the peaks across the glacier. A quick breakfast and another look at the route photos and we are off, heading for the first ramp of the advised route, which forms a large 'Z'. Again, the snow is firm and lovely to climb. Navigating the shoulder past Mt Mabel, we then need to descend around bluffs below Mt Rosa, where the pass reveals itself high above a large bowl. The views down the entire Hooker Glacier are incredible, with Mt Sefton poking lance-like through the clouds like some wild, jagged eyrie in a Tolkien fantasy.

Crossing the bowl, we zigzag our way to the top of the pass at 7000ft (2130m) and strip down to one layer in the reflective heat

© Steve Waters

From left: snow lingers on upper slopes long into the Austral spring; a lack of huts necessitates tent camping. Previous page: trudging towards Ball Pass

of mid-morning. The snow is becoming slushy. We take obligatory selfies then bid a fond goodbye to the awesome Hooker as we turn our focus to the Tasman, where the pass drops away steeply. We traverse gingerly over to our descent route along Ball Ridge. The snow is pretty wet by this stage, the going more tiresome and sometimes downright scary – unnervingly, I punch one foot through a cornice. On the second such occurrence we leave the spine of the ridge and manoeuvre below and around the hidden crags. It takes hours to make it down to the private Caroline Hut, at around 5900ft (1800m), for a well-earned tea break on the open veranda.

Upon leaving, we pick up some snowshoe tracks indicating the correct line to avoid the ridge's rocky spires. It is the first sign of other people we've seen since leaving the lake the day before. Eventually, we drop below the snow line again and can pack away our ice gear. The route soon leaves the bare ridge altogether, descending a steep tussock and scree-filled gully, before ultimately landing on the flats to the north of Ball Hut.

The light is fading and, all of a sudden, a second night out here doesn't seem like such a good idea. But we're keen to push on and not let nagging injuries get the better of us. We continue the route along the valley, negotiating more storm damage and gully erosion before picking up an old 4WD track. Walking in the dark now, we're in good spirits on the flat road until we finally make the car park. While I'm scanning for a spot to bed down, my companion hits up an elderly Dark Sky photographer from the US who agrees to drive us back to the village. **SW**

DIRECTIONS

Best time to go // September to December.
Gear required // Crampons, ice-axe, four-season tent, good sleeping bag.
Nearest town // Mt Cook Village.
Getting there // Buses from Queenstown or Christchurch take between four and 5.5 hours.
Where to stay // The historic Hermitage Hotel if you have the money; the YHA, Unwin Lodge or White Horse Hill campground if you don't. The Hermitage's all-you-can-eat buffet breakfast should not to be missed regardless of where you stay.
Things to know // The local Department of Conservation (DOC) office has photos of the correct 'Z-route' through the bluffs above the Playing Fields – take copies! The pass is always snow-covered, but most of the approaches are snow-free by midsummer. Check www.avalanche.net.nz before you depart. Expect the weather to turn atrocious at any time.

Opposite: heli-ski operations in and around Queenstown have easy access to world-class backcountry lines

MORE LIKE THIS
EXTREME NEW ZEALAND

BACKCOUNTRY HELI-SKIING, QUEENSTOWN

Kiwis use helicopters like taxis in the backcountry, and with a favourable exchange rate, it's little wonder that NZ is one of the best places in the world for remote skiing and snowboarding. Most operators are based in Queenstown, which means you can be getting a face full of virgin powder not long after stepping off your international flight. Packages can be tailored for duration, location and skill levels, with or without a guide, and this makes it easy for those with less-than-expert technique to make the jump to heli-skiing. Operations are usually centred on the nearby Harris Mountains where both snow cover and weather are more reliable than elsewhere in the country. You can sign up for fully guided, multi-run days with a gourmet buffet lunch, or just a one-off drop into some hell-chasm beyond the edge of civilisation. Similar deals are also available in nearby Wanaka.

Nearest town // Queenstown

ICE CLIMBING, WYE CREEK

This adventure starts where most others end. NZ's most accessible and consistent ice-climbing area is a two- to three-hour journey on foot from The Remarkables ski resort high above Queenstown. From the top car park, take the Lake Alta chairlift to the top station then head south through the obvious col to drop down into the upper valley of Wye Creek. Follow the creek downstream past several tarns and you will eventually find the ice. July and August are the best months for ice quality, when the frozen waterfalls and stunning alpine scenery will leave you totally amped. You will need snowshoes or XC skis to get in, and most groups snow camp, spending several nights in the area. Or you could skip the walk by taking a commercial tour by chopper. Every year, The Remarkables Ice & Mixed climbing festival is held in August with a series of competitions and workshops close to the resort.

Nearest town // Queenstown

CLIMBING TITITEA/MT ASPIRING

Twenty-three of New Zealand's 3000m peaks are all in the Aoraki/Mt Cook area. The 24th, Tititea/Mt Aspiring (9951ft/3033m), is further south in its own wilderness national park outside the postcard-perfect party town of Wanaka. Known as the 'Glistening Peak' by Māori and sometimes marketed as the 'Matterhorn of the South', this beautiful pyramid is one of NZ's most popular mountaineering excursions. Several routes of varying difficulty and duration lead to the exquisite summit, though all are technical and dependent on the season and snow conditions. The peak is surrounded by crevassed glaciers and there are two huts to use as base camps above the treeline: Colin Todd for the North West Ridge, which is favoured by guiding companies; and French Ridge for the harder South West Ridge approach. Expect a very long summit day from either. Tititea/Mt Aspiring is often packaged as a guided climb at the end of local Alpine Skills courses.

Nearest town // Wanaka

TOURING IN TASMANIA

An overnight backcountry ski tour on the edge of the Tasmanian wilderness requires just the right conditions. But when they're good, they're world-class.

Australia's most southerly ski resort lies on the edge of Tasmania's Wilderness, a Unesco World Heritage-listed area covering 3.9 million acres (1.5 million hectares), or roughly a fifth of the mountainous island that hangs off the bottom of the continent, right in the path of the 'Roaring Forties' weather behemoth. It's a wild landscape of jagged peaks, forgotten tarns, lonely moors, bogs, terrible weather and endemic Tasmanian fauna and flora found nowhere else on Earth. And it can all be reached in a two-hour drive from the island's charmingly picturesque capital, Hobart.

Naturally, summer is the most popular time to visit. Decent snow is unreliable, and that's being generous. Which is why, when there is a solid dusting, Hobart snowhounds like myself exit the capital by late Friday afternoon in order to reach the park's entrance in enough time to get a good-night's sleep and start skiing first thing in the morning.

When forecasts whipped up excitement again, I heeded the call, hastily packed for a weekend of ski touring, and drove through the night. The last 30 minutes to Lake Dobson at the end of the road was a low-gear crawl up narrow switchbacks, through primeval mountain ash and tree fern forest onto snowgum-fringed sub-alpine heathlands. The snow sparkled silently on the pandani (giant grass trees) as I rounded icy Lake Dobson, the early morning light awash with rising mist. Passing a swanky-looking ski lodge, I reflected that my own accommodation had been much humbler – a rustic worker's cabin, 10 minutes back down the access road.

Mount Mawson, the only official ski 'resort' in Southern Tasmania, is a 30-minute hike above the lake. It has a handful of rope tows and several historic lodges, and is actually a club field (resort), providing affordable skiing to members, with a ski patrol run by volunteers from

the seven ski and outdoor clubs populating the region. The rope tows, which only run on weekends or holidays, are, of course, the main attraction here for downhill skiers, but it's the adjoining snow-covered wilderness expanse of wide plateaus, windswept peaks and barren ridges that begs further exploration for a more serious winter enthusiast, offering many overnight touring possibilities. And I'd brought bivvy gear for just such an occasion.

I shouldered my skis and continued climbing past the uniquely Tasmanian flora until the narrow short-cut track exited onto a wide, steep, snow-covered – if somewhat icy – fire trail. I pulled on my skins and started grunting up the hill. I'd chosen lightweight alpine

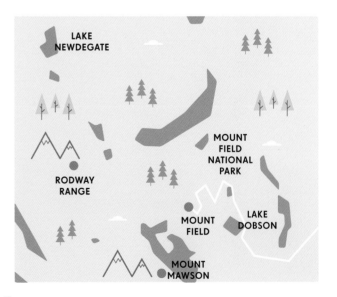

GRASS ROOTS

Tasmania's World Heritage habitats contain diverse endemic flora, including pandani, the world's tallest heath, which can grow to 40ft (12m). These 'Dr Seuss plants' have sharp, serrated leaves, narrow trunks and a palm-like canopy. The Pencil pine, meanwhile, is actually a cypress. These slow-growing, slender trees are often found on the edge of mountain tarns and are susceptible to fire. The fagus, or tanglefoot, is a small, straggly, deciduous beech with leaves that turn a brilliant red in the autumn.

From left: the kangaroo-like pademelon; the Mt Anne track is a wild outing not far from Mt Field. Previous page: Australia's frontier island is wide open and wild

"The Mawson Plateau was now transformed by decent snow depth into a delightful alpine skiing playground"

touring skis with hybrid bindings for added downhill fun, and despite my relatively light overnight pack, I'd worked up a decent sweat even by the time I'd reached the 'resort' area. The rope tows lay still and the modern day-use shelter was empty, still too early for the volunteers. The sun was just dragging itself above McAulays Ridge.

I stopped to remove my skins after sidling up a slope by a still-inactive tow. The Mawson Plateau in summer is a bog-filled, boulder-strewn meadow, but was now transformed by decent snow depth into a delightful alpine skiing playground. It was rare to see such wonderful whiteness here under a clear blue winter's sky. After a short glance towards Mt Mawson's summit, I decided to head in the opposite direction, northwest across the plateau to the Rodway Range. The snow was lovely for touring – firm but not too icy or powdery – and soon I passed the junction to Tarn Shelf below, my following day's return route if the weather held.

Remaining as high as possible, I easily ascended the range, leaving the deep, scary eastern slopes for skiers with a greater need for adrenaline than myself. I passed by the top of the steep Rodway Tow, perhaps the most daunting 'nutcracker' lift in Australia; not one you really want to fall from. After crossing the Rodway, I contemplated leaving my pack at K Col for the out-and-back run to Mt Field West, the highest peak in Mount Field National Park, at 4705ft (1434m). Deciding to keep my survival gear close, I steadily ascended the sloping ridge leading to the wide, high shelf under Naturalist Peak. This was backcountry skiing at its finest and I still couldn't believe how good the snow and the weather was.

I finally reached my goal at the far end of the shelf and laid out a well-deserved lunch on the high point. Soaking up the view of the Tasmanian Wilderness World Heritage Area, I felt remarkably remote. Then I noticed a dark smudge on the southwest horizon – my cue to pack up and move on. Weather can turn quickly in southwest

Tassie and I was taking no chances. I had a fantastic, if harried, ski alone back across the gleaming white plateau and down to K Col, where I turned north to make a run along the Rodway Range. Normally a heaving mass of boulders, the deep snow had plugged all the gaps in the long, airy ridge and I made good time, although I was beginning to feel rather weary. And dark clouds were gathering and growing.

I skied quickly down through snowgums to Lake Newdegate, where an old iron hut, surrounded by pandani, fagus and pencil pines, served as emergency shelter. With the top of the Rodway Range disappearing into the clouds, the old hut was looking pretty good. Besides, winter days are short in southern Tasmania and I was dog-tired. I made a quick dinner then settled into my bivvy bag on the hut floor, hopefully safe from any nocturnal varmints.

But the storm never came. Or, at least, it went somewhere else. Answering a call of nature outside later that night, I was amazed to see stars overhead – and then something else: an eerie green shimmer racing across the frozen lake surface. The hairs on my neck stood up as I looked up and saw green clouds rolling across the top of the Rodway Range. It was the southern lights – aurora australis – and I was blown away. I'd read about the phenomena, but had never witnessed it. As if the skiing hadn't been brilliant enough, nature just turned it up another notch. **SW**

DIRECTIONS

Best time to go // July and August.
Gear required // Lightweight touring skis, a four-season tent and a good sleeping bag.
Nearest town // Hobart.
Getting there // Mount Field Visitor Centre is 55 miles (90km) from Hobart International Airport, but you'll need your own car. The Lake Dobson trailhead is a further nine miles (15km) on; snow chains are required for winter access.
Where to stay // Tourist cabins are available outside the park boundary and at nearby Westerway. Inside the park, the Government Huts are a cheap, rustic alternative, only a 10-minute walk from the trailhead.
Things to know // Grab a copy of TASMAP's Mount Field National Park map from the visitor centre when you pay for your park permit. There's also a small cafe on-site.

MORE LIKE THIS
OZ'S MOST EPIC SKI TOURS

HOTHAM TO FALLS CREEK, VICTORIA

The most famous Victorian backcountry traverse links two of the state's premier ski resorts in an exciting and remote two-day crossing. From Hotham, follow snow poles down ungroomed Swindler's Spur, past several historic huts to Cobungra Gap, then ascend through snowgums onto the Bogong High Plains, a stark, empty, exposed Alpine plateau populated only by wild brumbies (horses) and legends. Wonderful backcountry skiing in fine weather can turn dismal and downright dangerous once conditions tank on the treeless Plains. Follow the numbered poles to number 333, where a track junction offers several possibilities. The north branch leads to shelter at Tawonga Huts, nestled below Mt Jaithmathang, then on to Pretty Valley and the start of the groomed trails to Falls. Alternatively, veer right across the High Plains to camp at Ryders Yards or cosy Cope Hut, where a groomed trail winds towards the resort. Consider returning to Hotham by the opposite route to complete the circuit.
Nearest city // Melbourne

MT JAGUNGAL, NEW SOUTH WALES

Sitting aloft in its own wilderness area in the north of Kosciuszko National Park, prominent 6762ft (2061m) Mt Jagungal is a coveted, almost mythical destination for the most serious Aussie backcountry skiers. It's approachable from several directions, but the most consistent snow cover will be from the south, and a return trip will take anywhere from six to 10 days along a well-defined route heading north from Guthega Power Station. Follow Schlink Pass Rd along the Munyang Valley before joining the Valentine and Grey Mare fire trails. Rustic High Country huts appear sporadically, providing campsites and emergency shelter. In good weather, excellent navigational skills will get you up onto the high open plateaus of the Rolling Grounds and the Kerries for breathtaking skiing in sparkling winter sunshine, though beware the lack of obvious landmarks. Beyond Jagungal, a through route leads to Kiandra. But as you lose elevation past Mackey's Hut, the snow tends to become patchier, the trees denser and you may spend a lot of time walking and fording creeks before reaching the tarmac.
Nearest town // Jindabyne

MAIN RANGE SKYLINE TRAVERSE, NEW SOUTH WALES

This expert three-to-five-day route along the 'Roof of Australia' should only be attempted in fine weather by skilled backcountry navigators. From Thredbo Top Station, climb onto the Ramshead Range (extra points if you start from Dead Horse Gap) and ski the crest, avoiding the crags until joining the well-trodden Kosciuszko walking track east of Lake Cootapatamba. Tick off the highest summits in the country and several Alpine tarns before leaving the track after Carruthers Peak. Ascend the broad ridge to Mt Twynam, then continue peak-hopping to Mt Tate. Locate Consett Stephens Pass to the north and cross to the long, beautiful plateau of the Rolling Grounds. Dicky Cooper Bogong marks the end of the Main Range and an exhilarating descent brings you to the inaptly named Schlink Hilton hut. From here, head south along the well-marked trail through the Munyang Valley to Guthega Power Station.
Nearest town // Thredbo

© Ashley Whitworth / Shutterstock, Theo Clark / Gettyimages, Jason_L / Shutterstock

Clockwise from top: clouds settle over
Mt Bogong in Victoria; sunset near
Hotham ski resort; locals along the
Skyline Traverse

MOM-AND-POP MOUNTAINS

*For a skiing or riding experience that's more quirky and quiet than at the famous resorts,
it doesn't get much better than New Zealand's tiny, family-owned 'club' ski fields.*

Rope tows are an endangered species. But they are cheap, fast and simple. A rope moves in a continual loop, powered as often as not by some ancient tractor engine or similar. The idea is to grab the moving rope with one hand until you are moving with the rope. Then you flick what is known as a 'nutcracker' under the rope, clamp it down by holding on – and up you go. The strain is taken by the nutcracker being attached to you by a belt or climbing harness. It all feels a little overly complicated and outdated, but such is the charm of New Zealand's 'club' ski fields.

The major New Zealand resorts are well known for a Southern Hemisphere winter blast. But scattered across the Southern Alps are a dozen or more small areas whose charms and challenges are spread through whisper, not billboard blast. They offer a very different, very varied experience, laced with infectious Kiwi charm. Most are owned and run by volunteer clubs and, while the members might get cheaper prices, all are open to skiers and boarders, and still offer superb value.

The Selwyn Six – Porters, Temple Basin, Broken River, Craigieburn Valley, Mt Cheeseman and Mt Olympus – hide in the mountains west of Christchurch, the second largest city in NZ. They are close enough for a day out; you could take in two or three in a weekend; or a week's road trip will see you cracking the full half dozen, which is

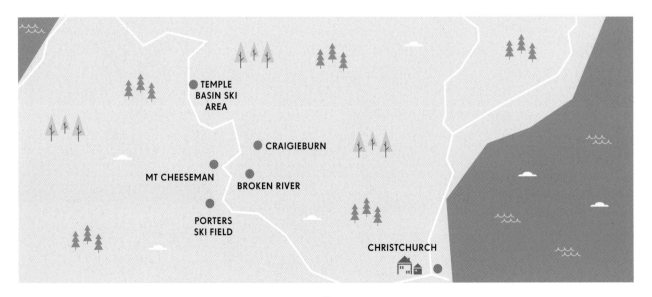

TEMPLE
BASIN SKI
AREA

CRAIGIEBURN

MT CHEESEMAN

BROKEN RIVER

PORTERS
SKI FIELD

CHRISTCHURCH

exactly what I had in mind (there is also an option, for those with the skill and fitness, to ski tour between four of them).

Porters leads you gently into the delights and is a grand place to start. With rare easy road access, a quad chairlift and a line of three T-bars stepping up the mountain, a vast area opens up for all levels of skiers, whether they're cruising the cat track taking in the views, or plunging down seemingly bottomless Big Mama. Jason, an old biking mate, led me into Crystal Valley, a near 3000ft (900m) 'slackcountry' descent of mountain face and gulley that delivered us to within a spit of Porters Lodge, the only accommodation nearby.

The following day, I went on to Temple Basin, which is hidden, even by club field standards, and is the closest ski area to the main divide of the Southern Alps. I clambered up a snowy, at times icy, trail into the clouds. After 90 minutes and 1600ft (500m) of altitude gain, I found the ski area sitting in the mist. Fortunately, a goods lift carries your luggage to the heavens. Nothing is easy about Temple Basin, neither access nor skiing. It is protected by an amphitheatre of mountains and pays its respects to the sentinel of Mt Rolleston opposite. Rope tows here probe into bowls unseen from the lodges and hiking between them is the deal. A band, The Eastern, entertained us on the divide and the party went on until long after the sun had set in the western sky and, for some, almost until it rose again in the east. The next morning, the lifts were unsurprisingly quiet and the snow was firm. Laurence and I found powder stashes down Bills and Cassidy, and laughed at the madness and beauty of it all.

Next, we were on to Broken River, another 'walk-in' ski area. The ski field has a rather funky tramway that, when it works, transports skiers and gear. If not, it's a 20-minute trudge up the access road. Getting to the rope tows from the three accommodation lodges here involves a hike up a long line of wooden steps to the Access Tow. Thus, mastery of the rope is a prerequisite just to reach the day lodge and main ski area.

The day lodge is central to the vibe at Broken River and, as with most of these areas, it's totally accepted that some people will bring their own food and drink. If you want to fire up the barbecue on the deck, go for it. After lunch, steep runs were had off Nervous Knob, long drops into Allan's Basin and much fun off Main Tow. Then, with fresh snow and improving visibility, it was run after run down the ridge to the base of Access Tow, hollering at our good fortune.

Just along the Craigieburn Range from Broken River is Craigieburn Valley itself. After driving up another winding, icy access road, our plan was to stay overnight, ski some runs in the morning and then tour along the range to Mt Olympus. In the bar that night, club president Phil told us how, decades earlier, some members had lovingly built their own T-bar lift, eschewing the commercially available versions. Piece by piece it was transported to Craigieburn, then installed. Dramatically, after less than a season, the towers buckled. So now Craigieburn defiantly remains a grooming-free and rope-tow-only area.

With more snow overnight and ropes to unfreeze, Craigieburn opened late that morning. We traversed beneath Hamilton Peak

WHITE KNUCKLE

Driving to many of the ski fields in New Zealand is part of the adventure – and that applies to many of the main resorts too. On narrow and tight dirt roads, steep corners abound and crash barriers don't. Skiers and boarders who wouldn't blink before a double black may close their eyes as their car teeters on the edge of some icy switchback. 4WD hire cars will give you some confidence, but snow chains are often required. Shuttle buses may be preferable for your own sanity and security.

Clockwise from top: off-piste in the Selwyn region; stoked at Cheeseman; après at Mt Olympus. Previous page: Broken River rope tow

"The ski field has a funky tramway that, when it works, transports skiers and gear"

and boot-packed up onto Hamilton Saddle. A sublime run in deep powder took us back into Allan's Basin and on to Broken River in time for pizza. Soon we were on our way again, taking the main tow up and then booting up a peak overlooking Yukon Bowl. We were tempted, but were late and Mt Cheeseman was calling. A narrow ridge, which would be challenging in bad weather or ice, led us to the climb of Mt Wall and across to Mt Cockayne.

Mt Cheeseman, with two T-bars, is a family favourite. There were no rope tows to deal with, so the only nutcracker required was for the walnut bowl on our dinner table. Alas, we didn't get to ski Cheeseman at its best, as more thick, icy fog wrapped the mountain the following morning. The weather also thwarted our plan to continue touring across the range to Mt Olympus. After a few blind runs, we left early in the afternoon to drive to Mt Olympus instead.

The road to Olympus wound through rocky hills and past a sign that instructed: 'Snow chains and courage should be carried at all times'. Upwards we went on the narrow road, where occasional crumbling edges, snow and fading light added further interest. The Top Hut, the accommodation lodge, was perched halfway up the slopes, necessitating a journey on two rope tows with all our gear. The next morning, in clearing skies, the two upper rope tows gave up some beautiful skiing before we hiked up Little Alaska for a soft snow return to lunch. We gobbled down more runs before boot-packing up to the Sphinx for one final off-piste celebration. Partway down the access road, we saw another sign, perhaps less useful than the first. 'Back to Reality', it proclaimed. **HK**

DIRECTIONS

Best time to go // The season generally runs from July to late September. August and September are usually reliable but check the snow reports and prepare to move around.

Gear required // You'll get everything from sublime powder to savage ice, so be prepared. If you plan any backcountry excursions then take suitable skis/boards and safety gear.

Nearest town // Christchurch is 1-2 hours from the Selwyn Six. Springfield is the last town you'll pass before you hit the mountains; Darfield the closest with a ski shop.

Getting there // Christchurch has an international airport with direct flights from Australia and elsewhere, plus regular connections to Auckland, NZ's largest international airport.

Where to stay // All six of the fields have limited accommodation, usually a mix of catered and self-catered.

Things to know // The Southern Alps are big mountains with variable weather and the inherent dangers all such ranges possess. In winter, avalanche awareness is essential.

MORE LIKE THIS
KIWI CLUB FIELDS

ROUNDHILL

Twenty-five miles (40km) from the town of Tekapo, Roundhill's two T-bars and a platter (overhead tow) access some wide-open runs, ensuring it's a real family favourite. Many park up to the snow, with their tailgates open, setting up barbecues, tables and chairs for the day. But, as the Roundhill website puts it: 'For the more adventurous, head up the world's longest and steepest rope tow and see what Australasia's biggest vertical drop (2569ft/783m) is all about.' The Heritage rope tow goes on and on. It's nearly 5000ft (1500m) long, averages 30 degrees and tops out at 6998ft (2133m), opening up some steep, challenging runs, contrasting with the mellowness of much of the ski field. The most spectacular picture-book views – over aquamarine Lake Tekapo to Aoraki/Mt Cook, New Zealand's highest mountain – demand a drink at the tiny Von Brown cafe.
Nearest town // Tekapo

ŌHAU

Privately owned rather than club run, but with a similar vibe, Ōhau never fails to provide a fine stay and a full stomach, summer or winter (at the Lake Ōhau Lodge, order the pumpkin and orange soup followed by salmon on potato bake with caramelised onions, and plum cake with raspberry sauce for desert). Such indulgence demands a decent workout. And with a handy 10in (25cm) of fresh stuff dropping on Ōhau the day before, I timed my visit well. Access is focused around a double chairlift heading up the guts of the bowl. There's plenty to keep you busy inbounds, but for those well equipped with skins, safety gear and a knowledge of mountain travel, Ōhau has an array of sidecountry excursions. Just watch out for the famous Ōhau rocks that can ruin both run and base. The vistas from the ridge on a blue-sky day are mindblowing. Hemi's run, named after a local Māori ski tourer, drops into a series of bowls and narrow valleys, finishing on the access road just below Ōhau.
Nearest town // Omarama

FOX PEAK

Fox Peak, on the Two Thumb Range, is Kiwi club skiing in the raw. When we visited, a tiny wooden 'Ski field' arrow, with lichen growing on it, showed the way and our car was soon bumping up a farm track, dodging heavily pregnant ewes. In fading light we arrived at Fox Lodge, a proper old mountain hut, perched below the ski area. The Southern Alps were cooking up a storm but weather is localised in these parts and when one ski area gets a dump, another nearby may get nothing. Fox had been unlucky this time and the snow was thinning, but I could see the potential of the three fast-moving rope tows. A tiny hut serves as both ticket office and snack bar in a ski area staffed entirely by club volunteers – and it is usually only open on weekends. A hike up to 7650ft (2350m) Fox Peak offers excellent long off-piste runs into North and South Basin, with 3200ft (1000m) of vertical to the base station. We were among perhaps only 40 people there on a peak season Sunday.
Nearest town // Fairlie

Clockwise from top: epic runs, epic views atop Ohau; the T-bar at Roundhill; Lake Ohau road and the peaks of Ohau

AN ALPINE ODYSSEY IN OZ

Australia's Main Range is one of the finest stretches for multi-day backcountry touring in the Southern Hemisphere – but it offers much more than just a ski tour.

I strapped skis and a carbon violin case to my already bulging pack. It was late on a Sunday afternoon, mid-September, misty and drizzling, in Guthega's car park at the road's end. Winter had played its own tune that season with snowstorms few and far between. The season of 2020, like the year of 2020, was less than average. A ridiculously warm September had played havoc with the snow and a virus had done the same with humanity. Pete, Richard, Mal and I were eager to escape.

Hiking on grass and wet snow, we moved up towards the Main Range, Australia's highest ground. Crossing the swing bridge over the Snowy River, the violin case's strap caught on a stanchion. Fortunately, I caught it before it dropped into the swollen river. More fortunately, I was not carrying Richard's priceless Guarneri concert piece. Once across, we put on our skis and continued, almost until dark, to camp below Mt Twynam, the bronze medallist among Australia's tallest mountains.

The bad weather blew itself out overnight and blue sky greeted beanie-clad heads emerging from tiny tents. Strong coffee brewed as a stream of enthusiastic skiers passed our camp en route to the tops. Fully caffeinated and with porridge lining our stomachs, Pete, Richard, Mal and I skied first to Twynam's summit before taking a steep, still-icy gully down to Blue Lake, mainland Australia's largest glacial lake. We picked our way around the rim of the lake's thinning ice, which, in the thaw of spring, can appear as true blue as its name suggests. Although avalanches are uncommon in Australia, a large slide had recently brought car-sized snow blocks cascading to the lake's edge.

Sticking skins back onto skis, we climbed back onto the defining ridge of the Main Range. From here, waters flow west into the greens of the state of Victoria and on down the Murray River, starting its 1550-mile (2500km) journey to the sea; or east towards the browns of the Monaro plains in New South Wales to continue down the Snowy River. Australia's highest land, on the world's flattest continent, is a very special place. A wombat might shuffle nonchalantly across the snow and, while he does, a pair of colourful parrots flash across the marbled, ice-rimmed trunk of a snowgum, surely the most beautiful trees in the world to ski among.

For decades I've loved that colour contrast, the rain shadow effect so often blocking moisture from reaching further into the Monaro. But, in this winter of 2020, I felt a different contrast. Each time

© juancsanchezherrera / Shutterstock

⚞ FROM THE ASHES

In the far northern reaches of what is now Kosciuszko National Park sit a few ruined heritage buildings. This is the town of Kiandra, torched and blackened in Australia's fiery Black Summer of 2019-20. The fires also destroyed the nearby Selwyn Snow Resort. Kiandra, a frozen but bustling gold-rush town in the mid 1800s, held ski races as early as 1861 when the Kiandra Snow Shoe Club was formed, believed to be the world's oldest ski club. Selwyn Snow Resort, meanwhile, has been rebuilt.

"Two years later, I embarked on my Alpine Odyssey, a second winter traverse of the Main Range"

I stood on those high peaks, I felt both lucky and guilty to be in one of my favourite places while, 6500ft (2000m) below, Victoria sat out the winter in a grim lockdown. For a while, its capital, Melbourne, would claim the dubious title of the most locked-down city in the world. It was a poignant trip in more ways than one.

I'd started guiding Pete in the backcountry over 20 years ago. He had become a great friend and a great supporter of my various expeditions and fundraisers. His enthusiasm was impressive and endless. Regardless of time or temperature, he'd be out to dance in the full moon shadows on Mt Townsend's slopes, or to ski to Mt Tate's summit for sunset.

The first time I took Pete out on the Main Range was a couple of seasons after I'd skied nearly the full 400-mile (650km) length of this Alpine country in 1997. It was an auspicious start as we lay in our sleeping bags for 48 hours while a blizzard raged, eventually bailing when the wind dropped a touch. Once, only once, I heard him complain. Indeed, I even sensed panic in his voice when he realised I might have skimped a little on the quantity of cheap red wine I'd carried for our ski camp. Quality is of no consequence when you have a foam mat as your garden seat, the peaks of the Sentinel and Watsons Crags as backyard rockeries and the billowing cumulus below your feet as an unkempt lawn.

Navigating carefully on a compass bearing during that trip, we scrabbled our way across the Ramshead Range to the top chairlift station at Thredbo resort, the southern gateway to the Main Range. Then, descending towards the village, I slipped and slid 30ft down the hill, skittling Pete below me. The guide taking out the client is never a good look.

Pete was a passionate snowboarder. I'd actively discouraged him from wasting his time, and mine, on a splitboard. But in more recent years, due to much improved technology, I couldn't resist. For sure, I'd laugh as he hiked or hopped along or found himself too low on a long traverse. But seeing him ride, hearing him holler on the steep stuff off Carruthers Peak, made me laugh too, in a more respectful way.

On our 2020 trip, Pete, Richard, Mal and I continued along the range towards the Western Faces – an array of ridges, gullies and creeks that drops off the top of the Main Range and offers the most challenging and extensive backcountry descents in Australia. We dropped runs on glorious, sun-softened snow, then, from the summit of Mt Anderson, Richard swapped ski poles for violin bow. As a serenade to skiing, in surely one of the finest venues he had ever played, he took off, linking turn after tune after turn. Here was one of the world's most famous violinists playing Vivaldi's 'Winter' to the wind.

Two years later, in 2022, I embarked on what I called my Alpine Odyssey, a second winter traverse of the mountainous land a quarter of a century after my first. A journey crossing the country of nine traditional owners (Aboriginal groups), through three states and territories. In 1997, I didn't see or speak to another soul for the first 18 days of that winter traverse. The first person I met told me about

the death of Princess Diana. Twenty-five years on, the day after I finished my latest journey, the world was tuned into the burial of her mother-in-law, Queen Elizabeth II. Soon after, my own mother-in-law, Eira, whose name means snow in Welsh, passed away.

This time I was repeating the route, with the added twist of diverting to ski at each of the 11 snow resorts dotted across the Alps. When I arrived at Thredbo at the beginning of September 2022, I was 40 days and nights into my journey. I had planned to meet Pete there, to ski the resort and then head off to summit 7310ft (2228m) Mt Kosciuszko, Australia's highest mountain. But Pete was not well and did not show up.

It's a hot summer day as I write this, just a couple of months since I completed my 50-day Alpine Odyssey. Through the window I can see distant snowdrifts still clinging to the southern and eastern gullies of the Main Range. Earlier this same day I penned a eulogy for Pete, who was taken not by the C word that has held sway over our world these past few years, but by that other rotten one. 'Carpe Diem [seize the day],' people often say after such losses. It actually translates more fully as make the most of the present and give little thought to the future. Perhaps we lovers of snow should better say, 'Carpe Ski'em'. **HK**

Clockwise from top: the tor at Mt Kosciuszko; mingling with the masses at Thredbo. Previous page: Thredbo ski resort

DIRECTIONS

Best time to go // The most reliable time for snow is late July into September. Backcountry touring on the Main Range runs well into October; and there are gully runs into November.

Gear required // Cross-country skis and telemark set-ups once dominated. But lighter AT gear and the rise of the splitboard has drawn new groups of skiers and boarders here.

Nearest town // Access points include the resorts of Thredbo, Guthega and tiny Charlotte Pass. All feed 20 miles (30km) or so down to the snowline hub town of Jindabyne.

Getting there // Jindabyne is roughly a two-hour drive from Australia's capital, Canberra, and five hours from Sydney.

Where to stay // All the resorts have accommodation, but this can be hard to find in peak season. Jindabyne is a good base. Up on the Main Range, tents are the only option.

Things to know // Day forays onto the Main Range are possible, but allow three days for a full traverse; much longer to enjoy its many delights.

Opposite from top: the popular slopes of Mt Buller; Jagungal Wilderness is wild indeed

MORE LIKE THIS
OZ'S BIGGEST BACKCOUNTRY

FALLS CREEK & MT BOGONG, VICTORIA

Falls Creek – or Falls as it is often shortened to (the perfect name for this sport) – is a resort in the Victorian Alps, one of Australia's Big Five, along with Hotham and Mt Buller, also in Victoria, and Thredbo and Perisher in New South Wales. With loads of beginner and intermediate terrain and a great village, Falls is also the pre-eminent XC (cross-country) ski resort in Australia. Some 30 miles (50km) of groomed trails head onto the Bogong High Plains and, at the end of August every year, the long-distance Kangaroo Hoppet attracts about 1000 skiers as part of the global Worldloppet series. Beyond the trails, the High Plains offer easy touring terrain and an array of atmospheric old huts. An overnight trip will see you at Hotham, with perhaps the most consistently challenging resort skiing in Oz. In the other direction is Victoria's highest peak, Mt Bogong, at 6515ft (1986m). The delights of this bold mountain, standing separate and aloof from its surroundings, are hard won from the High Plains (allow a couple of days), but there are endless gullies and faces to explore on its summit plateau.
Nearest city // Melbourne

MT BULLER & MT STIRLING, VICTORIA

A tale of two mountains that are not really twins, more distant cousins living next door. Rowdy Mt Buller is the closest large Alpine resort to Melbourne and, when the snow conditions hit it well, offers as varied and fun skiing and boarding as anywhere else in Australia. And with its stack of fast, modern lifts, Buller moves people if not mountains. Six miles (9km) away is Mt Stirling, out for a quiet life. Eschewing lodges and lifts, Stirling is all about ski-touring, generally easy touring for the most part, on marked trails. That's not to say that challenges can't be had at Stirling. Head to the Stanley Bowl for some steeper backcountry runs or take a trip out towards the Monument and Craig's Hut. Countless thousands of Victorian XC skiers and tourers have cut their teeth here. A smattering of basic huts allows for simple, self-catered accommodation. For a real contrast, spend a day at Stirling then tour across to Buller – perhaps even ask them to keep the noise down.
Nearest city // Melbourne

JAGUNGAL WILDERNESS, NEW SOUTH WALES

As a light does to a moth, solitary Mt Jagungal (the Big Bogong) – the most northerly of Australia's 2000m peaks – calls you in. And most people head straight for the summit. But the terrain surrounding this popular peak is vast and can take days to explore. North of the Main Range, on through the massive expanse of Kosciuszko National Park, you'll find stands of gnarled snowgum trees, occasional groves of straight mountain ash, granite monoliths, creeks, tarns and hidden old huts. It's never too challenging, except when the blizzards blow and disorientation takes hold in this up/down country. If you come to the Jagungal Wilderness looking for steep stuff, you might be disappointed. But if you come for some winter wilderness wandering, you'll rejoice.
Nearest city // Canberra

A SOUTH ISLAND SKI HUB

New Zealand has more beauty, adventure, wonder and thrills per square mile
than any country in the world. It's no wonder Cardrona ski resort is so epic.

The view from the shared kitchen in Queenstown's Absoloot Hostel was serene. The windows framed Lake Wakatipu, which in turn was framed by the snow-capped Remarkables and Kaikoura mountain ranges. It was beautiful and otherworldly, and, as my effervescent guide Nick explained in an inflected, clipped Kiwi accent, the backdrop for several scenes in The Lord of the Rings movie trilogy.

Yet Nick hadn't come here to sell serenity. Queenstown, on New Zealand's South Island, isn't known as the Adventure Capital of the World for its ability to slow the heart rate. Today, Nick explained, we could execute 360-degree spins in the world's fastest passenger speedboat. Or ski dive from 15,000ft (4500m) over New Zealand's highest mountain, Aoraki/Mt Cook. What about 15 minutes piloting the world's only hydro shark, a two-person jet ski that can submerge at high speed? I sensed a bungee-jump offer was coming.

All, except for the hydro shark, sounded like A-grade adventure fun. But halfway through the spiel, my eyes and thoughts had returned to those snow-topped mountains. The just-risen sun had coloured the sky a pure, clear, powdery blue. The deep, grey-blue lake was unruffled; the wind a soft kiss. Nick, seeing my attention wander, suddenly grabbed it back. 'Or, we could go snowboarding,' he said. 'It's been puking. It's bluebird. And we have the choice of skiing Coronet Peak, Treble Cone or Cardrona.'

'You had me at snowboarding,' I replied.

Now, let's face it, New Zealand is a long way from anywhere except New Zealand. Getting there takes considerable time and money. Looking for advice on whether to take the plunge in the first place, I'd sounded out Ed Leigh, a British-born ex-pro snowboarder turned TV and Olympic Games broadcaster. Having spent two decades living in the European Alps, he'd moved to the South Island three years ago with his Kiwi wife and two skiing-mad children. 'It might not be able to match the steeps of Europe, the tree runs of North America, or the powder stashes of Japan,' Ed started cautiously, 'but there is some incredible snow and even better scenery. I'd add that no one builds better terrain parks or offers more genuine hospitality than the Kiwis. Look, I'll never get used to calling the resorts ski fields, but there's nothing like it anywhere in the world.'

It was Ed who had advised me to base myself in Queenstown, for more than just the adrenaline offerings. It lives up to its

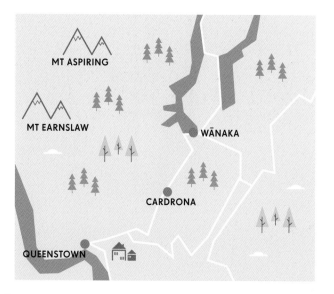

⚒🎿 STAYING POWER

The Cardrona Hotel, established in 1863, is one of New Zealand's oldest, and one of only two buildings still standing from the Cardrona Valley gold rush era. The town was a prosperous settlement in its heyday as well as a significant commercial hub for the area. Featured in a famous New Zealand beer commercial in the 1980s, it lays claim to being the most photographed pub in the country.

Below, from left: clear skies and slopes at Cardrona; it's a dream resort for snowboarders. Previous page: freestyle skiers flock here too

reputation as a global tourist hub and one of the best winter party towns. And its proximity to a range of New Zealand's best ski fields practically makes it a ski town. When I asked Ed which resort he would choose if he only had one day to ride, his response was emphatic: 'Cardrona – it has the best of everything that skiing in New Zealand has to offer.'

And so I found myself with Nick in his early 1990s Land Rover, making the 45-minute drive from Queenstown to Cardrona. The drive itself was almost worth the price of the lift pass. We first skirted the shores of Lake Wakatipu, before tackling the country's highest road along the Crown Range, full of tight curves and sweeping vistas over remote, sheep-dotted fields, mountains, valleys and lakes. As with most ski fields in New Zealand, access to Cardrona itself is along a long, steep unsealed access road that ends in countless switchbacks. Nick's trusty 4WD meant we could skip past all the cars putting on the chains required for the ice- and snow-covered final section. With Cardrona only having nine lifts and 25 miles (40km) of pistes, every minute counted if we were to get the best of the new snow. We grabbed a flat white from Little Meg Café, which was expertly made by a young barista wearing a T-shirt that read: 'Cardrona – promoting sick days since 1980.'

On the hill, we took in the bluebird skies and a fresh 10in (25cm) layer of snow that allowed most of the piste and off-piste Cardrona combinations. 'It's pretty much perfect conditions,' said Nick, whose easy riding style had the flair of a man brought up in the parks and mountains around Queenstown. I tried to keep up with him as he raced to rinse any untracked powder. His local

knowledge led us to the Keg and Arcadia areas, where there was a variety of snow-gathering gullies and plenty of rocks to throw ourselves off; Arcadia's chutes offer the steepest terrain on the mountain. For un-extreme riders such as myself, the runs that peeled off Captain's lift provided mellow turns on the groomed slopes.

For lunch, we hit Captain's Pizzeria. This is located at the base of the Highway 89 blue run and offers some of the best views on the mountain, alongside locally brewed craft beer and what the owners call the 'world-famous-at-Cardrona pizza'. Given the venue has been running since 1986, I had to back their call. Over a sweet

> *"No one builds better terrain parks or offers more genuine hospitality than the Kiwis"*

potato, feta and chorizo pizza, Nick introduced me to local skiing legend Jossi Wells. Jossi was raised in the Cardrona patrol room, where his father was head of ski patrol. At 16 years of age, Jossi was the youngest person ever to compete in the X-Games, going on to win five medals, including slopestyle gold in 2016. 'You have to hit the park,' he advised. 'It rivals [US resorts] Breckenridge, Keystone and Mammoth for resort features.'

Cardrona's terrain park is overseen by John Melville, the eminent head shaper at some of the biggest snowboard contests around the world. Its 22ft (6.7m) Olympic Superpipe is the only one in the Southern Hemisphere to be assigned by the FIS as World Cup standard. After a few hours of mainly watching freckly eight-year-olds sticking incredible tricks, we hit the pistes for the last hour. The final run, the Queenstown Return, was a scenic glide along the cat track on the Cardrona boundary, with breathtaking panoramas of row-upon-row of the Southern Alps and the entire Wakatipu Basin.

Cardrona is unique in New Zealand in that it is the only ski area with accommodation on the mountain. However, with only 15 self-contained apartments and one restaurant, it's no après ski hotspot. Many of the locals will drive down the hill for a glass or two of Glühwein beside the roaring outside fire at the Cardrona Hotel, one of New Zealand's oldest. Yet the beauty of staying in the heart of Queenstown meant that in 45 minutes Nick and I would have the pick of traditional pubs with live music or quirky hole-in-the-wall wine bars and then be able to walk home. By 10pm, I was deliriously, uproariously happy. I'd assigned Nick as a BFF and assured him that I may have just had one of the best mountain days of my life. Granted, the mezcal may have played a part in my exuberance.

Nick patted me on the back, raised a tequila and headed for the exit before turning back to me. 'Just wait for tomorrow,' he said. 'Tomorrow, we ride the hydro shark.' **BM**

DIRECTIONS

Best time to go // The season runs from June to October, depending on conditions. The best snow is usually July and August, but many locals swear September is your best bet.

Gear required // Trusted skis and snowboards that can handle a mix of off-piste, groomed runs and park terrain. There are a couple of ski rental shops located at the base of the mountain and many in Wanaka and Queenstown.

Nearest town // Cardrona is 14 miles (22km) from the town of Wanaka and 28 miles (45km) from Queenstown.

Getting there // Queenstown Airport receives daily direct flights from Auckland, Wellington and Christchurch. Shuttle buses go daily from Wanaka and Queenstown to Cardrona.

Where to stay // Queenstown has everything from luxury stays with incredible views to cheap fun and exciting hostels.

Things to know // Cardrona has great all-rounder skiing, with 25% of the terrain suitable for beginners, 25% for intermediates, 30% for advanced and 20% for experts.

MORE LIKE THIS
GREAT RESORTS DOWN UNDER

TREBLE CONE, NEW ZEALAND

Treble Cone, 30 miles (50km) from Cardrona, close to the town of Wanaka, is the largest ski area – with the longest vertical rise and one of the longest groomed runs – in NZ's South Island. The resort sits on the side of a steep mountain, giving you the feeling of standing on the edge of the world as you look out across Lake Wanaka and to Mt Aspiring. With beginner slopes few and far between, the resort's reputation is built on the open powder faces and natural half-pipes in the Saddle Basin and on the summit slopes. On powder days, the Motutapu Chutes offer some of the steepest and most challenging terrain in the country, and perhaps the only skiing that comes close to the best of the Rockies or European Alps.
Nearest town // Wanaka

MT HUTT, NEW ZEALAND

Mt Hutt Ski Area, just a 90-minute drive from Christchurch, makes for a more laid-back and inexpensive ski holiday than the Queenstown resorts. It does, however, offer substantial thigh burn by NZ standards, with its impressive vertical drop. This, combined with the steep pitch, makes it prime racing terrain and has led to Mt Hutt being called the 'capital of speed'. On a clear day, views extend through the Canterbury Plains to the Pacific. From the back of the mountain, there are equally amazing views of the snow-covered Southern Alps, which stretch almost to the Tasman Sea. However, although the resort's exposed, tree-less location means that it catches the snow like a baseball glove, it can often be shut down because of wind.
Nearest town // Methven

PERISHER, AUSTRALIA

Owned by Vail Resorts, Perisher Ski Resort in New South Wales has the largest skiable terrain and the greatest number of lifts in the Southern Hemisphere. Like its New Zealand counterparts, its short season and limited altitude and snowfall are offset by a unique, family-friendly ski environment and world-class pipe and parks designed for differing abilities. It's neither steep, deep nor cheap, but if you get a rare powder day, skiing among the Snowy Mountains' eucalyptus trees, you will remember it for some time. Limited mountain hotels and lodges means most of the après-ski action and accommodation happens in the town of Jindabyne, an often-busy 30-minute drive from the resort base.
Nearest town // Jindabyne

*Clockwise from top: going off-piste
on Mt Hutt; Perisher is the Southern
Hemisphere's largest ski resort; Treble
Cone is New Zealand's largest*

BULGARIA'S BACKCOUNTRY COULOIRS

An unlikely ski scene has grown out of Bulgaria's extraordinary terrain —
you'll find some of the country's best beyond the lifts of Malyovitsa.

The heart of Bulgarian skiing is a bar under an overpass in Sofia. I didn't believe it until I saw it, but it's true. It's where, hidden in plain sight just a few hundred yards from the National Palace of Culture in the country's capital city, the Bulgaria Extreme and Freestyle Ski Association (BEFSA) meets year-round. OK, it's not an association in the traditional sense of the word, more a gathering of middle-aged men who like to drink Kamenitza beer and watch ski movies. Nevertheless, every Tuesday, a collection of 20 to 30 of Bulgaria's most ambitious skiers convene here, planning missions throughout the country's snowy – but very under-the-radar – mountain ranges, as US hip-hop blasts in the background.

I wasn't even in the country to ski. I love skiing and I ski any chance I get, but I was actually in Bulgaria waiting for my Schengen Zone tourist visa to reset. I'd read about the bar in an old article in *The Ski Journal* and, as a skier without a single connection in the area, drinking beers with other skiers seemed like the best way to kill the time.

Having wandered into the bar, I almost bumped directly into Lyubomir Gadjev, a lager-toting fortysomething with a propensity for fast motorcycles and, yes, skiing. The shiny-faced Lyubomir extended a meaty hand before my eyes could even adjust to the room. 'You're new here,' he said in near-perfect English. Taken aback, I offered my hand and a nod. 'Well, when are we going skiing?' he asked.

It was May. I was in a bar surrounded by Soviet-era concrete, wearing shorts and a sweaty T-shirt. And sure, I was working as a ski journalist, but I didn't have even a pair of ski socks in my bag, much less any actual gear. Besides, does Bulgaria even have

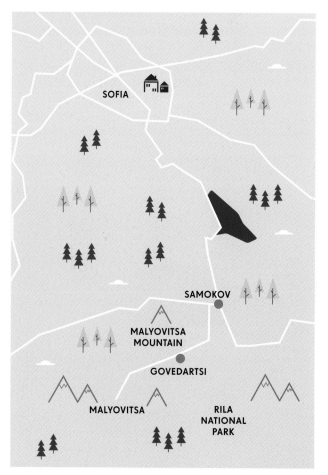

legitimate skiing, I wondered. And who is this guy? Lyubomir's smile widened. 'OK then, this Saturday.'

At the hinge of Southern Europe and the Middle East, Bulgaria was once a major agricultural resource for the Soviet Union, fed by moisture-laden storms blowing off the Black Sea. Those same systems plaster Bulgaria's mountainous terrain (roughly 60 percent of the country's total area) with white in winter, and have even given rise to many ski areas up and down the western flank of the country, from Bansko – Bulgaria's most well-known resort and a former FIS World Cup site – to Borovets, a ski area born out of the former hunting grounds of Bulgarian royalty. Day tickets at these resorts cost a fraction of those at their Alpine neighbours.

It was in the shadow of Vitosha ski resort that I found Lyubomir on that misty Saturday morning, parked outside an aging apartment complex cut directly from a Soviet community activation poster. He told me that in good years he's skied from Vitosha's 7520ft (2292m) peak down to the road near his house. But the peak was draped in morning fog, so it was pretty clear those lines weren't on the table this late in the season. Plus, added Lyubomir, Vitosha hadn't opened yet this year. But he told me not to worry as we were heading to Malyovitsa, a two-hour drive down the road.

After picking up fellow BEFSA member Dimitar Kambarev and a pair of extra skis, poles and boots, Lyubomir pointed his dusty, Russian-built SUV south, out of the city. Soundgarden and Nirvana crackled over the radio. Bulgarians love their grunge and early 1990s music, said Dimitar, as it reminds them of revolution and the fall of the Iron Curtain. Grey blocks of apartments cut from the Soviet era quickly gave way to rolling waves of green peaks as we plunged deeper into the Rila mountains.

The ski area at Malyovitsa is nothing impressive, only offering 2.5 miles (4km) of skiable terrain with a wooden base lodge and five surface lifts, but its access to higher alpine slopes has made it a favourite of mountaineers and backcountry skiers alike. Malyovitsa's peak extends to 8953ft (2729m), and a series of winding couloirs snake down its steeper northern face, often holding snow until late May or early June. These couloirs are precisely why we came here.

After loading skis onto my pack – another essential loan in addition to a beacon, shovel and probe – I shoved down some bread spread with *lutenitsa* (a Bulgarian vegetable relish) and began following a well-worn path along a forested drainage area. Within 30 minutes, trees gave way to sub-alpine rock and unobstructed views of the mountain above. Tantalising ribbons of snow wove between rocks and ended in a massive basin just above our trail. I struggled to keep up, sucking in wind behind Dimitar and Lyubomir, who are surely Bulgaria's top endurance athletes. Finally stopping to take a break at the base of the snowfield, the latter looked back with a wide grin. 'Sorry,' he said. 'We are racing the sun.'

Eventually transitioning to ski boots, we agreed to head up Malyovitsa's middle couloir, a twisty hallway of snow that tops out

⚐ HEAVEN SENT

It's a common belief in Bulgaria that when God created the world he gave different elements to each country, with some taking the mountains and pastures, others the coasts and seas. When it came to their country, there was nothing left – so God took a piece of paradise and gave it to Bulgaria.

Clockwise from top: hiking upwards on Rila Mountain near Malyovitsa peak; Rila Mountain's summit. Previous page: Musala peak in the Rila mountains

"Lyubomir told me that in good years he's skied from Vitosha's 7520ft (2292m) peak down to the road near his house"

at a small ridge, 1700ft (520m) above. We kicked into frozen walls of snow as we made our way up the steepening grade, the rock walls leaning in closer and closer as we gained ground. The heat of the day settled in as we reached the top of our line. Spread out in front of us, the Rilas rose and fell in a dramatic panorama. Far below, Rila Monastery, a 10th-century Eastern Orthodox monastery and Unesco World Heritage Site, poked out of the sea of awakening green. 'You're up,' said Lyubomir, nearly knocking the wind out of me with a hefty palm to my back. 'Guests drop first.'

I sensed the hint of urgency and hustled to click into my skis. Pulling a pair of goggles over my snapback cap, I adjusted straps, tapped my poles and dropped back towards the snowfield. As out of my element as I'd been on the approach, the skis felt familiar underfoot. I cut small turns through the rock choke point at the top of the line and then opened up into the apron at trhe bottom, connecting high-speed arcs through fast corn snow (small clumps formed by repeated melting and freezing). Looking back over my shoulder, I eyed my handiwork as Dimitar and Lyubomir burst out onto the apron (the broad area just below the couloir) behind me.

I couldn't believe it. I'd scored some of my best (and surely last) turns of the season with a couple of guys I'd chanced upon at a bar meet-up in Bulgaria's capital. **KK**

DIRECTIONS

Best time to go // People ski the couloirs off Malyovitsa from early winter until late spring, but for the most stable snow conditions, wait until early April.

Gear required // Beacon, shovel, probe (and AIARE avalanche training or equivalent – or a guide). From there, a standard AT (Alpine Touring) setup should suffice.

Nearest town // Govedartsi (8 miles/13km away).

Getting there // From Sofia, a drive to the car park at Malyovitsa ski area takes a little under two hours.

Where to stay // Govedartsi has accommodation year-round, and Hotel Mechit offers a great value, cosy stay for weary travellers. It also hosts a legendary karaoke night.

Things to know // Bulgaria has snowy winters, and wind blows off the Black Sea and sweeps down from the frigid Russian north. Keep an eye on forecasts. The country is outside the EU Schengen Zone but does not require a visa for US travellers staying for fewer than 90 days.

Opposite, from top: Slovenia's Planica at Ratece near Kranjska Gora in the Julian Alps; Mt Parnassos in Greece

MORE LIKE THIS
OVERLOOKED EUROPE

GREECE

Gracing Bulgaria's southern border, Greece may not seem like a destination for scoring deep powder turns, but the Mediterranean nation is actually home to more than 20 ski resorts. While the white-washed villages spread throughout the country's rocky coastline distract most of the tourist hordes, Greece's varied array of white-capped mountains have attracted skiers since as early as the 1920s. About 125 miles (200km) from both Athens and Patras, Parnassos Ski Resort, the country's largest ski area, offers high-altitude thrills over 17 miles (27km) of ski terrain. Most of Greece's ski hills are smaller, more local affairs, offering intimate accommodation and home-cooked meals of spiced lamb and *patsa* (tripe soup). The cost of skiing in Greece is a fraction of that in its Western European neighbours, and the country's skiers also benefit from powerful storms blowing up from the south, providing powder days with views of the Aegean Sea.

Nearest town // Athens

NORTH MACEDONIA

Lesser known than its Balkan neighbours, this relatively new country (it became the Republic of Macedonia in 1991 and then North Macedonia in 2019) is one of the most mountainous in the world. Still, after years of shifting borders and rulers, the country only has nine established ski resorts, few of which are equipped with the modern amenities of destinations in the Alps or Dolomites. But what the country lacks in bubble-heated six-packs, it makes up for in charm and affordability, providing a unique mix of Slavic, Greek and Turkish culture and heavy pours of locally grown wine. The country's ski scene really thrives beyond resort ropes, with ample backcountry offerings and a handful of cat-skiing operations shuttling visitors to the top of craggy lines. SharOutdoors runs winter tours along the border of North Macedonia, Kosovo and Albania, right outside the country's premier ski area, Popova Sapka, connecting skiers with local guides to access rural and isolated lines in this unlikely powder paradise.

Nearest town // Skopje

SLOVENIA

Bulgaria may have brought the FIS World Cup to Bansko, but Slovenia has become a regular stop on the tour, hosting contests at Kranjska Gora in the Julian Alps. Though many skiers might think this lesser-known ski nation is in the shadow of the Alps, it is technically part of that massive mountain range, as the Julian forms a snowy cradle at its eastern edge. The country's 50 or so ski areas capture maritime moisture before it moves inland, blessing the region with consistent (and often deep) snowfall from December through March. Slovenia is gaining popularity among Western Europeans looking to cut costs, but by and large it remains hidden from the greater skiing mainstream, allowing for days of quality skiing after storms, and few queues away from the most popular resorts, Kranjska Gora and Krvavec (just 20 miles/30km from Slovenia's capital, Ljubljana). For those looking for unspoilt wilderness, Vogel Ski Resort, tucked inside Triglav National Park, is protected from development and boasts panoramic views of Lake Bohinj.

Nearest town // Ljubljana

AN ICY SLUMBER

There are now several ice hotels all over the world, but Sweden has the original, with an impressive design that guarantees an immersive Arctic sleepover.

At Kiruna Airport, in northern Sweden, far beyond the Arctic Circle, I'm beckoned by a man holding up a sign with my name on; he's the musher – my taxi. Outside the airport building, surrounded by snow-covered forest, I'm immediately hit by a blast of cold air and my exposed nose starts to turn numb; it feels at least -30°C (-22°F). I'm surprised and delighted in equal measure to discover that there's a separate pick-up/drop-off area for dogsleds. 'In Jukkasjärvi, there are more dogs than people,' the musher informs me cheerfully. 'Being picked up by dogsled is very normal around here.' But dogsledding is not why I've come. I'm here to stay in a hotel room made entirely of

ice, in a hotel made entirely of ice – Sweden's legendary Icehotel, which was the first of its kind in the world.

Once I'm wrapped up in my Icehotel-issued snowsuit, boots, balaclava and mittens, I board my sled and our eight-dog team takes off along a well-trodden snow trail. Just over an hour later, we finally pull into the Icehotel's parking area in the tiny village of Jukkasjärvi. I see two orderly lines of single-storey, snow-bedecked cottages and a standalone gateway made up of three overlapping concrete arches, through which I can see the actual Icehotel. What's visible is rather understated: from the outside, it doesn't look like a grand palace of ice, but rather like a large, low-slung

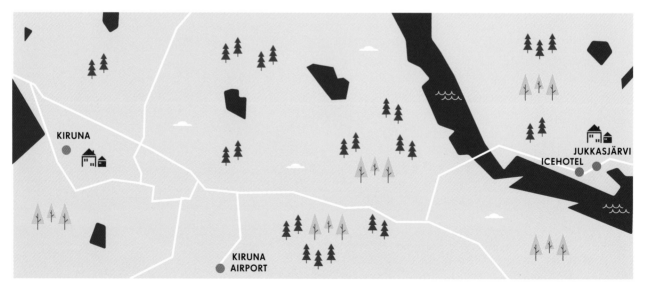

igloo. The ice bricks surrounding the metal door are so translucent that they seem to glow from within.

The Icehotel property is deceptively large, and divided into 'cold' and 'warm' sections, the latter made up of heated cottages and pastel-coloured hotel rooms. The cold section comprises the original Icehotel, created anew every year. When temperatures in Jukkasjärvi drop below zero in early November, the Icehotel's builders construct the skeleton of the hotel using custom-made steel frames, which are blasted with 'snice' (a mixture of snow and ice, so reflected sunlight will slow the hotel's spring melt) from snow blowers. After three days, once the snice has hardened around the steel frame, the frame is removed, leaving behind a shell of ice and snow. During the last week of November, once the skeleton of the hotel is in place, the ice artists move in for a couple of weeks to sculpt each of the individually designed Art Suites.

I hadn't realised how numb the strip of exposed skin on my face had turned during our dogsled ride, which is why it's a great shock to the system when I step into the reception area next to freestanding arches, and am blasted with heat from the roaring fireplace. However, my thawing is short-lived – it seems that I wandered into the reception area for *warm* accommodation by mistake. I'm directed outside and through the freestanding gateway to find the cold-room reception.

The reception is spacious and heated, with easy chairs, a fireplace and a gift shop. Behind the seating area is a corridor with a metal door leading into the Icehotel itself, as well as communal bathrooms, a large sauna (for thawing out after an icy night's sleep) and lockers. The receptionist hands me the key to my dressing room. 'Leave everything here overnight,' they warn me. 'The temperature in the ice rooms is below zero, so anything left outside your sleeping bag will turn to ice.'

I head out to find my room. The huge doors swing open with a hiss, letting me into a grand entrance hall, with ice chandeliers above, and a 'Welcome to Torneland' sign next to a doorman in a top hat, who's also carved from ice, of course. Some guests are propping up the original Icebar, cocktails in hand. The glasses are made of ice. A single corridor branches off to one side, with metal doors opening into Art and Deluxe suites.

Once I find my Art Suite – 'Flow', it's called – I am struck by how eerily silent it is, how the thick snice walls muffle any sound. Beneath the round skylight (the only source of light besides the rectangular LEDs in front of the bed) is the centrepiece: my bed. A thick, normal mattress, it's covered in two sets of reindeer hides, sitting atop a ridged, gently undulating, icy platform. I study my bed's angles and colours. The ice is remarkably clear, with a single branch of waterweed plant deliberately suspended in its icy prison.

When it's finally time to turn in for the night, I wonder how I'll keep warm. Besides my thermal military-issue sleeping bag and liner, warm enough to withstand temperatures down to -20°C (allegedly), and my thermal undergarments, I add socks and a woolly hat to my overnight ensemble. But the designer of one of

⛷ GUEST ARTISTS

Each year, Swedish and international artists wanting to work on the Icehotel's rooms use the open application system to send in their designs. They can work with ice, snow, or a mixture of the two, and have free rein, design-wise. The only thing that they have to include is an ice-bed frame that fits a double mattress. In May, a committee chooses the best designs, then, in mid-November, the winners arrive at the hotel to transform the ice and snice into otherworldly designs and sculptures.

"The temperature in the ice rooms is below zero, so anything left outside your sleeping bag will turn to ice"

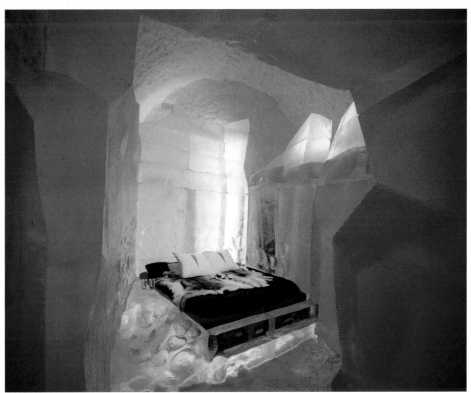

Clockwise from left: chef's table at the Icehotel's Veranda restaurant; the 34 Meters deluxe suite; on-site wilderness survival skills classes. Previous page: Rhythm of the Arctic deluxe suite

the ice rooms gave me some much-needed advice for a good night's sleep: 'Don't wear too many clothes,' he said. 'Just one layer of merino wool will do, along with a hat and woolly socks. The sleeping bags are designed to reflect body heat, so if you're wearing multiple layers, there's no heat to reflect.'

As I flip the LED switch by the bed and the room plunges into complete darkness, I try not to think about potentially waking up in the middle of the night and having to make a frigid 4am bathroom trip. I do wake up briefly a couple of times because the exposed skin on my face is beginning to feel numb. But I pull my scarf up over it and fall back to sleep, and the night passes relatively uneventfully – until I'm startled into wakefulness by a knock on my door, the lights come on and one of the Icehotel staff arrives with a glass of hot lingonberry juice on a tray.

Blearily, I look at my watch. It's 8am, and at 10am, visitors will be arriving to look at the rooms (day-trippers are allowed to tour rooms once guests have checked out). Trudging into the reception area, I leave my woolly layers in the dressing room, gratefully accept a cup of hot coffee, and settle down sleepily on my sauna perch, trying to remember what snowy adventure awaits me: snowmobiling beneath the northern lights or cross-country skiing in the nearby mountains. **AK**

DIRECTIONS

Best time to go // You can now check into Icehotel 365 year-round, but the original Icehotel building is open from mid-December to April, when you can view the northern lights and take part in wintry activities.

Gear required // Icehotel provides all the necessary equipment for husky sledding, snowmobiling, snowshoeing and other activities, but your own warm layers are a must.

Nearest town // Kiruna.

Getting there // From Kiruna Airport, it's a 20-minute drive to the village of Jukkasjärvi; you can also opt for a husky-sled transfer to the hotel in winter months.

Where to stay // The Icehotel, of course.

Things to know // Bring thermal underwear.

*Opposite, clockwise from top: igloos
at Kakslauttanen Arctic Resort
in Finland; admiring the view at
Finland's SnowCastle Resort; Hotel de
Glâce, Canada*

MORE LIKE THIS
INTERNATIONAL ICE HOTELS

HÔTEL DE GLACE, CANADA

North America's sole ice hotel, the luxe igloo Hôtel de Glace, a short drive from Québec City, welcomes guests into its 30 individually sculpted ice rooms and suites from January until March. The ice room arrangement is pretty standard: you sleep on an ice bed atop warm blankets, inside an Arctic sleeping bag, and thaw out by the fireplace in the lounge in the morning. If you get cold feet about staying in icy accommodation, traditional hotel rooms are reserved for all guests at the nearby Hôtel Valcartier. Other guest perks include welcome drinks served in ice glasses, an ice bar, a private ice-skating path, and hot tubs in an outdoor part of the spa, so you can sizzle as you contemplate the raw beauty of your wintry surroundings.
Nearest town: Québec City

KAKSLAUTTANEN ARCTIC RESORT, FINLAND

A genuine wilderness resort in the north of Finnish Lapland, Kakslauttanen Arctic Resort lets you choose between residing in intimate, thick-walled snow igloos – where temperatures hover around zero and you wrap up in an Arctic sleeping bag – or glass-domed igloos that open up the surrounding wilderness to you without your setting foot outside, so you can lie in bed and watch the ethereal, eerie spectacle of the northern lights overhead. In the smoke saunas by the river, the steam from the stove mingles with smoky scents of the birch twigs with which you flagellate yourself to stimulate blood circulation, while periodically taking frigid dips in the river. Although Rovaniemi, further south, claims to be the official home of Santa, Kakslauttanen features Santa's Home – a vast log building where the jolly man welcomes families with children.
Nearest town: Saariselskä

SNOWCASTLE RESORT, FINLAND

Appealing to *Frozen* fans and dyed-in-the-wool romantics alike, this fortress-like ice hotel wouldn't look out of place in the Disney animation. Built from blocks of ice from the Gulf of Bothnia, it comprises ice rooms where you sleep on furs and blankets beneath gently tinkling ice chandeliers while surrounded by elaborate ice art. There's also a restaurant where the furniture is sculpted from the cold stuff, and an indoor ice-sculpture exhibition. Icebreaker cruises and a tube slide for kids are fun extras. You can push the boat out by taking in the Baltic Sea from floor-to-ceiling windows in one of the plush ice villas, or make a lifetime commitment to your sweetie in the SnowChapel.
Nearest town: Kemi

VICTOR DE LE RUE ON ARÊCHES BEAUFORT

French pro snowboarder Victor de Le Rue might be known for dropping steep lines, but he began his career building perfect jumps at very un-extreme resort Arêches Beaufort.

Some of my best memories are from the early part of my snowboarding career, when I was riding at a tiny ski resort in the French Alps called Arêches Beaufort. The town was famous for its cheese – related to Gruyere – and there were maybe a thousand people living there, with this small family-style ski resort. It didn't have many lifts, and the lifts that it had were slow; there was a lot of tree-skiing. But it had great snow – the clouds kind of got stuck there and it snowed *a lot*.

About 10 years ago, when I was more focused on making great video parts for films and for sponsors, we wanted to find a place that was quiet, where we could go with our crew, and just build some jumps and film some tricks. We would rent an apartment and, each morning, drive 10 minutes to Arêches Beaufort. We'd bring a packed lunch – with a bunch of great cheese, of course – and then just spend all day building the jump. We'd take a break, have this nice picnic, and then get back to work. We shovelled so hard. And then we'd come back down. The next day we'd head up super early and have these great sessions for the whole day, get some great shots. Then we'd go looking for the next spot.

Before that, I'd never thought too much about becoming a pro snowboarder, or about being sponsored by this or that brand. I just did the best I could every year and my parents just let me do my thing. But I'm the youngest of a five-kid family. We grew up near a ski resort in the Pyrenees called Saint-Lary-Soulan. My parents owned the big ski shop in front of the gondola and were always super busy, so they wanted us to be outside and not just inside watching TV or whatever.

I was in ski club, but my older brothers and sisters were all snowboarders and I wanted to do what they were doing. I got my first snowboard when I was six, and by the time I was 11 I'd stopped skiing to focus on snowboarding. Having successful older siblings [pro snowboarder Xavier de Le Rue and boardercross Olympic bronze medallist Paul-Henri de Le Rue] meant it just felt natural: if you snowboard and you're good then you become a pro. Some parents might think it's crazy to stop school, but when you have people in the family winning stuff, earning good money, getting opportunities in life, it just makes sense. I was inspired by them and that helped me so much. I've never really had a backup plan.

I started to enter a lot of boardercross competitions because my whole family was into boardercross. But then I started doing more

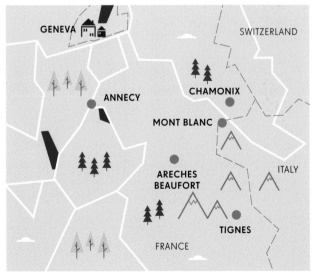

freestyle riding at the snow park — I started spending all my days at the snow park doing so many laps a day. I even picked up a few small sponsors. And then I got sponsored by Rip Curl.

Rip Curl was making great films so I just started spending my entire winter filming and travelling. This was around the time I started trying to organise and film some of my own projects, some at Arêches Beaufort. The small resort was perfect for getting beautiful shots. There were areas they didn't groom (where snow has been prepped for skiers) and the backcountry was amazing. You would just hike for a little bit and come across a zone with no people. We'd have these big rollers to ourselves and just have a sick session without any tracks around. We did some great tricks for our video parts. We knew this place was special because the snow was good, the light was good, and you wouldn't have people tracking out the landings. Now, I love organising films myself and am currently working on a couple.

Then I started going on more extreme trips, doing bigger lines. I went to Alaska and I felt pretty good in the steep terrain. I was able to add tricks in the middle of my descents, and my profile in the snowboard world kept growing. I won the Freeride World Tour twice, which gave me quite a bit of credibility.

Eventually, I made the decision to leave Rip Curl and join The North Face like my brother, Xavier. I had a secure spot at Rip Curl so it was a bit of a gamble. It was kind of ambitious because you have so many crazy athletes on The North Face team and it's an American brand. It's huge. But I knew that if I ever wanted to propose the kind of crazy trips I had in my imagination — like going to Antarctica — they could support something like that. It was the best decision I've ever made. I'm going to Antarctica next year with my brother.

I've always dreamed of snowboarding down a huge iceberg. You know, being on the boat, then jumping on to the huge floating ice cube, climbing it hurriedly with my ice axe and crampons. What a beautiful shot it could be: a hand plant or a trick on an iceberg.

But I need to be careful. I'm 33 now and, maybe it's old guy talk, but these days I just love being in the mountains with fewer people, good friends, people I trust. My wife and I now live in a town called Val Thorens, where she is a ski instructor. It's about two hours from Arêches Beaufort. But now I am also a dad. Our son is two and a half, he's already really used to being out in the mountains and on the snow, and today he took his first chairlift. But, time is more limited. And that's when I rush it a little too much — that's how I broke my foot in December.

My wife had told me I had a week to go do whatever I wanted. And I tried to do it all. I love Chamonix. People always assume if you are French you have been to Chamonix, but I only discovered it around 2017. I was like, wow, these mountains are insane, all the people are crazy — I realised that this place was something that was super specific and wild. And this is where I can do all the things I *really* love right now. I love riding, I love climbing, I love paragliding — when I can do them all together, I am happiest.

So, I drove to Chamonix, which is about eight hours away from Val Thorens and immediately I decided on a very big objective — no acclimatisation and straight up to 12,500ft (3800m). The idea was to take off in my paraglider from the top of the Aiguille du Midi, land at the bottom of an Alpine climbing route, climb and sleep in the middle of the wall, keep climbing another day, and then fly back to the valley. But I crashed on my first landing and broke my foot. I didn't know it was broken, so I thought: 'Let's just go for a couple of pitches and we'll see how it goes.' It didn't go too well.

And so today was my first day snowboarding and it went well, so I'm super excited. **VDLR**

"These days I just love being in the mountains with fewer people, good friends, people I trust"

ARÊCHES CLOSE-UP

For a glimpse of the photogenic terrain of Arêches Beaufort, and what Victor and his friends were able to pull off there, DIY-style, check out snowboard films like Transworld's *Origins* and *Dopamine*, made by Absinthe Films. De Le Rue's parts in both films feature footage taken in Arêches Beaufort on jumps he built himself.

Clockwise, from left: Arêches Beaufort, known for its aromatic cheese; Victor de le Rue was recently added to the prestigious Jones Snowboards team; on-piste at Arêches. Previous page: De Le Rue, doing his thing in Wyoming

DIRECTIONS

Best time to go // The ski season in the Alps typically runs from January to April, with spring being prime season for bluebird days, so long as the snowpack holds up.

Gear required // Your usual resort kit will do. There are multiple rental options in the town itself.

Nearest town // Annecy, France

Getting there // Arêches Beaufort in the Savoie region of France is about two-hours drive from Geneva, Switzerland and three hours from Turin, Italy.

Where to stay // Being a spa getaway means Arêches Beaufort does have some high-end options, but mostly smaller, Alpine-style *pensiones* and hotels. The Auberge de Poncellamont is known for its hospitality, top food *and* accessibility to the slopes.

Things to know // Shaded north-facing terrain keeps snow quality very high at Arêches Beaufort, making it a good bet after storms, when other resorts are getting tracked out.

Opposite, from top: Switzerland's Saas Fee glacier at first light; Pla d'Adet ski resort, Saint-Lary-Soulan in the French Pyrenees

MORE LIKE THIS
EUROPE'S UNSUNG SKI SPOTS

SAINT-LARY-SOULAN, FRANCE

This is the resort that Victor de Le Rue grew up near. It is the biggest in the Pyrenees, but still somewhat under the radar in Europe. Perched at 8200ft (2500m), it is incredibly popular with families and anyone who comes for a mix of quaint French country living – the town is also a spa town – family-friendly adventures such as tobogganing, and snow sports. But that doesn't mean the skiing and riding is underwhelming for experts. There are still 60 miles (97km) of marked trails and 28 lifts and gondolas (including a new one that links the village of Saint-Lary-Soulan with the ski slopes). Like a lot of the terrain in the Pyrenees, most of the runs up high are tree-free and the views are epic.
Nearest town // Toulouse

SAAS FEE, SWITZERLAND

Often overshadowed by its neighbour Zermatt, Saas Fee punches way above its weight in terms of terrain, while also offering a more intimate and casual vibe. The village of Saas Fee itself is car-free, charming, and devoid of the crowds of nearby giants, making it popular with families. The ski areas are split into three – with a total of 40 lifts – and connected by local buses. The lifts will take you to a hypoxic 11,500ft (3500m). Saas Fee holds snow for longer than most European ski resorts and is surrounded by high jagged 13,000ft (4000m) peaks and vast glaciers.
Nearest town // Geneva

ELLMAU, AUSTRIA

Austria itself flies somewhat under the radar as a ski destination in Europe, but Ellmau even flies under the radar in Austria. For one, Austria is known for its raucous après scene, but Ellmau is more family-oriented, with few options for binge drinking. The village of Ellmau sits at the feet of a big, well-known area called the SkiWelt, where you can challenge yourself a bit if the smaller surrounding resorts get stale. But the charmingly low-key town of Ellmau also has its own tiny, affordable, lift system, where 95 percent of the runs are beginner or intermediate. Yet, there are uncrowded steeps and impressive backcountry zones. Beginner terrain, affordability and the option to fall asleep before 10pm make this a standout in the Tyrolean Alps, and also all of Europe.
Nearest town // Salzburg

MUSHING IN LAPLAND

In the blues of the polar night, Lapland on the Arctic frontier is like a scene from a Christmas card — especially when you're flying with huskies through the great white wilderness.

The Alaskan huskies howled frantically with excitement, hungry for the run. It's not jarring; it's a sound that belongs utterly to Lapland in the far north of Finland, a region that is the real-life winter wonderland of childhood imagination. Snow was spread out before me like a pristine white sheet. I pushed off with the lightest of steps and the toboggan sled began to glide. We gathered momentum and it felt a little like flying — weightless, effortless, free — with a six-strong team of huskies powering my flight.

Nudging above the Arctic Circle, the wilderness immediately north of Lapland's busiest hub, Rovaniemi, feels a world away in spirit. There are no Santa-seeking crowds here, no glitzy grottos or tourist tack — just mile after mile of downy snow and forest. Bar the soft panting of the dogs and an occasional yelp, the only sound was ringing silence and the crunch of snow.

You quickly learn that mushing is not so much about taking control as relinquishing it by intuitively trusting another creature. Spending time with these huskies, striking up a rapport with them and falling into *their* rhythm, was as close as I'll ever get to the true call of the wild. Negotiating the contours of the glittering tundra and picking up speed as we headed up and over frozen lakes, swamps and hills, I momentarily struggled to keep my balance on the increasingly slippery track, gripping the handlebars tightly, one foot hovering over the break. I imagined myself tumbling headfirst into a huge snowdrift. Leaning forwards with my body weight on the runners of the locally made toboggan sled — similar to the sleds they use in Alaska, but slightly wider and more rigid for better traction — I tried to control it. 'Relax,' came a friendly muffled shout from behind me. 'You've got to put your trust in the huskies, they know exactly what they're doing. And rule number one: never let go. The dogs will just keep running!'

Although many companies in Lapland will take you for a quick hour-long spin on a husky-driven sleigh during the winter months, doing your own mushing elevates the experience to a whole new level of adventure. For a few precious hours, you can switch off from the white noise of the modern world, tune into nature and feel what my guide, Valentijn, described as the 'raw power of the dogs'. Even dogsledding day tours have an element of expedition about them, but for a full-on mushing experience, nothing beats Bearhill Husky Tours' 17-hour Black Dog 90 excursion: an extreme day-trip whipping you 56 miles (90km) on a racing sled through the savagely white and wild landscapes of the Arctic.

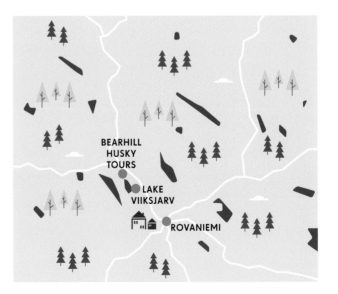

LONG RUNNING

Despite dogsledding being relatively new as a sport in Finnish Lapland, there's historical evidence that the tradition is a rich and old one: runners have been discovered dating back 5000 years, and it is believed that these sleds would have been pushed and pulled by both humans and dogs. For the isolated communities of the Arctic north, mushing was a lifeline – pack dogs were used to herd reindeer and transport goods and food.

"In Lapland, the connection between guide and husky runs deep"

'Our extreme trips are more challenging,' enthused Valentijn. 'This is dogsledding as we do it ourselves, in small groups or alone. The tours involve mushing in the dark, long distances and fewer breaks. But the bonus is there is more chance to work with your dogs, preparing the teams and providing food and water for them.'

Valentijn explained that Lapland has thousands of working huskies. But, although the region is now synonymous with the dogsledding culture, it's a relatively recent activity. It started with racing for fun in the 1970s and evolved into tourism in the 1980s. 'Husky sledding is not indigenous to Lapland the way it is to some other parts of Scandinavia,' he said.

We were just a couple of hours into our own seven-hour tour, which would take us 25 miles (40km) into the snowy wilderness, and already I could feel the burn in my core after spending so much time balancing on the sled. The temperature was around -12°C (10°F), but a brutal wind, whipping off the snow and sending it flying into the sky like sparks, made it feel much colder. Tears froze to my eyelashes.

I wanted it to go on forever, but also felt relief when we drew to a halt for a break. Valentijn tended to the dogs with a love that was palpable, with cuddles, strokes and tender words. We melted snow over a stove for the huskies and they were given a hearty, fat-rich lunch to boost their energy for the run back to camp. Huskies are born long-distance runners, easily able to run up to 100 miles (160km) or more a day.

Hot berry juice and cookies gave my body a sugar boost, and I began to slowly thaw out as we chatted about huskies and mushing faux pas by the hiss of a campfire in a *lavvu* tent, a traditional teepee shelter of the indigenous Sámi people. 'We prefer Alaskan huskies as their characters are perfectly suited to mushing and working together as a team,' said Valentijn. Here the connection between guide and husky runs deep and this is reflected in Bearhill's sustainable ethics: modern, dry, no-chain kennels and a no-kill policy that means older dogs are rehomed when their sprinting days are over, as opposed to being put down.

As we rumbled on through the downy snow and over the icy tundra, the light began to change. January during the polar night means that by 3pm there is already the flare of a would-be sunset on the horizon, with powdery pinks and purples streaking the sky.

When we arrived back at camp, I crouched down to say goodbye to the dogs. I ran my fingers through their thick fur and looked into their blue eyes. The first winter stars were already populating the sky as I reached my toasty log cabin. Like any good Finn, I decided that the best way to conclude a day at the helm of a sled was by stripping off for a steam in a wood-fired sauna and reflecting on the day's experiences. In a burst of madness, I headed down to the private jetty wearing nothing but a towel, holding my breath as I jumped into the *avanto* (ice hole) with a gasp and euphoric holler. The cold was like an electric shock to every fibre of my being.

The next morning, I woke up in darkness to a husky's howl and the previous day's mushing adventure came flooding back to me – in muscle and memory alike. **KC**

Clockwise from left: Bearhill Husky Tours prefers Alsakan huskies because they work as a team; 'trust the huskies!'; northern lights over Lapland. Previous page: Lapland has thousands of working huskies

DIRECTIONS

Best time to go // Dogsledding in Lapland happens when the trails are properly frozen, usually late November to April.

Gear required // Most companies (Bearhill included) provide winter clothing, but check when booking. You should dress warmly regardless, with merino thermals and a good fleece. Temperatures swing from 0°C to -35°C in winter.

Nearest town // Bearhill Husky Tours is located on the shore of Lake Viiksjärvi, 14 miles (22km) north of Rovaniemi.

Getting there // Transfers to and from Rovaniemi are included and arranged when booking.

Where to stay // The rustic lakeside cabin on-site is perfect and a practical choice if you've opted for a full-day or sunrise tour. There's also plenty of accommodation in Rovaniemi.

Things to know // Three-hour sunrise/sunset tours are special, but to ramp up the thrill, sign up for more extreme adventures, such as Black Dog Midnight Madness, and Black Dog 90, a 17-hour expedition to the Swedish border.

© Joel Forsman / Bearhill Husky

Opposite: the polar night on Kvaløya ('Whale Island'), just west of Tromsø in Norway

MORE LIKE THIS
NORDIC DOGSLEDDING PLAYGROUNDS

ENONTEKIÖ, FINLAND

Close to Sweden and Norway in Finland's forgotten northwest, Hetta Huskies in Enontekiö takes you dogsledding in a great white wilderness, 125 miles (200km) into the Arctic Circle, where the heartbeat of Finland's indigenous, reindeer-herding Sámi is strongest. Mushing here is magic – narrow, undulating tracks, snowy bends, dips and rises take you sledding through sparkling taiga forests, across the high tundra and over frozen Lake Ounasjärvi.

Hetta Huskies' safaris vary in length and intensity – from brief 1.25-mile (2km) rides to five-day, expedition-style tours into the remote wilds – but a genuine passion for dogs shines through in all of them. The owners, Finn Pasi Ikonen and his British wife, Anna McCormack (both former professional athletes/explorers), found their spiritual home here in 2005. They set up camp with 200 huskies, mostly Alaskan, and their ethos remains an incredibly responsible one. Dogsledding here is more than just a thrill, it's a deep dive into the world of the husky, from meeting the pack at camp to learning how to harness; from post-run cuddles to trip preparation. Overnight safaris ramp up your chances of seeing the northern lights.
Nearest town: Enontekiö

SPITSBERGEN, SVALBARD

Home to more polar bears than people, Svalbard is both the largest continuous wilderness in Europe and the final frontier before the North Pole. The main island of Spitsbergen (the only glimmer of civilisation for miles) is a place of stark, heartbreaking beauty and brutal cold, especially during the dark months of winter. Dogsledding here fully immerses you in the High Arctic and lets you slip into the role of polar explorer. It's savage, lonely and silent here, but for the sound of husky yelps and pants.

Wrap up *very* warm (temperatures regularly notch -20°C/-4°F or lower) and unleash your inner musher at family-run Green Dog, where half-day tours whisk you into the Bolterdalen valley to sweep around bowls and crest rises as pearly white mountains rise up like the prows of great ships. The dogs are a cross between Greenland dogs and Alaskan huskies, a mix that makes for a robust, friendly breed. Keep an eye out for wild reindeer and ptarmigan as you sled on by. Other Green Dog tours chase the northern lights, head to an ice cave in a glacier and embark on a three-day expedition to a trapper's cabin in the wilds. You can meet, greet and harness the dogs before setting out.
Nearest town: Spitsbergen

KVALØYA, NORWAY

Husky sledding in the blues of the polar night on Kvaløya ('Whale Island'), just west of Tromsø, is a never-to-be-forgotten experience. As you fly through the white valley, with Alaskan huskies guiding the way, the northern lights come out to play more often than not. Here you can really tune into legendary Norwegian polar explorers such as Nansen and Amundsen, who achieved some of their success by using sled dogs.

At Kvaløya Husky, Tommy, your experienced guide, knows his huskies and these trails like the back of his hand. Small-group, five-hour day trips plunge you into the white wonderland of the High Arctic, leading you through forests, past frozen creeks and ragged mountains. Wildlife is prevalent and reindeer, moose, fox, snow grouse and eagles are regularly spotted. For more of a challenge, hook on to the overnight mushing tour, which throws you properly into the white wilds, where you'll negotiate some steep, difficult terrain, set up camp (bring own camping gear) and have dinner by an open fire as the stars and – if you're lucky – aurora shine above. The camp is situated in Straumsbukta, a 45-minute drive north of Tromsø (pick-ups can be arranged).
Nearest town: Tromsø

FRANCE'S FINEST SKI RESORT

*Val d'Isère is huge, loud and, at times, ostentatious –
but, boy, does it have the terrain and snow to back it up.*

When I lined up for the first lift at Le Fornet in Val d'Isère – holding my ground and crossing tips with a mix of British bankers, Italian influencers and hardcore French freeskiers – the plight of 5th-century Piedmontese shepherds couldn't have been further from my mind. But it was all I could think about a few hours later. Even more unexpected was that after about half an hour of snowboarding, and 2000ft (610m) of vertical powder-filled descent, we would be whisked from what felt like the Middle Ages into a high-tech future.

The morning had started with a breakfast of warm coffee and hot croissants with my two mates Roger and Dan. We'd all met working as 'dishpigs' in a restaurant when doing a season here in 'Val' in our early twenties and had managed at least one ski trip back each winter in the 15 years since. After the *petit déjeuner*, we received some avalanche transceiver training for our backcountry adventure and an off-piste gear-check from our guide, Chris from Val Heli Ski. We then took the lift to Col de l'Iseran and on to the Glacier du Pisaillas. On the glacier, we hit the chairlift to des Cascades and finally all the way up to the summit of du Montets. That was 45 minutes of travel time that included a few warm-up runs, where Chris did an ability assessment. Despite our annual reunion dinner at our favourite restaurant La Baraque the night before, we managed to pass.

This approach elevated us to 11,300ft (3400m) above the Mediterranean Sea, and the highest point of Val d'Isère ski area. The panoramic views that took in the French Alps and bordering Vanoise and Italian Gran Paradiso National Parks were breathtaking. In the distance, we could also make out the Grande Motte glacier located at Tignes. The two ski areas are linked and,

until 2015, were known as Espace Killy, after celebrated French ski racer Jean-Claude Killy. Now the current name of Val d'Isère-Tignes isn't exactly a creative moniker, but it sure does what it says on the tin – and it's huge.

The two resorts are very individual, but they do share Europe's most snow-sure skiing from late November until May and immediate access to one of the greatest playgrounds in the Alps. From our vaulted position, we had 165 runs served by 90 modern, fast, lifts available at our ski tips. The combined on- and off-piste area comes in at a whopping 25,000 acres (10,000 hectares) – three times the size of Whistler, the biggest ski area in North America.

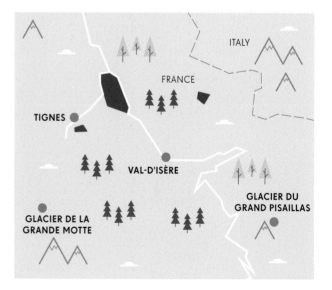

"There were so many possible routes it was like a Choose Your Own Adventure"

But the quantity of terrain is one thing, quality is another. Val ticks both boxes like few other resorts in the world. It is enormous and exciting. For advanced and expert skiers especially, there's a scintillating array of runs on offer: swooping World Cup pistes, big open powder fields, tight little chutes, and long off-piste itineraries. Yes, Val is expensive, but there is also a deep core of Alpine buzz that cuts through the bling.

However, that morning, we turned our back on one of Europe's – heck, the world's – most iconic resorts and its lifts, in order to instead skin up to the peak at L'Ouille Noire to access untouched and out-of-bounds terrain. What we were doing was essentially reverse heli-skiing, where a chopper picks you up in otherwise inaccessible terrain after your run and returns you to civilisation. It allows for huge vertical meterage and untracked snow without forking out for heli-ski day prices. It's a fairly new offering in the valley, but has become more common in the past five years.

Assured of a ride home, we dropped in, down into the back bowl towards the beautiful and empty Vallon des Montets. With the snow still deep and untracked from a dump a few nights before, there were so many possible routes it was like a Choose Your Own Adventure book. Luckily, we had Chris on hand to make sure we didn't end up

in any narrative, or Alpine, cul-de-sacs. After skirting the 10,000ft (3000m) Ouille des Reys peak, we stopped in the time-frozen village of L'Ecot, often described as one of France's most beautiful and remote villages. It was here that our guide Chris described how for centuries the shepherds and their families lived in the stone-walled, caulked slate-roofed houses of the hamlet. We had been riding and traversing for over an hour. That's when the future arrived.

A helicopter descended, loudly but gently, and whisked us back to Val d'Isère, scooting less than a mile above the stunning Vanoise National Park. The heli-trip home meant that, by lunch, we were back in the central village of Val d'Isère. It was just another example that even though we'd all spent years skiing here, its capacity to surprise remained, well, endlessly surprising. And we still had the afternoon to scratch the surface of the resort itself. While eating our croque monsieurs, we couldn't keep our eyes off La face de Bellevarde and its majestic omnipresence, rising above the Olympique gondola. We all agreed it was time to tackle the famous black run.

Starting at 9500ft (2900m) and dropping to 5100ft (1500m) at the bottom, it is known for its steepness and challenging terrain – but it is pure Val. It is sometimes icy, sometimes mogul-y, and often both.

THE SNOW FACTORY

While Val d'Isère's high altitudes and two glaciers help guarantee snow from November to May, the resort also has the largest snowmaking facility in Europe. Called the Snow Factory, it cost $5m to build and can produce 88,000ft^3 (2500m^3) of artificial snow in just one hour, enough to cover a football pitch in 6.5ft (2m) of snow.

From left: flying high above the village of Val d'Isère; the French Alps are an extreme skier's dream. Previous page: when the mountain sleeps, the town comes alive

Its legendary status and pace come from its inception as the 1992 Olympic men's downhill track. Afterwards, with our adrenal glands buffeted enough for one day, we rinsed a few of the 'easier' greens, blues and reds that run skiers left off the Olympique gondola. By the third run, the pumping house music that soundtracked our descents became too much to ignore.

With our arrested development increasing in line with vertical feet travelled, the infamous Folie Douce was the obvious choice to end an epic day. This celebrated après-ski bar is situated at the top of the Daille cable car and is perhaps the most famous mountain clubbing hotspot in the Alps. When live cabaret lunch starts at 1pm, and 'clubbing' starts at 2.30pm, you soak in the pure decadence and fun that La Folie has served up since the mid-1980s.

It was actually this venue that helped cement both our friendship and Val's reputation as one of the best après-ski and nightlife resorts in the world. As the Ibiza-style tunes rained down through the crisp Alpine air and Mt Blanc gleamed in the distance in the lowering sun, my two friends and I raised a toast to another new experience in one of the greatest skiing resorts on the planet. Just what the Piedmontese shepherds would make of it was another matter entirely. **BM**

DIRECTIONS

Best time to go // Val d'Isère's season typically runs from early December to the end of April. Tignes tends to open a week earlier and close a week later.

Gear required // Will vary from full backcountry packs to basic ski wear. Sharp edges are also recommended.

Nearest town // Bourg-Saint-Maurice is a 20-minute drive.

Getting there // Chambéry airport (CMF) is a two-hour transfer from Val d'Isère, but it can be weather affected. Bigger international airports such as Lyon-Saint Exupéry (LYS) and Geneva (GVA) are often safer options.

Where to stay // For ski-to-door options, look around Le Joseray, La Légettaz and Le Châtelard. To be in the heart of the action, try Val d'Isère centre; Le Crêt for a more traditional village; and La Daille for the best value.

Things to know // The better you use and learn the bus network, the better skiing trip you'll have.

MORE LIKE THIS
EUROPE'S BIGGEST AND BEST

COURCHEVEL, FRANCE

There are several interlinked ski resorts known as Les Trois Vallées (Three Valleys), which form the largest ski area in Europe. Courchevel is the largest and most famous of them. We're talking 93 miles (150km) of Alpine runs accessible from Courchevel's 60 lifts alone, and these allow access to 370 miles (600km) of interconnected ski runs (including terrain at the resorts of Méribel and Val Thorens). Courchevel is known for its variety of world-class terrain, including off-piste areas, tree-skiing, couloirs and mogul-studded steeps. Each of Courchevel's five separate villages has plenty of terrain for beginners and intermediates too. One of those villages, Courchevel 1850, is often called the world's most luxurious ski resort – it makes Aspen look like Arizona's Snowball.
Nearest town // Albertville

ZERMATT, SWITZERLAND

Zermatt is an iconic town at the foot of one of the world's most iconic mountains, the Matterhorn. Understandably, it's a popular destination for skiers and climbers, and it never disappoints on either front. Like Val d'Isère, the skiing here is on a grand scale and attracts a high percentage of advanced skiers. The highest lift is above the 13,000ft (4000m) mark, while the Klein Matterhorn ski area has a sequence of gondolas and cable cars that climb from the southern end of Zermatt to the highest pistes in Europe. These are linked with the ski area of Cervinia in Italy, so pack your passport. The car-free village oozes traditional chocolate-box charm. Locals like to say that in Zermatt, après-ski begins at noon, which sums up the nightlife, restaurant and bar scene. Best of all, the Matterhorn itself is visible from much of the surrounding 220-mile (350km) trail system.
Nearest town // Zermatt

ST ANTON AM ARLBERG, AUSTRIA

Austria may be less popular for skiing than France or Switzerland, but serious skiers in-the-know rave about this jewel in the country's Arlberg region. The terrain is notoriously challenging – and fun – and the scenic traffic-free village of traditional Tyrolean lodges and inns has a raucous and unique après-ski scene. St Anton could actually compete with Val for the title of 'the ski resort with the most under-classified slopes'. Red runs can suddenly turn into super-steep blacks by any other resort's standards. St Anton was always known for its relative lack of crowds, and in 2016/17 things got even better as it was linked to the similar-sized resorts of Lech and Zürs – and the terrain grew far beyond the number of skiers. It is now part of Austria's largest linked ski area.
Nearest town // Innsbruck

Clockwise from top: mid-mountain at Courchevel, France; hucking cliffs near St Anton am Arlberg, Austria; Zermatt, Switzerland, with the famous Matterhorn peak in the distance

THE DEEP FREEZE DIP

In Arctic Finland, a hole in the ice, called an avanto, is like a portal to heaven and hell all at once – and the locals can't get enough of it.

During my trip to Arctic Finland I had zero intention of undressing and plunging into an outdoor pool, where the water is merely a fraction above freezing. Apparently, however, the activity a pretty major part of the country's winter traditions.

I was in Arctic Finland to experience a bit of outdoor adventure amid the elements (husky sledding and a stay in an ice hotel had already featured on the itinerary). But then I found myself on the edge of Urho Kekkonen National Park – home of Father Christmas, according to Finnish culture – a vast slice of wilderness that's sequestered away about 600 miles (1000km) north of Helsinki and just 25 miles (40km) shy of the Russian border. I was overnighting at Fell Centre Kiilopää in order to do a spot of hiking around Kiilopää – one of the park's highest fells at 1760ft (537m) – the following day (even if I didn't get to see Santa). And with darkness falling just after 2pm, I soon learned that disrobing and dipping into the icy water was in fact the de facto way of passing Lapland's rather long winter evenings.

The plunge holes are called *avantos* and can be found in the ice and snow all over Finland, where conditions allow. Some of them are man-made, some are natural, and there is never a shortage of people prepared to dunk themselves in one. This is a nation where embracing extremes is deeply ingrained in both psyche and tradition, and I was curious enough to work up the courage to try it out. The ritual typically begins by absorbing the heat of a wood-fired smoke sauna. This is followed by the cold plunge – a very quick one. Even hardy Finns only brave the *avanto* for a maximum of a minute or two at a time, before core body temperatures start plummeting dangerously. Yet, combine the sauna sweat-up with

avanto submersion and you can not only survive, but gain some major health benefits from the experience.

The sauna experience was surprisingly pleasurable. Sauna-going is more atmospheric here because it is done within the very high standards of Finnish steam rooms: the smoke sauna. Here, the smoke from a fire, lit with dried birch twigs, aromatically permeates the interior. Finnish sauna etiquette entails showering, undressing and sitting in quiet contemplation on a bench – naked as the day you were born – in 80°C (170°F) steam until your body has had enough, which can take anything from five minutes to a maximum of 25.

© Mikko Ryhönen / Visit Finland

According to the numerous experts who have published studies on sauna-going, the benefits of the steam for the body include the flushing out of toxins and cleansing of the skin. I managed 15 minutes: a point at which I felt nicely mellow and probably about 10 minutes before I would have collapsed in a fainting puddle of perspiration. So far, so great, I thought, why can't it just end here, perhaps with a nice refreshing beer. No such luck.

Gluttons for pleasure through punishment, Finns do not settle for one extreme activity when there is another, still more drastic one, on offer nearby. Donning trunks and clutching a towel, I made my way out onto the sauna veranda where the *avanto* awaited. Through each of their long, long winters, which, this far north, last from November to April, Finns take to these icy pools regularly to feel the boost to their metabolism, circulation, memory and energy levels that immersion can bring.

Mine was a particularly fetching *avanto*, even by the high standards of lake-studded Finland, where there are thousands of similar winter-time ice holes. It was illuminated by a string of veranda lights and surrounded by snow-bowed forest that lent it a fairy-tale aspect. If Santa was inclined to go for a dunk in an *avanto*, I am quite sure it would be somewhere like that. But as it was well below zero outside, my body had already experienced an air temperature drop of almost 100°C (212°F) in a couple of minutes. At that point, I was mostly concerned with survival. I must admit, I was wavering. To make matters worse, there were no other plucky people jumping in ahead of me with encouraging shouts of: 'Come on in.'

I stood there on the edge, thinking that my 11th-hour reticence was just cultural and born of inexperience. If I *were* Finnish, I thought, I would regard this as a standard December activity. I focused hard on an image I recalled of an old lady stepping into an *avanto* with a blissful smile on her face: if she could do it, so could I. Apparently, wearing any protection defeats the purpose of the cold-water immersion; *avanto* bathers should strive for ultimate contact between their skin and the frigid water. As a stalling technique, I began running through other *avanto* trivia I'd learned. Finally, reasoning that easing myself into the water via the ladder would only present another opportunity for me to wimp out, I decided on a different tactic: I jumped in.

Needless to say, it was as cold as anything I'd ever felt. A skin-prickling cold. A searing cold. A cold so cold it required a whole new spectrum of adjectives to be coined in order to accurately describe it. But more than the chill, what I felt in that instant of hitting the water, and in the moments immediately after, was euphoria. There is no greater way of embracing the Arctic nature than this. I remained for a few seconds, gazing out into the night-time forest, muffled under its blankets of white. And, when the time had expired (30 seconds is good for beginners and even hardened *avanto* bathers never do more than three minutes) and I was back on dry land, I did not, strangely, feel relief. I felt a little sad that I couldn't linger in the *avanto* for a bit longer.

> "Finally, reasoning that easing myself into the water via the ladder would only present another opportunity for me to wimp out, I decided on a different tactic: I jumped in"

I felt as though we'd clicked, that ice hole and me. Stripped of everything that cosseted me in everyday existence for a brief while, I saw the surrounding wilderness afresh as well. It was no longer the dark, slightly otherworldly thing it had appeared when viewed from the car or restaurant window, because while I had been in that water, I was temporarily part of it, part of some raw elemental ancientness. **LW**

Former Finnish president Urho Kekkonen, after whom the national park around Kiilopää is named, was famous for discussing his country's affairs of state in the sauna. He formed the Tamminiemi Sauna Club in Helsinki for this purpose. The sauna can still be rented for certain events.

Clockwise from top: Finns use avantos to boost metabolism; a steam usually precedes a plunge; the spiritual home of St Nick. Previous page: there are hundreds of avantos in Lapland

DIRECTIONS

Best time to go // From November to April. Snow and ice linger long up in the Arctic.
Gear required // A towel and courage.
Nearest town // Ivalo, Finland.
Getting there // Fly to Ivalo (the most northerly airport in the EU), then take a taxi/rental car to Fell Centre Kiilopää.
Where to stay // Fell Centre Kiilopää.
Things to know // A dip in an *avanto* can be dangerous. It should only last for a moment, followed up by some sauna time to warm up again. Ensure you seek advice before trying it if you have any health conditions.

Opposite, from top: Antarctic cruises often offer an optional polar plunge; master cold-water dips with the 'Ice Man', Wim Hof, in Poland

MORE LIKE THIS
POLAR-BEAR CLUB MEDS

POLAR PLUNGE, ANTARCTICA

This one of the globe's most exclusive cold-water dunks. Whereas the northern polar region is straightforward enough to visit – brushed by easily accessible parts of Europe and North America – the southern polar region is a different animal. You can only set off for Antarctica by boat from southern Argentina or New Zealand, which is what you need to do to take an Antarctic polar plunge. Most Antarctica-bound expeditions and vessels accepting tourists schedule one polar plunge during the voyage, weather permitting. You're only allowed in the water for a moment, wearing a safety harness and with the ship's doctor close at hand just in case. Check the itinerary when booking your adventure.
Nearest town // McMurdo Station, Antarctica

WIM HOF METHOD WINTER EXPEDITION, POLAND

This experience is as much about the man who leads it as it is the destination. Charismatic extreme athlete Wim Hof – the holder of several snow- and ice-related world records – is also known as the Iceman for his ability to endure low temperatures. He is your guide and mentor for this venture. Over the course of a week in southern Poland's hills and valleys, you will learn how to withstand the icy cold through a combination of specific breathing techniques and good old-fashioned dedication, enabling you to gradually increase your immersion times. How and why would you do all this? Well, there is a gamut of health benefits that result from exposure to intense cold, from lower stress levels to reduced inflammation. The week culminates in a climb up 5259ft (1603m) Mt Śnieżka on the Polish-Czech border. The peak's name translates as 'snow-covered' – no wonder it's a Wim Hof favourite.
Nearest town // Wroclaw

KNEIPP BATHS, BAD WÖRISHOFEN, GERMANY

The gentle, picture-perfect settlement of Bad Wörishofen in Bavaria doesn't look as though it would necessarily be the spiritual home of cold-water immersion for health purposes, but you will find a distinctly chilly aspect to the array of treatments at the 40 or so spa hotels in and around this little town. The reason why? One Sebastian Kneipp, who, while serving as a priest at the Catholic monastery, began offering treatments that included bathing in ice-cold water and walking barefoot in the snow. Soon enough, Archduke Franz Ferdinand of Austria became Kneipp's client and the Kneipp-inspired cold-water treatments were adopted across Europe. Today, Kneipp's healing methods have been given Unesco Intangible Cultural Heritage status, and you won't find more ways to get intimately acquainted with cold water anywhere else on Earth. At the town's Sebastian Kneipp Akademie, you can discover more about how to implement Kneippism, the founding principles of which also include movement, inner balance and phytotherapy (medicinal, plant-based therapy).
Nearest town // Munich

ON THE EDGE IN CHAMONIX

*In the spiritual home of alpinism, glacier harnesses are as ubiquitous
as ski goggles. Chamonix is the ski town you visit to scare yourself.*

When we stepped off the Mont-Blanc Express train in Chamonix, France, the wheels of our overweight ski bag rumbled across the centuries-old cobblestones. It was early spring, and espresso-sipping tourists and tiny hatchbacks sprinkled the streets. The sound was of ski boots clunking on the feet of mountaineers, who were strolling through town with climbing gear and ice screws jangling from their glacier harnesses. The sun had already disappeared behind the skyscraping valley walls and a chill from the incoming storm was setting in.

It was one of the snowiest seasons in Chamonix for almost 50 years and the previous day's ski tracks in the high peaks were filling up again daily. My buddy Ryan and I lugged our stuff past the legendary après bar, Elevation 1904, where an electric current of stoke – that almost physical sense of excitement – was buzzing among hardcore alpinists and pro skiers. The scene was intimidating, foreshadowing the intensity of our month-long trip into this hub of extreme, steep, high-stakes ski mountaineering. I'd been living on the front range of Colorado for a few years and my own home runs had come to feel passé. Here, there would be no easing in.

But I'd been looking to feel that thrill of hanging on the edge of comfort in a way that demands intense focus. Chamonix is the perfect place for that fix. You don't necessarily have to throw yourself

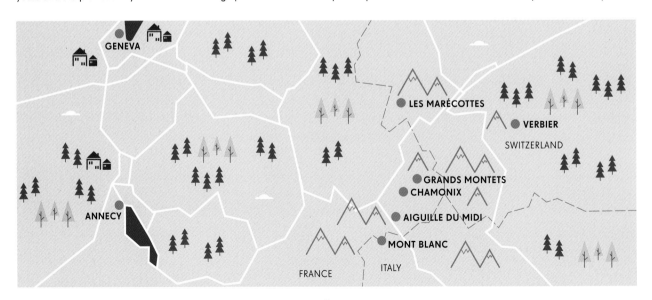

GRAVE TIDINGS

When the weather's against you, it's worth a stroll through the Chamonix Cemetery at the foot of the mountains where more than five generations of legendary mountaineers have been laid to rest. There you can recognise the names of pioneers including Edward Whymper (first to ascend the Matterhorn, in 1865) and Maurice Herzog (first to climb Annapurna, in 1950) alongside graves adorned with ice axes, crossed skis, and coiled ropes.

'You don't necessarily have to throw yourself down a cliff every morning to taste the wonders of the Chamonix Valley'

From top: there are more mountain guides than school teachers in Chamonix; the resort offers a respite from scarier terrain. Previous page: signature steeps

down a cliff every morning to taste the wonders of the Chamonix Valley on skis or a snowboard, and hiring a guide is always an option. You can arrange one in the morning, and discuss your goals and intentions ahead of time to match your level of skiing.

It's never a bad idea to start with an accessible ski down the Vallée Blanche – a descent of 9200ft (2800m) over 14 miles (23km), which can feel like standing on a conveyor belt with panoramic views of the Mt Blanc massif and its surrounding peaks – while scoping out potential lines and linking up alternative descents in your mind. Expert skiers with avalanche safety training can brush up on basic crevasse knowledge and drop off the back side of the Grand Montets ski area onto the Argentière Glacier, where steep, sustained powder runs await just outside the rope boundary, and a boundless amphitheatre of couloirs in all directions funnels down another long glacier descent to the valley floor.

But if you're looking for more serious fun in Chamonix, it is best to buddy up with someone familiar with the terrain. One who's comfortable with basic glacier rescue techniques in the event of a crevasse fall, or something more serious. On just our second day riding, we linked up with a young British alpinist named Luke, who was nursing some frostbitten fingers and living in his van, when not crashing at his girlfriend's flat. A storm had come in right side up and coated the steep runs with fresh, high Alpine powder.

We shuffled into line with all the other hungry snow hippos packing the first tram of the day, which would take us in 20 minutes from the centre of town at an elevation of 3400ft (1035m), to the top of the Aiguille du Midi peak at over 12,600ft (3800m). Built in 1955, the cable car still holds the record for the world's highest vertical ascent. The top of the tram station has a museum, a panoramic viewing platform and a gift shop for sightseers, but we hustled to the top of our first classic line: the Cosmiques Couloir, a 45- to 50-degree sustained 2900ft (900m) run on the west face of the Midi, exiting onto the Glacier des Bossons. It is a test-piece line with the steepest section over a small, exposed cliff band.

As Luke set up the first 200ft (60m) rappel into the couloir from the bolted belay at the entrance, two Frenchmen dropped in above us, skipping the rope work thanks to ample snow coverage and snaking fresh tracks from under us. It made little difference. Every one of our turns was perfect: deep, fluffy, fast and powerful, throwing up rooster tails that put us in the white room for a moment – where our vision was obscured by all that snow – before the clouds parted to reveal a wide-open view of the glacier valley below. This we repeated until we couldn't scream any more without choking on snow and we eventually regrouped in a safe spot mid-couloir, shrieking in disbelief at what was waiting for us on arrival. We were only halfway down, and the second half was of equal transcendence, rolling over a mostly covered bergschrund (a crack caused by moving glacier ice) and through a vast crevasse field before wrapping around a moraine bench at the bottom of a rocky spur.

After the Cosmiques descent, we rode down to the entrance of the Tunnel du Mont-Blanc and hitched a ride to town before hopping

right back on the Midi and hustling over to the Glacier Rond, another powder-stacked couloir with an exposed, 1300ft (400m) entrance traversing left onto a shoulder that exits the same way as the Cosmiques. There are few tracks in it and, like its neighbour, it's an ideal entry point for this type of extreme skiing, with rappels, cliffs, hazardous exposure and crevasses. But in good snow conditions it's not too hairy a line, with some calculated risk.

This double-header of adjacent lines is what locals call the 'Home Run' and to get both in such optimal conditions shatters any notion of prerequisite patience. It's quite the opposite: when Chamonix gives you the goods, you have to be ready to receive them or you might miss your shot. We lived this mantra for weeks, waking up early and cramming into the first tram to follow various gung-ho lunatics onto some of the most aggressive and memorable lines of our lives, calming our nerves each afternoon with a round of tall beers.

As much as Chamonix can be about testing one's mettle and getting rad, it's just as much about savouring a warm, flaky pastry in the morning and stopping mid-glacier to slice up a meat and cheese charcuterie snack while toasting your giddy, powder-stoked friends. There's a lifetime of skiing to keep you engaged and on your toes, but if you get too caught up in the thrills and don't stop to gaze at the mountain landscape and absorb it all on a daily basis, then you're missing your shot at receiving the gifts that Chamonix has to give. **SY**

DIRECTIONS

Best time to go // March

Gear required // Skis with touring-capable bindings or a splitboard and skins, avalanche safety gear, glacier harness with an ice screw and 3-to-1 pulley system.

Nearest town // Chamonix

Getting there // Fly to Geneva, Switzerland and either take the scenic, Mont-Blanc Express train from Geneva Cornavin station, which takes around three hours, or a quicker van shuttle from the airport with Alpybus (www.alpybus.com/chamonix).

Where to stay // Hôtel Le Morgane

Things to know // Le Mulet bus takes you all over town for free and runs every 10 minutes, while other buses will take you up-valley to La Flegere and Les Grand Montets for a few euros or free with your ski pass. The Grand Montets tram station was gutted by fire in 2018 and is being repaired.

Opposite: on the pistes of Verbier, you're surrounded by famous peaks, including the Matterhorn and Dent d'Hérens

MORE LIKE THIS
TESTING EUROPEAN SKI TOWNS

VERBIER, SWITZERLAND

There's a reason that the annual grand finale of the Freeride World Tour is held in the Swiss resort of Verbier, having originated in 1996 on the 40- to 60-degree north face of the Bec des Rosses, where there's a near 2000ft (600m) drop through a rocky maze of cliffs and couloirs. The occasionally high-consequence terrain is massive and scoops snowfall out of the sky, but doesn't require as much rope work or put you over as much hazardous exposure as other more extreme areas of the Alps. It's also accessible, with an advanced network of lifts connecting a vast amount of terrain. Many skiers will show up and head straight to the Col de Chassoure to test their skills on the Chassoure-Tortin 'wall', or up to the peak of the imposing Mont-Gelé, where options abound from its 9918ft (3023m) summit. Regardless of what you decide to ski, make sure raclette is on the après menu.

Nearest town // Martigny

LA GRAVE, FRANCE

'Sorry, no rescue.' You might hear this phrase in France's La Grave, though hopefully not when you're in dire straits. With no ski patrol, grooming, avalanche control or marked runs, La Grave epitomises extreme skiing. A 48-mile (77km) drive southeast of Grenoble, off a sketchy road cut through the Romanche valley, the 12th-century farming village is home to some of the world's most accessible no fall zones (where there's nothing to stop you if you tumble), where some of the best skiers in history have misstepped and lost their lives. The two-part gondola ride will bump you up to over 7000 vertical feet (2100m) of steep, technical skiing down glaciers and couloirs, but don't just ride it up and follow tracks – some will lead you off cliffs that others have jumped with a parachute strapped to their back. It's best to hire a guide here to take you down lines off the Glacier de la Girose and other classics.

Nearest town // Grenoble

LES MARÉCOTTES, SWITZERLAND

This small resort village in the Martigny region of Switzerland sucks deep powder out of passing storms thanks to the lake effect produced by several nearby bodies of water. Beyond the piste, sheer peaks and knife-edge rides shoot up and cut the sky with bold spine lines and deep chutes (narrow sections between two rock walls). Steep-skiing and freeride star Jérémie Heitz has called these surrounding peaks home his entire life and it's where he learned to race his Alpine giant-slalom turns on the open faces of 55-degree slopes. Head to Les Marécottes during the right storm cycle, watch the snow coat the terrain and you'll see why some folks call it 'Little Alaska'. Martigny train station – which connects to Geneva in less than two hours on a scenic ride – is nearby, and the resort itself has spectacular views, from Mont Blanc to Grand Combin.

Nearest town // Martigny

ARIANNA TRICOMI ON ALTA BADIA

Freeride World Tour champion Arianna Tricomi has competed all over the world, but her home village in the Dolomites is still among her favourite terrain. Here she tells us why.

I had been looking at Val Scura for years, trying to figure out how to ski it. It's a couloir – a thin, narrow chute of snow – on a peak known as Sassongher, in my village of Corvara. A unique shape, the line of snow is 2600ft (800m) long in the middle of a big wall. It makes it look as if the wall is cut in two. You have to rappel off a cliff at the end, using ropes, so you have to know what you're doing when you get there.

I'd been wanting to ski it since I was young, but I was too excited about getting out of the valley and skiing in other places. When Covid hit, I was back home and everything was shut down, so it was the perfect opportunity to ski it. It was one of the best winters we'd ever had – it was beautiful. If you ski out of the couloir, you end up in my village. It feels so powerful.

I grew up in Corvara, which is one of the villages in the ski resort of Alta Badia, in the middle of the Tyrolean Dolomites. South Tyrol, the most northerly province in Italy, shares a border with Austria, so the region is characterised by Italian flair with an Austrian influence – the two cultures come together. It's Italian but less loose than Italy usually is; the Austrian aspect makes everything clean and functional. There's a strong culture in our valley. We have our own food, our own music, our traditional clothes. It's very fancy in Alta Badia, but also very welcoming. Some restaurants have Michelin stars and the hotels are very high end. You can't bring your own sandwich into the lodge, it's not that kind of place.

I am so lucky. It takes me 30 seconds to walk from my house to the first gondola. At times the Dolomites have incredible colours when the mountains turn pink and yellow and orange. We call this moment, when the sun sets, *enrosadira*. It's a Ladin term – the

ancient language of the people of the Dolomites – that means 'turning pink'. The shapes of the mountains are unique, too; a gentle, fairy-tale kind of landscape. All the towns are connected through mountain passes. You can be in the middle of big and dramatic mountains, while on very mellow slopes. That's really what Alta Badia is known for. But the most famous run here is the Gran Risa piste, the site of the men's alpine World Cup race each December, which drops down into the village of La Villa.

Corvara is close to the Dolomites' massive Sella Plateau. There aren't many such places in the world where you can go through so many valleys without taking your skis off.

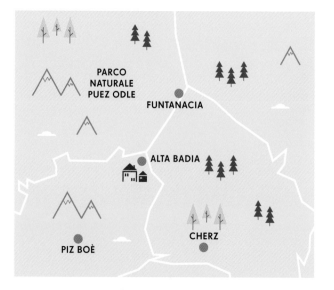

HOME ON THE RANGE

The Ladin people, who were the original settlers of the Dolomite Mountains, speak a traditional Romance language called Ladin, also known as Dolomitic Ladin. It's spoken by around 30,000 people across the five valleys of the Sella Group massif. Ladin is recognised as one of the three official languages of the South Tyrol region of northern Italy, along with German and Italian. Although the Ladin people are Italian, they remain most closely connected with the culture of Austria's Tyrol, and they take great pride in their culture and cuisine.

From left: winter in the Dolomites; on the slopes at the Alta Badia ski resort; the village of Corvara, where Arianna Tricomi grew up. Previous page: Arianna Tricomi is a three-time world freeskiing champion

My mum used to ski in the Olympic downhill races. She's very passionate about the sport and she put me on skis when I was about three. I was an alpine ski racer for more than 10 years, but at the beginning I wasn't very good. I was the worst kid in the group – and my mum was the ski teacher! I didn't win anything. But then I went through some sort of a turning point and I started winning races. It took me some time to figure it out. But I quit alpine skiing aged 16 because of the vibe and the rules. It was too strict. I did four years of slope-style competitions after I quit racing, but I always went powder skiing on the side.

I was going around my village with a friend of mine, a ski instructor who was competing in freeride competitions. I had no idea what freeride was. But he took me out in the forest, on tree runs in deep powder. For me, it was like: what is this? My heart

was beating like crazy. I couldn't believe that sort of terrain was right outside my door. He was skiing in a different way. After that, I started freeriding in my village; skiing off-piste, on bigger, steeper terrain. Nobody here really knew about freeriding or what it meant. But I grew up powder skiing with my mum and she showed me many different aspects of skiing, such as hiking uphill on skis with skins on.

My first freeride competition was in March 2013 in a very small place in Austria. I didn't have a clue what I was doing. I got there and everybody was checking the mountain face with binoculars. I didn't understand what they were doing. I was like: what are they looking at? It turned out that they were looking at the mountain to plan what line they were going to ski down. I didn't do that.

I dropped into the mountain face the next day. I didn't have a plan other than to just ski down the middle. I decided to do

*"I couldn't believe that
sort of terrain was
right outside my door"*

a switch 180 off a cliff, which is basically going backwards and
then spinning forwards in mid-air. I crashed and lost everything,
including both my skis and poles. It was embarrassing. Somehow,
though, the judges were impressed with my skiing and thought
I was worthy of a second chance, so they gave me a wildcard to
enter another competition.

It took me two winters to qualify for the Freeride World Tour,
which is the most elite freeride competition in the world. During my
first two years on the tour, when I got third place overall, I was also
at university. In 2018, I was done with education and decided to
take a year off and just ski. That was the first year I won the overall
title on the Freeride World Tour. I won in 2019 – and 2020 too.

You have to stay humble. I'm 30 years old now and I understand
how powerful the mountains are. **MM**

DIRECTIONS

When to go // December to April.
Nearest town // Bolzano.
Gear required // Your favourite resort skis or snowboard.
Getting there // Fly into Venice, Innsbruck, Milan or
Munich. The nearest train station is in Brunico, 24 miles
(38km) away, from where taxis and coaches are available.
Where to stay // Hotel Arkadia in Corvara.
Things to know // Alta Badia has 53 lifts and 80 miles
(130km) of groomed terrain, the majority of which is made up
of beginner and intermediate slopes. Smack in the middle
of the Unesco World Heritage-listed Dolomites range, Alta
Badia is part of the massive Dolomiti Superski, a connection
of ski resorts that includes 450 lifts and some 750 miles
(1200km) of groomed terrain. One ski pass gets you access
to all of that. If you want to explore off-piste, your best bet is
to hire a guide with Alta Badia Guides.

Opposite, from top: Cortina d'Ampezzo is prepped to host the 2026 Winter Olympics; wide open pistes at Livigno ski resort

MORE LIKE THIS
THE BEST OF ITALY

CORTINA D'AMPEZZO

The host site of the 2026 Winter Olympics – and also where Italy hosted its first Games in 1956 – Cortina d'Ampezzo is one of the Dolomites' most stunning ski areas. Two hours north of Venice in the Ampezzo Valley, Cortina offers a wide array of winter activities for skiers and non-skiers alike, from downhill and cross-country to snowshoeing. There's also an Olympic-sized ice skating rink and a bobsled track. Made up of a series of interconnected ski areas, Cortina has a whopping 36 lifts, all of which are part of the Dolomiti Superski pass, which also allows access to more than a dozen other ski resorts. Roughly half of Cortina's terrain is geared towards intermediate skiers and riders, making it a great spot for families or those looking for mellow, groomed slopes. Experts should head to the Tofane area, which has hosted World Cup ski races in the past and has steeper runs and ample off-piste terrain. The slopes are set under the towering Cinque Torri, a rugged backdrop of five rocky peaks that offer long, meandering runs back to the lively village.

Nearest town // Belluno

COURMAYEUR

If you're heading to Italy from legendary French ski resort Chamonix, you'll drive through the Mont Blanc Tunnel and arrive in the gorgeous Aosta Valley at the slopes of Courmayeur, around 135 miles (220km) west of Milan and 60 miles (100km) east of Geneva, Switzerland. Skiers can even cross the international border back into France from the slopes of Courmayeur. The views of Mt Blanc from the cable cars and mountain summits are outstanding. Hire a guide if you want to ski off-piste – this resort has heaps of steep skiing and backcountry-style terrain, but with the risk of avalanches or ending up atop a cliff, you'll want an expert to show you around. You'll find 12 miles (20km) of cross-country ski trails in nearby Val Ferret. The town of Courmayeur, an Alpine hamlet at the base of the ski area, is known for its high-end hotels, boutiques and Italian charm, but you can still find a farmstay on a budget.

Nearest town // Turin

LIVIGNO

Livigno has made a name for itself in recent years as a hub for freestyle and freeride skiers and snowboarders, drawn to the jumps in the terrain park and the powdery steeps of big mountain faces. Livigno's remote location in the Alta Valtellina valley near the Swiss border makes it less crowded than some of Italy's other popular resorts, and it's more affordable and low-key than its luxury destination counterparts elsewhere in the Dolomites. Innsbruck Airport in Austria is about 110 miles (180km) away, making it one of the nearest to fly into. Livigno's world-class terrain parks will be the site of the snowboarding and freestyle ski events at the 2026 Winter Olympics. For hardy skiers and riders, the resort's spiky, snow-covered peaks are reminiscent of the Himalaya, earning Livigno the nickname 'Little Tibet'. Heli-skiing and backcountry skiing are also on offer here – ask around to hire a guide – while the town's duty-free status makes it a great-value spot for souvenir shopping.

Nearest town // Bormio

© Boerescu / Shutterstock; Shutterstock; tomtsya / Shutterstock

SERIOUS SLEDDING IN SWITZERLAND

Not quite a sport, not quite an adventure, too extreme for small children and perhaps too silly for adults, tobogganing Swiss-style is winter's most overlooked joy.

I'd decided to experience the least touristy thing that can be done in the mightily touristy Jungfrau region. Tramping through the slushy snow of Grindelwald, one of the many charming Swiss mountain villages, I passed prettily painted chalets, fondue restaurants and winter sports stores. I took a cable car crammed with skiers and their paraphernalia up over the Alpine meadows, which rose steeply through conifer forests and over crags. I disembarked at another top station, brimming with high-altitude adventure possibilities from skiing to zip-lining, where big signs pointed the way to everything you could hope for in such a complex: places to eat, slopes to ski, summits to climb. But there were no signs for what I'd come for: Big Pintenfritz, the planet's longest toboggan run.

My steed for the nine-mile (15km) cruise was a wooden Alpine Davos racing sled, which is steered by digging your foot in. Tugging my sled behind me, I ascended towards the starting point of the run, the 8800ft (2680m) peak of Faulhorn. It was a 3.5 mile, 2.5 hour climb, which actually heightened the anticipation. For many of the winter thrill-seekers around me, that's way too much of a prequel.

The mountain was under thick snow cover in February, the third month of Switzerland's winter sports high season. It was packed with the day's other visitors, variously bound for the ski lift, the viewpoint or the ski bar. However, when I reached the ski bar, I became slightly concerned, as the only other person I had seen with a toboggan thus far was a small child. I refused to believe he was about to trek 3.5 miles through the snow by himself. Clutching a cockle-warming Glühwein, I checked I was on the right track. 'Yes,' said the man ladling my drink. 'Keep going up all the way – it's a long pull.'

But what a pull. Ahead, as the path coiled up beyond one of the only two remaining buildings I could see – the tiny Gummi-

Hütte refuge – I was treated to a preview of the type of mountain scenery I could expect: panoramas of those blockbuster peaks near Grindelwald, including the fang-like summit of Rötihorn with Faulhorn peeping out beyond, and the Eiger to the south. I was starting to feel the effects of lugging a toboggan this far up just as I also became keenly aware of the elements. At that moment I was proud of my clothing selection: thermal under-layer, ski trousers, ski boots, a Fjällräven padded jacket and double-lined ski gloves.

I reached a junction in the path, gritted my teeth and kept going up another dauntingly steep climb. I was struck by Faulhorn's photogenic preposterousness: it resembled a big, lopsided

"At last I was swooshing back down towards the saddle, ice shards showering into my face from the force with which I was digging in my heels to brake"

blancmange teetering out above the ridgeline, with Berghotel Faulhorn appearing to be the dollop on top. Switzerland's highest mountain hotel was buried up to its eaves by snow, and was shut. I spotted some other tobogganers careening down the mountainside from the saddle. They'd chosen to start their Big Pintenfritz run from there, rather than climb the extra 100 metres or so up to the aforementioned closed hotel. To my weary, altitude-addled brain, it seemed like a pretty good idea, so I did the same.

At last I was swooshing back down towards the saddle, ice shards showering into my face from the force with which I was digging in my heels to brake. Sledding in many parts of the world is considered child's play, perhaps an alternative for those who cannot ski. Big Pintenfritz is not child's play – but it is serious fun.

The runs themselves are basically summer hiking trails that are transformed into sled runs once the snow falls. The valley and the civilisation from where I had set out that morning was now just a vague smudge below. The initial descent was steep in sections too – sufficient to hit speeds of up to 25mph (40km/h), which felt much faster because of how close to the ground I was. There is no

equivalent of a ski school for sledders – you can tackle the run of your choice just as soon as you can kick yourself off on it. Training comes on the run itself.

There was a long arc on a gentler gradient that enabled me to relax a little. I had enough time to imagine the scene as it might have seemed to an onlooker: one fully grown man, clothes wet from rolling about in the snow, proudly steering a mode of transport most commonly associated with children's story books at Christmas. But by the time I approached Bussalp, a mountain restaurant halfway down, I felt like a seasoned professional. The few tumbles I did take were more comical than dangerous. Although Big Pintenfritz is certainly steep at times, it's not going to make you plunge off into any abysses.

Tobogganing isn't just fun, it is downright funny. It's perhaps most suited for adults who wish to find their inner child. I was, however, freezing, as ice shards were seeping through my thermals. The novelty of being able to stop off part of the way through an adventure activity for a hot drink in the middle of nowhere was a thrill in itself – the Swiss are experts in getting impeccable

NAME GAME

The Big Pintenfritz is so called after the nickname of Fritz Bohren, who ran the hotel atop Faulhorn in the late 19th and early 20th centuries. Bohren was renowned for his hospitality and sense of humour, the combination of which made guests flock from afar.

From left: Big Pintenfritz toboggan run; get a bird's-eye view from the First Cliff Walk in Grindelwald. Previous page: rush hour on the slopes

infrastructure up and out onto their remote mountainsides. I paused at Bussalp for another Glühwein (this wasn't drinking and driving, it was de-thawing).

Back on my toboggan, I headed into the forest for more two-bladed delight. The lower echelons of Big Pintenfritz are more challenging than the upper ones, because there are roads with occasional pedestrians and vehicles to avoid, while tree cover obscures the view ahead. Nevertheless, I soon spied houses in the valley below and began thinking about warm baths, warm fires... *anything* warm.

Then I remembered something: snow slush. Grindelwald had been *full* of snow slush. But it was too late. Rounding a bend, the snow suddenly wasn't there any more and I was scraping along icy asphalt, unable to stop. Finally, I managed to do so in a rather ungainly manner, outside a wayside cafe. It was a low snow year so I ended up walking the last half mile in the Grindelwald dusk down towards the lights of the chalets and fondue restaurants.

'How was it?' asked the man in the toboggan rental store.

'I want to go again,' I said, grinning like a little kid. **LW**

DIRECTIONS

Best time to go // December to March. Conditions are best several days after a snowfall – when temperatures are low enough to prevent melting – and early in the morning.
Gear required // Sled, thermal base layer, warm coat, ski trousers, hat, gloves and snow boots.
Nearest town // Grindelwald.
Getting there // Fly into Basel, Geneva or Zürich, then take a train to Interlaken Ost and change for the 45-minute journey to Grindelwald. From the Grindelwald Firstbahn cable car, walk 3.7 miles (6km) to the start of Big Pintenfritz.
Where to stay // Grindelwald has plenty of options.
Things to know // You need to be fit for the hike up to the saddle just below Faulhorn.

Opposite, from top: year-round toboggan fun on the Alpine Coaster in Switzerland; racing is encouraged at Courchevel Moriond

MORE LIKE THIS
EUROPE'S BEST SLED RUNS

WILDKOGEL ARENA, AUSTRIA

From the town of Bramberg am Wildkogel, the Smaragbahn cable car runs up the slopes of Wildkogel mountain to around 6900ft (2100m), for an 8.5 mile (14km) thrill ride on the world's longest floodlit sled track. It takes between 30 and 50 minutes to drop a massive 4265ft (1300m) in altitude to the finish line. Sledding some or all of the Wildkogel Arena run by night is an unforgettable experience, as lights illuminate settlements in the valley below, and the darkness emphasises the wildness and vastness of the surrounding Kitzbühel Alps. The last cable car of the day ascends at 4.15pm but the course stays open until 10pm, allowing time for refreshments at loveably rustic mountain restaurant Zwischenzeit on the way back down.

Nearest town // Bramberg am Wildkogel

ALPINE COASTER – GLACIER 3000, SWITZERLAND

The Alpine Coaster offers tobogganers a slightly different form of fun: a year-round run mounted on rails that will have you twisting and turning for 0.6 miles (1km), high up among the snow-daubed peaks of the Diablerets massif. Straddling the border between the Swiss cantons of Vaud and Valais, Les Diablerets are a group of summits between 9148ft (2789m) and 10,530ft (3210m) high. The Glacier 3000 development is spreadeagled between several of them. An epic cable car ride from Col du Pillon delivers you up to top station Scex Rouge at 9646ft (2940m), where the Alpine Coaster begins making it the world's highest-elevation toboggan run. Your vessel for this Alpine action is a toboggan fixed to rails mounted up to 20ft (6m) above the mountainside. The course hurtles along heart-in-mouth curves, waves and jumps at speeds of up to 25mph (40km/h) – you determine exactly how fast you go by using the brake pedal. While you're up here, other adventures to try include ski runs and the Peak Walk, a suspension bridge connecting two mountain summits.

Nearest town // Gstaad

MORIOND RACING TOBOGGAN, COURCHEVEL MORIOND, FRANCE

The Courchevel resort complex has a reputation for being one of the world's swankiest ski destinations, but Courchevel Moriond is a more down-to-earth and budget-friendly place than its high-class (and higher-elevation) sister resort. Formerly known as Courchevel 1650 due to its altitude in metres above sea level, Courchevel Moriond has an atmosphere more reminiscent of an Alpine village, and it's the starting point for a high-adrenaline toboggan ride, during which you are actively encouraged to race and, as the organisers say, 'put your F1 driving skills to the test'. You'll be speeding around hairpins from the off, zooming through tunnels and down straights, and taking on the tricky switchbacks of the 'double serpent' on 1.8 miles (3km) of sheer snowy exhilaration.

Nearest town // Courchevel

SKY TO SEA IN ICELAND

Skiing usually takes place only on high-elevation, snow-capped mountains. But in Iceland, you can ski from the tops of peaks all the way down to your very own berth on a sailing boat.

Iceland has become a popular destination for adventure travellers from all over the world, who flock for its rugged hiking trails, scenic waterfalls and hot springs, as well as the unique lodges and farmstays. Most travellers visit Iceland in the warmer months, for hiking among volcanoes or snorkelling in a continental divide. It's one of those places where summer looks and feels a little like winter. And in winter... well, the name sort of says it all. My friends and I wanted to see *that* Iceland. We wanted to explore a snow-covered landscape on skis, without anyone else around.

A friend, who is a certified mountain guide, mentioned to us that she'd got a gig guiding for Ice Axe Expeditions, which included six nights aboard a sailing boat in Iceland's remote Westfjords, and six days of guided ski touring. So we decided to embark on a backcountry ski adventure that would be unlike anything we'd done before. We wanted to ski in a place that felt like the ends of the Earth, seemingly untouched by humans and so far from civilisation that it would feel like it was just us and the seals. I had no trouble enlisting five of my most experienced backcountry-skier friends from around the US.

So we set off via Reykjavík for the town of Ísafjörður ('ice fjord'), the largest settlement in the Westfjords in the northwest of Iceland. On the plane into Ísafjörður, an Icelandic man asked us what was in the long bags he saw us hauling through the airport. When we told him they were for skis, he looked confused. 'Why are you bringing skis to Ísafjörður?' he said. "There is no snow here."

We all knew that skiers don't come to Iceland for quality snow of the sort you'll find in Alaska or the Alps. Skiers come here for the beauty of the place, the wonder and magic of doing things like skiing from summit to sea, to experience snow underfoot and

the smell of saltwater in the air. Iceland is not exactly a known ski destination, though the island has about a dozen small ski areas, most of them small and family-oriented. Two heli-ski outfitters operate on the Troll Peninsula. I've had a long-term fascination with the idea of skiing to the ocean – there are only a handful of places in the world where this is possible.

Unpredictable conditions, though, become part of the adventure here. It was early May, the tail end of the snowy season and prime time for spring ski touring. But there just wasn't a whole lot of snow. Thankfully, there was just enough for what we came to do: explore on skis and have a fun-filled adventure where we didn't quite know what would happen next.

Our home for the next week was waiting for us, floating in the Ísafjörður marina – an elegant 6oft expedition sailing boat named *Aurora Arktika*, painted cherry red and with the distinct don't-mess-with-me vibe of a pirate ship. In its past life as a racing boat, the *Aurora Arktika* was owned by Sir Robin Knox-Johnston, a British sailor who was the first man to single-handedly sail around the world non-stop. Now the boat is enjoying a quiet life of shuttling skiers across calm fjords as part of a local business that runs guided sail-and-ski trips a handful of times throughout the year. There are a few outfitters that lead guided boat trips year-round – for hiking and skiing – in this area.

We loaded our gear and set sail across deep and choppy waters. Sea sickness subsided upon reaching the Hornstrandir Nature Reserve, on a remote, finger-shaped peninsula, where the waters within the fjords are relatively calm. The 220 sq mile (580 sq km) Hornstrandir is a true wilderness. Although this area was once home to a handful of farmsteads, fishing villages and summer cottages, accessible only via horse or boat, nobody has inhabited the land since the 1950s. In 1975, the government designated it a protected nature reserve. With more Arctic foxes than people, this uninhabited land mass has no roads, next to no infrastructure, and is capped by the ethereal-looking Drangajökull glacier, a shrinking chunk of ice that's been called Iceland's loneliest glacier.

We spent our first night anchored just offshore, dining on cod we had caught along the way, and staring at maps with our guides, Lel and Erin. Our all-female group of skiers settled on a route up and over into the next fjord over, a crossing that would require us to hike uphill on dirt for about 500 vertical feet (150m) before reaching the snow line. The following morning, our first on the boat – after a breakfast of toast and butter with tiny shrimp mixed in – our crew geared up. To get to shore, our captain, a bearded man named Óli, had to drive us over in a rubber Zodiac boat, depositing us on slippery rocks covered in seaweed – not what you need when wearing ski boots.

We climbed a couple of thousand vertical feet into the clouds and into zero visibility – but there was snow. And it felt soft and skiable. We dropped in and made our first glorious (if a little scratchy) ski turns. When we landed back on the boat in the late afternoon, it was time for après-ski snacks (more fish, naturally) and

"*With more Arctic foxes than people, this uninhabited land mass has no roads, next to no infrastructure, and is capped by the ethereal-looking Drangajökull glacier*"

a plunge into the Arctic waters. The Arctic Circle is only 30 nautical miles (55km) to the north, so this water is always cold. Our cook aboard the boat, a mermaid-like woman by the name of Rebekka, had a personal goal to swim in the water every day, for longer than the day before. By the end of the week, she was in the water for four whole minutes. The rest of us could barely handle four seconds.

We spent the rest of the week skiing similarly spectacular lines, collecting mussels off the beach during downtime and watching Rebekka swim. But our final run was the most memorable. After skiing up to one of the highest points in the Westfjords, the rocky 2086ft (636m) summit of Bolafjall, we could see the Drangajökull glacier in the distance and ocean on both sides of us. We felt like the only people in Iceland. From there, it was a very long ski back down to the salty sea. **MM**

In the past, the Hornstrandir was known as a refuge for outlaws, who were running from the law with the hope of hopping aboard a passing foreign ship. The outlaws also had to watch out for polar bears, who would occasionally reach the peninsula on drift ice from Greenland.

Clockwise from left: snowfall can be hit and miss, but adventure is guaranteed; ski guide Erin Laine rides the Zodiac to shore for a day of ski-touring; the Aurora Arktika sailboat. Previous page: Skiers find a ribbon of snow to the ocean

DIRECTIONS

Best time to go // The best time for backcountry skiing from a sailing boat in Iceland is from late March to late May.

Gear required // You'll need backcountry touring skis or a splitboard, as well as avalanche safety kit: a beacon, shovel and probe. On the boat, you'll need a sleeping bag, warm layers and a swimsuit for the coldest plunge of your life.

Nearest town // The historic fishing town of Ísafjörður.

Getting there // Fly to Reykjavík, then get a domestic flight to Ísafjörður. The sailing boat cruise from there to reach the Hornstrandir Nature Reserve takes several hours.

Where to stay // Before or after you board the boat, stay in Ísafjörður at Hótel Ísafjörður or any of the guesthouses. Eat at Tjöruhúsið, a seafood restaurant in a tiny, old house in the town. It has no menu, just the freshest catch of the day.

Things to know // Jökull Bergmann, founder of Bergmenn Mountain Guides, leads ski touring trips into Hornstrandir, though you do need to be an experienced backcountry skier.

Opposite: the fiordlands of British Columbia are surprisingly reliable for a decent maritime snowpack

MORE LIKE THIS
SUMMIT-TO-SEA SKIING

ALYESKA, ALASKA

There aren't many ski resorts in the world where you can cruise a groomer or slay powder down the steeps while soaking in ocean views. Alyeska is a special place for a lot of reasons, but that panoramic view of the Turnagain Arm ocean inlet, part of the Gulf of Alaska, is definitely among them. Alyeska boasts that it's the only ski resort in North America with mountain, glacier and ocean views. Located a scenic 40 miles (65km) from Anchorage, Alyeska is a 1610-acre (650 hectare) ski area with seven lifts, including a mountaintop tram, and terrain for all abilities. Stay at the 304-room Hotel Alyeska, or any number of options in the nearby town of Girdwood. You might not be that far above sea level (the top of the mountain is 3939ft/1200m in elevation), but this place still gets loads of snow. Because daylight lingers so long in the Alaskan spring, the night skiing here is famously good. You can ski until 9pm.

Nearest town // Girdwood

LOFOTEN ISLANDS, NORWAY

If you've always dreamed of seeing the northern lights, put this place on your list. At the Lofoten Ski Lodge, on the secluded Lofoten Islands in Norway, you'll stay in a remodelled fisherman's cabin. By day, IFMGA-certified mountain guides from Northern Alpine Guides organise summit-to-sea ski adventures into snowy Arctic fjords; by night, you can watch the northern lights from the outdoor hot tub, relax in the sauna and enjoy chef-prepared two-course dinners. This is a backcountry ski trip, so you'll need ski touring experience and avalanche safety gear – and be prepared to climb for your turns. Guided ski-touring packages, which include room and board, range from private rental of the whole lodge for a long weekend or full week to renting a room or cabin with a group. The lodge takes bookings for ski packages from February to May; summer trips are available too.

Nearest town // Svolvaer

BRITISH COLUMBIA

If backcountry skiing from a sailing boat sounds novel and fun, British Columbia has its own version of that style of adventure. Sail Bainbridge, based south of the border in Bainbridge Island, Washington, offers a Sail 2 Ski trip into the fiordlands of British Columbia. This epic 10-day journey, for four to five people, comes with a boat captain and a ski guide, and takes place in March or April. You'll set sail on a 44ft schooner from Washington's San Juan Islands, crossing the border to BC's Princess Louisa Inlet, which is accessible only by boat, then hike your way up through a lush rainforest – with skis and camping gear on your back – until you reach the snowline. You'll set up an overnight base camp there and spend a few days ticking off ski descents that may or may not have ever been skied before, earning yourself coveted lines with views of the Salish Sea.

Nearest town // Nanaimo

SVALBARD BY SNOWMOBILE

The deeper you travel into the unforgiving Arctic wilderness, the fainter the lifeline to refuge.
A snowmobile tour in Svalbard is a thrilling ride into the unknown.

When the Svalbard archipelago first appeared after the three-hour flight north from Oslo, it was instantly apparent that this is a place apart. It is still a land where nature, not humankind, has the upper hand. Triangular white peaks rise above broad white valleys. Beyond them are more peaks, more valleys. On and on they stretch, receding to a hazy horizon. There was no evidence of life, nor even a patch of earth where life might support itself. From my window seat, Svalbard seemed of a scale and emptiness so vast it is hard to comprehend.

Svalbard has long drawn adventurers. The group of Norwegian islands lying far up into the Arctic Circle has exerted a magnetic pull on the curious and the foolhardy since it was first officially discovered in the 16th century. For me, Svalbard's appeal lies in the fact that it has changed so little since those early visitors first clamped eyes on it. The original pioneers had one thing in mind: to plunder seas brimming with whales, seals and walruses, as well as lands over-run with polar bears, foxes and reindeer. By the 20th century, attention had turned to what was in the ground: coal. Now, the prize lies not in what can be hunted or mined, but in the simple enjoyment of one of the world's purest environments.

Longyearbyen, where the plane landed, is the only settlement of any size. Would-be explorers trudge along its main street, calling

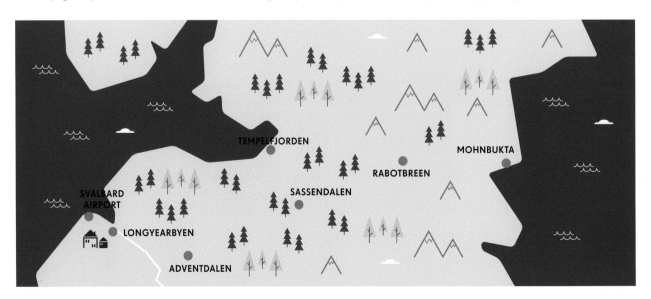

into stores to buy expedition food and wondering whether it might be sensible to get one more set of thermals. For all the trappings of civilisation, you're constantly reminded that people really shouldn't be here. It can drop to -25°C (-13°F) in winter, the sun doesn't rise for almost three months a year, and it's forbidden to leave town without an armed guide, to protect against polar-bear attack.

My guide, Nils, had the bone-crushing handshake of a man who knows what he's doing. We were about to embark on a snowmobile journey into the back of beyond, so this was reassuring. Humans have found a few ways to navigate the wilds of Svalbard – dogsleddding and ski-touring among them – but snowmobiles would allow us to roam further and deeper, and to traverse more of those fantastical peaks and troughs. Our aim was to travel all day to a remote camp.

By the time we left town, the storms of previous days had cleared and the sun was shining. We travelled through the wide glacial valley of Adventdalen as mountains swooped up on either side, their peaks crisp against the blue sky. Signs of human life faded. Nils led us up through a chasm in the rocks, and we emerged to find ourselves at the top of a mountain. Spread before us was the frozen river delta of Sassendalen and dark speckles of glacial moraine in the distance. By the time we bounced our way into the next valley, the weather had turned and Svalbard became mystical. Snow began whirling around us and black clouds loomed in the distance.

At Tempelfjorden, we arrived at the cabin of one of Svalbard's hardiest residents. Fur-trapper Hilmar Nøis built his home here in

> *"The sun doesn't rise for almost three months a year, and it's forbidden to leave town without an armed guide, to protect against polar bear attack"*

1912 and stayed for 38 years. It is little more than a shed, its sides clad in turf and driftwood, where chunks of sea ice the size of cars shift in the bay beyond. In the middle of winter, all alone, Hilmar's first wife, Ellen, gave birth to their first child here. Hilmar had set off on skis for Longyearbyen to fetch a doctor. 'Because of the bad weather, it took three weeks to get back,' said Nils.

There was little time to ponder the bleakness of Ellen's experience. In order to reach our own refuge by nightfall, we had to push on. Motoring through moraine to the top of Rabotbreen glacier, we skirted around blocks of ice as big as palaces, their surfaces as smooth to the touch as marble. Suspended within are tiny rocks and air bubbles, souvenirs from the last Ice Age. We took another break at the frozen sea of Mohnbukta, where the glacier's edge rises six storeys, a wall of blue ice scored with black and white grooves. While I lay back on my snowmobile and tucked into a bag of rehydrated spaghetti bolognese, Nils stood guard for the possibility of a polar bear crouching behind a rock,

RARE BEASTS

Venture out of Longyearbyen and you'll come across a Svalbard reindeer at some point, either standing alone in the snow or clustered in small herds. A distinct subspecies found only on the archipelago, they have short legs, stocky builds and small, round heads. They survive the long winter by storing up fat reserves over the summer, and picking through the snow for lichen. There are some 10,000 reindeer on Svalbard, compared with about 2600 humans and 1000 polar bears.

Clockwise from top: ice floes of Svalbard; polar bears will likely feature in tours around Longyearbyen; the village of Spitsbergen. Previous page: navigating the frozen waters of Mohnbukta Bay

assessing us as prey. We sat contentedly for a while, trying to work out if the white blobs in the distance were wind-whipped clumps of snow or an approaching predator.

Then Nils received a call on his radio – our camp, we learned, had blown away in the storms. We had no choice but to hare it back to Longyearbyen before the darkness and Arctic cold descended. But realistically, there weren't enough hours of daylight left for us to complete the journey. Even no-nonsense Nils seemed mildly anxious. With no concessions to my amateurish skills on a snowmobile, he set off like an F1 driver, as the clouds closed in around us. I could barely keep the back lights of his vehicle in sight through the gloom.

It was several hours before Nils allowed another short break. We arrived at a mountaintop just as the clouds broke. The last rays of the setting sun cast magic across the landscape – beneath us, the valley was bathed in pink light, the peaks beyond glowing the palest blue. There were still many miles to travel, but the sight stirred fresh enthusiasm for the journey. This was a proper adventure. As we sped onwards, a huge moon was rising. It hung an inch above the horizon for an hour before sinking back below the mountains.

We continued in the pitch black, the skies had cleared and were full of stars. When the lights of Longyearbyen appeared in the distance, it was a relief, but I wasn't quite ready to rejoin the world. Our plans may have failed, our arms and necks ached and our brains were frazzled from so many hours in the saddle, but Svalbard had once again shown that it, not us, was firmly in charge – which is exactly what drew me to it in the first place. **AC**

DIRECTIONS

Start/Finish // Longyearbyen, Svalbard.
Distance // 180 miles (290km).
Duration // One to two days.
Getting there // Fly to Longyearbyen via Oslo.
When to go // November to April.
What to wear // Good thermals and windproof winter gear; outfitters will provide snowsuits, boots and gloves.
What to pack // Lots of layers, including thermals, woollens, fleeces and waterproofs.
Where to stay // Basecamp Hotel is a cosy, atmospheric place in Longyearbyen, decked out like an old wooden trapper's cabin.
Where to eat // Longyearbyen's Huset serves a tasting menu of inventive Nordic dishes using local produce.
Tours // Basecamp Explorer offers a variety of trips in the archipelago. www.basecampexplorer.com
More info // www.visitsvalbard.com

MORE LIKE THIS
SVALBARD CROSS-COUNTRY ADVENTURES

DOGSLEDDING

Before there were snowmobiles, the only way to navigate Svalbard's terrain in winter was with a sled and a pack of dogs. It's possible to fancy yourself as an Arctic explorer of old and get behind your own team on a dogsledding adventure from Longyearbyen. There are various tours available, from brief forays out of the kennels and back, to romantic excursions that whisk you across frozen landscapes under the light of a full moon. The truly adventurous can embark on multi-day trips, with nights spent in fibreglass igloos, the dogs curled up outside. Mushing the animals and taking charge after instruction from your guide is an unforgettable experience. You get a whole new appreciation of the wilderness and your insignificance within it when it's just you, your dogs and one big expanse of snow. If you'd rather not have a go, just sit back on the sled and enjoy the ride.

Nearest town // Longyearbyen

VISITING AN ABANDONED TOWN

Once a thriving home to more than 1,000 residents who had a school, library, concert hall, heated pool and canteen at their disposal, the town of Pyramiden has been abandoned since 1998. The coal-mining settlement once belonged to the Soviets, who dug coal out of the surrounding mountains and shipped it back to the USSR. The facilities and infrastructure remain in place, as though the inhabitants have only just left, but tourists and the odd Arctic fox are the only signs of life now. When the sea ice has sufficiently thawed in spring, you can catch a ship to Pyramiden. There's a good chance you'll spot bearded seals, ringed seals and walruses en route. If the water's frozen, it's a two- or three-day trip on a snowmobile, with an overnight stay in the town's hotel where the adventure is capped off with a shot of Russian vodka in the bar.

Nearest town // Longyearbyen

HITCHING A RIDE IN A SNOWCAT

Dogsleds and snowmobiles aren't the only option for a snow-bound excursion on the archipelago. If you prefer leaving the driving to someone else, but still wish to see something of Svalbard beyond Longyearbyen, a trip in a Snowcat will get you out into the wild. It's a great choice for families with young children, the less physically able or those who just prefer to admire the scenery while staying warm and dry. The trucks trundle over the snow on rubber tracks, pulling passengers in a comfortable cabin behind. Beyond the windows are stirring views of ice-covered valleys and mountains, with the chance of spotting Svalbard's resident reindeer as they snuffle for food in the snow. There are various tours from Longyearbyen, with options to track the northern lights, watch the sunset from a mountain viewpoint or visit an ice cave cleft through a glacier.

Nearest town // Longyearbyen

Clockwise from top: Pyramiden, an abandoned Soviet mining town; what you get when you call an Uber in Svalbard; snowcats become city buses

A HIDDEN CATALONIAN GEM

Ski destinations that still feel remote, untracked, ancient and undiscovered are an endangered species in Europe. So ski the Val d'Aran while you can.

A friend of mine once returned from a trip to Europe with stories of the deepest skiing of his life – in a place I'd never heard of. The Spanish call it the 'Valley of Valleys'. Tucked in a mountainous cradle along Spain's border with France, Val d'Aran is ringed by a fortress of peaks. In fact, until the late Spanish dictator Francisco Franco built a tunnel on the backs of prison labourers in 1948, the mountain region was – aside from tobacco smugglers skiing through high alpine passes – cut off from its mother country for five snowy months each year.

Understandably, this northern nook of the Pyrenees has been off the public radar since before radar existed. But still, how could a ski town in Europe with incredible terrain and snow remain almost completely hidden from the rest of the world? I'd always wondered. A few years later I finally got the chance to see it for myself.

I had parked myself in Barcelona to be nearer someone I was dating, and I brought my ski bag along in the hope of scoring a freelance gig here and there (I was working as a ski writer at the

time). Despite Barcelona's sunny days and warm sea breezes, I'd heard that skiing opportunities weren't all that far off and, although committing to a life by the beach – for the time being – old habits die hard. I knew, for example, that ski options such as Masella were only around two hours from town. But I couldn't shake my curiosity for the Valley of Valleys. With the Alps so well-charted, there was still an air of mystery to the Pyrenees, and even more so with a place said to be one of its snowiest.

Even its name reflects the region's isolation and uniqueness. 'Val d'Aran' is neither Spanish nor French, but rather of a mountain-bound dialect called Aranese. Its traditional cuisine of cured boar, fresh yogurt and alpine honey adds to this sense of self-reliance. And despite residing within Catalonia's borders, the area does not view itself as part of Catalonia, which in turn is an autonomous region of Spain. Much like the Spanish Basque Country, Catalonia has developed its own government, speaks its own language (Catalan, compared with the Basque Country's *euskara*) and even flies its own flag, all while existing within Spain's internationally recognised borders.

I began my journey like all ski bums do, with a text to my friend who had been here before. Next thing I knew, I was receiving a text from Edu, a local ski instructor and freeskier at Val d'Aran's marquee ski area, Baqueira-Beret. He insisted I get there as soon as possible, insisting over and over again that he 'owed John' (for what, I still don't know). In the time it took me to pack my skis, backpack and a few extra layers, Edu had connected me with a bus from Barcelona's northern bus station to Lleida, an old Catalonian city at the southern foot of the Pyrenees. From there I hopped a smaller van into the belly of the mountains, with patches of white flying by as we cruised past jagged tectonic folds of limestone and breccia. When it seemed the van could go no further, the shuttle plunged into a three mile-long concrete portal, emerging the other side into a world of white.

Although Spain's former king, Juan Carlos I, frequented Val d'Aran and Baqueira-Beret until his four-decade reign ended in 2014, the ski area and its surrounding stone villages have managed to stay relatively secret on a global scale. That's changed a bit in recent years, with North American ski magazines slowly creeping deeper into Europe's 'other' mountain range and the Freeride World Tour adding a stop at Baqueira-Beret in 2022. But when Edu picked me up on an empty corner in Vielha, the Aranese capital of approximately 5500 inhabitants, Val d'Aran felt like anything but the next big thing in European resort destinations.

There were no flashing billboards, no nightclub bass pouring out into the streets, not a single fur collar or shiny puffy jacket in sight. A dark quiet hung above a maze of snowy alleyways. In a past life, Edu Carrera had been a promising alpine ski racer, but a freak motorcycle accident had left him partially paralysed as a teenager. These days, through extensive rehab and strength training, Edu has worked his way back up to competing for Spain in the Paralympics and it didn't take long for me to figure out I'd need to have my foot on the gas to keep up with my host.

⛷ A LAND APART

Val d'Aran is the only contiguous piece of Catalonia located on the north side of the Pyrenees and is home to the only Catalonian river that flows into the Atlantic Ocean (the Garonne River). It was also the site of a 1944 guerilla-led invasion from France, which had the aim of overthrowing the Franco dictatorship, but the efforts ultimately failed.

Right: village life in the Pyrenees of Catalonia is unlike that of other European ski towns. Previous page: Baqueira-Beret ski resort in the Val d'Aran

The next morning, the valley broke blue. A pop-up book of rocky peaks, mountain villages and Romanesque churches unfolded below as we rode up the Baqueira-Beret gondola. Historically, the Pyrenees have rested in the shadow of the mighty Alps since alpine skiing took hold in the early 1900s. France, the only country that boasts both ranges within its borders, says that the Alps account for 80 percent of its annual ski visits, while the rest are split between the Pyrenees and the nation's Massif Central. This often means is that Pyrenean skiing, despite technically forming part of Europe's larger ski community, has remained remarkably untamed.

After a short, 300ft (90m) hike from the Jorge Jordana lift, Edu perched on the ridgeline of 8200ft (2500m) Cap de Baqueira. With his back towards the expansive groomed pistes, he pointed into the gallery of chutes and couloirs leading towards Lacs de Baciver, a collection of shaded shots still holding fresh snow days after the last storm. I swept cold, light turns across an untouched canvas. As the

"Just when it seemed the van could go no further, the shuttle plunged into a three-mile-long concrete portal, emerging on the other side to a world of white"

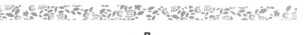

DIRECTIONS

Best time to go // Val d'Aran gets snow from November to late March, but late February and early March are when big northern storms bring buckets of snow to the valley.

Gear required // Skiers will be fine with a normal resort setup, but AT gear, a beacon, shovel and probe, and the proper avalanche training unlocks the backcountry terrain.

Nearest town // Vielha is the capital of Val d'Aran and is just 8.5 miles (14km) from Baqueira-Beret.

Getting there // From Barcelona's El Prat International Airport, the drive to Vielha takes about four hours on maintained roads. Daily buses travel between Barcelona and Lleida, with a connecting bus or shuttle to Vielha.

Where to stay // The Parador de Vielha is part of the state-run Parador hotel network and offers a palatial spa and dining area in the centre of town.

Things to know // The Pyrenees is full of national parks and pristine mountains, giving the range a wild, uninhabited feel.

pitch rolled over I picked up speed, boot-deep powder spinning up rooster tails in my wake. Edu took the local's approach, billy-goating his way between rocks and carving powerful giant-slalom turns into a wide, untouched powder trough.

Next, we hit one of Baqueira's more popular in-bounds freeride zones, a collection of tree shots and wide-open steeps that felt way more like Colorado or Utah than anything I'd seen in Europe. Edu relied on power and precision, skiing like he was making up for lost time. I struggled to keep up.

Finally, we skied over a wooded shoulder and into a hidden stash of glades. Emerging from the forest we popped out at an old stone cottage, miles from anything resembling a road. Still, smoke rose from the chimney stack as we clicked off our skis and walked in the front door. Sun seeped through curtain-shrouded windows as Edu ordered a round of Estrella Damm. We perched on a creaky wooden stool and sipped the beer. Development was underway here but, as the locals know, there are two sides to every valley. **KK**

*Opposite, from top: the popular
Aramón-Formigal in the Pyrenees;
Pradollano, the Sierra Nevada ski
resort, Spain*

MORE LIKE THIS
THE BEST OF IBERIA

ORDINO ARCALÍS, ANDORRA

Another stop on the Freeride World Tour, Ordino Arcalís shares a mountain range with Val d'Aran, but its home is the tiny European country of Andorra. Cut from the border of Spain and France, Andorra was established via a charter in 1278, which, until recently, included paying Spain a tribute in ham. It has three massive ski areas – all owned by the same conglomerate, Grandvalira Resorts – and the state boasts more miles of ski piste than main road. Ordino Arcalís is the smallest of the three resorts, but features steeper, more freeride-centric terrain. Although the resort offers well-groomed, winding terrain off its front and backside, the La Coma lift opens up a world of unmaintained chutes, big mountain faces and underexplored alpine basins. Drop back into the resort or take a lap off the ridgeline before catching a catwalk (gentle, narrow trail) back to the base. Once a two-lift journey, La Coma is now accessible via a new base gondola, taking skiers to the goods before Pyrenean sunshine heats up. When tired legs kick in, pop into Les Portelles Refuge for meatballs in mountain mushroom sauce served with a hefty pour of Catalonian grenache.
Nearest town // Andorra La Vella

SIERRA NEVADA, SPAIN

The Pyrenees may steal most of the headlines in Spain, but the country has several mountain ranges and more than two dozen ski areas. The furthest south of those areas in not only Spain, but all of Europe, is Sierra Nevada, a near-4000 vertical ft (1200m) resort on the country's third tallest peak, Veleta, offering views of Morocco on a clear day and the highest skiing in the country. Sierra Nevada provides nearly 70 miles (110km) of sunny, above-the-treeline ski terrain and has hosted everything from World Cup races to the 1996 FIS Alpine World Ski Championships and 2017 FIS Freestyle Ski and Snowboarding World Championships. But perhaps the greatest calling of this off-beat ski locale is the unrivalled cultural experience of skiing in the south of Spain. A little under 20 miles downhill, Granada is the beating heart of the country's vibrant south, home to not only the intricately beautiful Alhambra, but also to the gypsy caves of Sacromonte (from where, it's said, flamenco was born). There aren't many places on Earth where a day of skiing can be washed down with tapas tours down bustling cobblestoned sidestreets, but in Granada, you really can have it all.
Nearest town // Granada

ARAMÓN-FORMIGAL, SPAIN

While Spanish skiers are only slowly starting to catch on to Val d'Aran, Aramón-Formigal has been a favourite for decades. Located along the Aragonese Pyrenees, the northeastern Spanish ski area offers 147 runs across 109 miles (176km) of skiing, as well as a robust village of hotels, bars and Aragonese restaurants serving everything from grilled mountain trout to thick, marbled *chuletónes* steak. The resort even turns its base lodge into the après nightclub Marchica, consistently bringing out some of the country's best DJs to entertain crowds dressed in ski boots and faux-fur as they sip goblet-sized gin and tonics. For those who survive these festivities, Aramón-Formigal offers six distinct valleys of ski terrain connected by nearly 40 lifts, keeping crowds dispersed all day long. A free snowcat shuttles steep-seekers from the Espelunciecha lift to picturesque views of the monolithic peak of Anayet and the freeride terrain in Valle Portalet. If that isn't enough to whet the appetite, a mid-run stop at La Glera, with its selection of locally cured meats and cheeses, should do the trick.
Nearest town // Sallent de Gállego

© oksmit / Shutterstock; Antonio Luis Martínez Cano / Gettyimages

SKIING THE SCOTTISH HIGHLANDS

The Scottish are quick to defend the quality of their mountains, crags and couloirs. Indeed, some of the best mountaineers in the world have cut their teeth here. But skiing?

I was dragged up the final stretch of the 3636ft (1108m) summit of Meall a'Bhùiridh by a tired T-bar, while being pelted by piercing sideways sleet (there aren't many other kinds of sleet in Scotland). The clouds covering the rolling hills of the Highlands finally began to clear. I was able to lower my buff and breathe. I was on top of Glencoe Mountain Resort, the most beautiful of all of Scotland's ski resorts (yes, there are ski resorts in Scotland).

A lot of British skiers will tell you that skiing in Scotland is a novelty; a good way to get wet, cold and nothing more. It's true that it takes a certain level of stubbornness and opportunism to ski here. But the panorama before me on that day revealed another

side of the story. It answered the big question: why bother?

To the northwest of Meall a'Bhùiridh sits Buachaille Etive Mòr, a craggy mountain that rises steeply from the valley floor of Glencoe and dominates the bend of the glen. 'The Buckle', with its conical shape, is often cited as Scotland's most beautiful mountain. The character of the Scottish mountains is amplified in winter. Their crags look even more fearsome when jutting out of the snow. Their curves look even more graceful in a coat of white, and those curves take on a new form with every new snowfall. From the Etive Glades blue run on the west of the Glencoe resort, you have the best view of the mountain in Scotland. Around the corner lies Glen Etive and

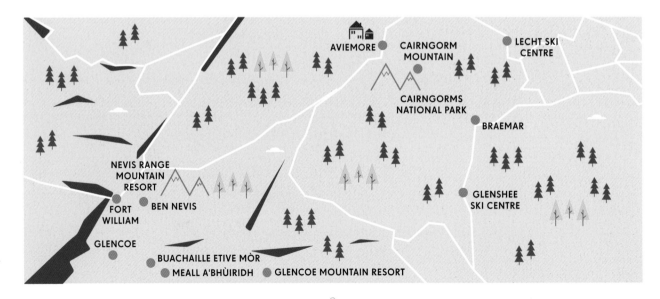

"Whether the snow will be champagne powder, slush or pure crust depends on the wind, the time, the temperature and, I'd bet, your behaviour in a past life"

the road that featured in the 2012 James Bond film *Skyfall*, which sent tourists flocking to the area.

Granted, Scottish skiing is an unpredictable endeavour, yet there are five ski resorts in the country: Cairngorm Mountain, The Lecht and Glenshee in Cairngorms National Park in the east; and Glencoe and Nevis Range on the west coast. Each resort is above the Highland boundary line, but none of them are snow sure. You don't plan to ski in advance here – you get up and go. If you're serious about skiing in Scotland, it requires monitoring the snowfall on social media and via webcams. When it starts to sprinkle with snow, webcam watchers move to full readiness, because what often follows is a full-force dump. The resorts will then confirm whether they're open or not. If you put it off for a few days the snow might get better – or it might disappear altogether. Whether it will be champagne powder, slush or pure crust depends on the wind, the time, the temperature and, I'd bet, your behaviour in a past life.

The drive to Glencoe is spectacular in itself. It takes just over two hours to reach the valley from the bustling central belt city of Glasgow, and en route you'll drive the length of Loch Lomond. Pull off the approach road to Glencoe on the valley floor, and you'll pass Blackrock Cottage – home to the pioneering Ladies' Scottish Climbing Club since 1947 – then spill out into the car park. The slopes themselves are only accessible by taking an old, slightly rickety access lift up a few hundred metres, passing frozen waterfalls as you go. I've been up here on bluebird days when the

powder is plenty, but I've also seen it during hailstones and sleet, and on days when the wind whips and whirls so ferociously that you're scared you're going to get blown off the mountain. On those days, it's best to give in to the elements, retire early and opt for a dram of whisky and an open fire instead.

Inevitably, all this anticipation does mean the mountains get busy. On an average day at Glencoe, you might wait 20 minutes for that first access lift, although once you've reached the plateau, the wait usually reduces to no more than five minutes per lift; particularly now that Glencoe has a new three-person chairlift. But it's the Cliffhanger Chairlift that will always get my heart racing on a windy day.

Ski resorts in Scotland are smaller and more antiquated than in other destinations. Andy Meldrum, owner of Glencoe Mountain Resort, once told me, 'people in Scotland see skiing as a sport, rather than as a holiday'. I often think it must be one of the most demanding jobs in the world to run a Scottish ski resort, a business relying on weather that may never come. Those involved in the trade are stoic and, as with most Scots, they meet whatever fate may come their way with their tongue planted firmly in their cheek. This is all part of the fun. When Glencoe's base-station restaurant burned down in 2019, on Christmas Day no less, Andy simply told the press: 'We'll keep skiing. We always keep going here. We plan to reopen tomorrow.' Andy also insists: 'On its day, the skiing in Scotland can be as good as anywhere in the world.' Among the skiing community, you'll often hear: 'It's just about finding that day.'

DRAM FINE

Roughly 50 percent of Scotland's whisky is made in the 50-plus distilleries in Speyside, a region just north of Cairngorms National Park. The Oban, Ben Nevis, and Dalwhinnie distilleries are classic stops.

From left: winter wildlife; catching air at Cairngorm Mountain; centuries-old cottages dot the Scottish Highlands. Previous page: the epic tranquillity of Glencoe under snow

On my most recent trip to Glencoe, the central chairlift had been hit by lightning and was out of action for the week, which gave me plenty of time to enjoy non-skiing activities. Skiing here is a passion, but it's the outdoors that's a way of life. If there's snow, they ski; if there's not, they make the most of the hiking and the world-class mountain-biking trails. Cairngorm Mountain Resort is around the corner from Aviemore, a Scottish trail town that's the gateway to Cairngorms National Park. Every second shop on the high street sells hiking equipment and, in the evenings, cosy bars host live folk music and serve single malt whiskies made nearby.

From the top of the highest chairlift at Cairngorm, it's a short hike to the summit of Cairn Gorm itself and there's terrific access to backcountry ski touring routes on the other side. A growing number of skiers will tell you that it's in these touring options that Scottish skiing comes into its own. These days, you get clips on social media that look like they could have been filmed on a powder day in Japan, restoking the debate on whether Scottish skiing is worthy or not.

It is occasionally suggested to me that skiing in Scotland is not *real* skiing. But I find it offers a uniquely authentic, natural and raw environment. We are proud of our mountains here in Scotland, as we are proud of our kilts, our haggis, our whisky, our warm welcomes and anything else that distinguishes us as a nation. And what you will get when you come to ski in Scotland is a distinctly Scottish experience – no heated chairlifts or piste maps. Or maybe it means champagne powder. It's just about finding that day. **SK**

DIRECTIONS

Best time to go // The best snow in Scotland tends to fall after February and sticks around until May.

Gear required // You can hire skis at each of the five Scottish resorts, often on a first come, first serve basis. Dress in layers with a weatherproof outer layer.

Nearest town // Cairngorm, Aviemore; Nevis Range, Fort William; Glenshee, Braemar; Lecht Ski Centre, Tomintoul; Glencoe, Kinlochleven or Fort William.

Getting there // Aviemore in the east and Fort William in the west are easily reachable by train from Glasgow or Edinburgh. The nearest airports are in Inverness or Glasgow.

Where to stay // The Cairngorm Hotel in Aviemore or Alexandra Hotel in Fort William are well-placed traditional hotels. There's a great youth hostel in Glen Nevis.

Things to know // If the weather does draw in, take a break and enjoy a hot chocolate. The mountain weather often passes through quickly in the Highlands.

Opposite, from top: the outdoorsy outpost of Fort William seen from the Nevis Range; Glenshee Sunnyside, poking through the clouds

MORE LIKE THIS
SKIING THE SCOTTISH HIGHLANDS

GLENSHEE SKI CENTRE

At the southern end of Cairngorms National Park – about an hour north of Dundee – Glenshee is the largest ski resort in Scotland and offers the greatest variety. With 25 miles (40km) of pistes, it boasts '3504ft of adventure' and prides itself on its steeps (the Tiger will challenge the best skier). But the resort is ideal for intermediates too, as you can go a long way on blues here, or an off-piste trip up Glas Maol will provide you with the best views in the area. Fantastic ski touring terrain can also be accessed via the Glenshee lift system. One claim to fame for the resort is that it hosted the very first British Snowboard championships in 2000 and still has fun terrain parks.

Nearest town // Braemar

LECHT 2090

At the northeastern end of Cairngorms National Park is Lecht 2090, named for its elevation in feet. Operating since the mid-1970s, Lecht 2090 is the pick of the bunch for families, with two travelators, a plethora of green runs and many easy blues. It is the smallest of Scotland's ski resorts, but punches above its weight. There's a racing piste and a freestyle park, and there's been good investment in snowmaking facilities here, making it slightly more reliable than other Scottish spots.

Nearest town // Tomintoul

NEVIS RANGE

Contrary to popular belief, Nevis Range is not actually on Ben Nevis, but the neighbouring mountain of Aonach Mòr (4005ft/1221m), though you do get a great view of the highest peak in the UK from the top of the summit rope-tow. The Nevis Range resort is a popular year-round attraction, but comes into its own during a heavy winter. As the highest ski resort in Scotland, there are 12.5 miles (20km) of pistes, accessed by Scotland's only ski gondola and 12 separate chairlifts and rope tows. The gondola is particularly helpful for backcountry access. The Goose is a brilliant red run, and the views out over lochs Eil and Linnhe back to nearby Fort William are beautiful.

Nearest town // Fort William

IN THE TRACKS OF
TELEMARK LEGENDS

Some of the greatest heroes of World War II were a tough-as-nails band of Norwegian winter soldiers – their legend lives on in the country's impressive hut system.

'**H**ei! Kan vi bli med dere?'
For 13 Brits huddled around a wood burning stove in a small hut, hearing Norwegian should not have been as surprising as it was. We were in the middle of the Hardangervidda in *Norway*, after all, on one of the largest and coldest plateaux in Europe. Nevertheless, it got our attention.

We had no idea what the man was saying, but the sentiment was clear. The two men who had entered the hut were unmistakably weary and weather beaten. It was cold, around -20°C/-4°F (disregarding the bitter wind chill we'd be facing all day). They looked every bit the callers you would anticipate – and almost expect – in a small hut on the Hardangervidda: athletic physiques and equipped with sharp cheek bones, deep blue eyes and frosted beards, they cut the image of what youthful explorers *should* look like, maybe the sort that joined Fridtjof Nansen and Roald Amundsen on their pioneering polar expeditions at the start of the 20th century.

We simply responded with, '*Ja ja*', and swiftly freed a space in our huddled circle by the stove. They didn't speak initially but straight away joined us in thawing out their fingers from the day's excursions. I asked them where they had come from and told them we were from the UK. 'Ah, OK,' one of them replied. 'Well, welcome to Norway.'

We were a team of 13 instructors from the Army Training Regiment Winchester who had embarked on this 'Adventurous Training' trip to Norway. Norway can be both beautiful and intolerant, sometimes interchangeably and amicably. In a country of five million people, a passion for the outdoors is at the core of Norwegian existence. From great polar explorers such as Nansen and Amundsen to modern day Olympic legends such as Marit Bjørgen and Ole Einar Bjørndalen, Norway and skiing in particular go hand-in-hand. Where better,

then, for a team of British amateurs to test their resolve than on an icy plateau? Our team aimed to ski across the Hardangervidda before heading into the Jotunheimen mountain range for a final challenge: summiting the highest mountain in Northern Europe. The logistics took shape long before we departed to refine an itinerary, procure the right equipment and prepare our skills. Almost half the team had never worn skis until a few months before our departure to Oslo. And yet, within a few months, we were breaking trail in knee-deep snow across steep terrain in a challenging environment.

We had begun the trip in Rjukan, a town in the county of Telemark (notable for being the birthplace of telemark skiing). Telemark

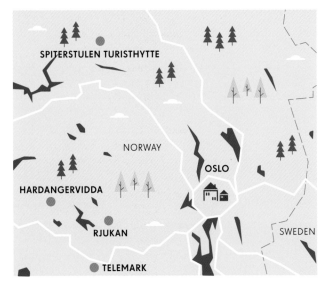

IX

GLORY OR DEATH

The Norwegian saboteurs' attack on the heavy water plant in Rjukan was codenamed Operation Gunnerside. Prior to the daring raid, Colonel Leif Tronstad informed his soldiers, 'I cannot tell you why this mission is so important, but if you succeed, it will live in Norway's memory for a hundred years.' Their escape, covering over 200 miles on skis in a Norwegian winter, does indeed continue to live on.

Clockwise from top: a fishing hut in Voss; Norwegian flag planted atop a mountain plateau; pulling sleds across the Hardangervidda plateau during the gruelling Expedition Amundsen ski race. Previous page: backcountry bliss

skiers are often known as 'free heelers', using boots that are clicked into toe bindings, leaving the heels free. It was the original way of getting around in Nordic countries – traditionally, hunters used to craft skis out of wood.

This form of travel was famously used by a group of Norwegian saboteurs in World War II, as dramatised in the film *The Heroes of Telemark* (Anthony Mann, 1965), starring Kirk Douglas. An essential German heavy water plant was located in Rjukan. The heavy water – also known as deuterium oxide – was a key component in the creation of an atomic bomb. Rather than bombing the plant, likely killing civilians, the Operation Gunnerside team instead parachuted in and made a daring raid on the plant. The mission was an audacious success – the entire inventory of heavy water was destroyed, along with equipment critical to create it. Not a shot was fired, nor a life lost. The escape across a frozen plateau was almost as audacious. Fully armed, in uniform and on skis, the Gunnerside group skied across hundreds of miles of challenging terrain to neighbouring Sweden, with 3000 dispatched German soldiers unable to locate them.

For the first four days of our trip we followed the 'Heroes of Telemark' route in the Hardangervidda, staying in both manned and unmanned Norwegian Trekking Association (DNT) huts. This wonderful system, unique to Norway, relies on membership and trust to support and encourage people to explore the natural beauty of

down Galdhøpiggen, the highest mountain in both Norway and Northern Europe. To our relief, the weather transformed into clear blue skies and all-day sunshine, albeit with a numbing -18°C (-0.4°F) base temperature. We were told at the DNT hut that we were the first team planning on skiing up Galdhøpiggen that season, which was both daunting and exciting.

A brisk morning welcomed us as we zigzagged our way up the lower slopes, slowly gaining altitude and escaping the chilly valley floor. Due to deep snow, our anticipated ascent time went out the window but onwards we ventured. Rocky outcrops meant we had to remove skis, attach them to the side of our rucksacks and head up on foot. There were a few brief meetings to discuss the option of turning around to ensure our safe descent, but ultimately summit-desire, the pristine weather conditions and a strong team meant we continued on.

As we kicked in steps up the steep upper slopes, we reached the 8100ft (2500m) summit of Galdhøpiggen in mid-afternoon and could have been easily persuaded we were in the Himalayas. Majestic snowy peaks spiked up around us as the sun bore down across the clear sky. A bracing wind and tough descent meant our time on the top was cut short. The skis came off the rucksacks, skins were removed, and a new test lay ahead – skiing down the mountain. Thankfully, all the team successfully gathered again at Spiterstulen to celebrate a thoroughly successful excursion. **GS**

'Operation Gunnerside was an audacious success'

the country by enabling their sustained living in that environment. It was intimate at times, with 13 of us cramped into a small hut awaiting sunrise to escape into the freedom of the snowy landscape.

Hardangervidda felt like a wilderness sometimes. A place where serenity and tranquillity were matched by bitter winds and whiteouts. Maps galore were spread across the tables under candlelight each evening, to judge the elevation and route profile of the following day and to evaluate our most efficient path. We were constantly tinkering with the itinerary and managing the mental arithmetic of time, distance and speed.

Six days on the bounce, totalling over 30 hours of skiing, was both physically and mentally demanding. Our distances increased as people's techniques and competency improved along with the weather, but the terrain became more undulating and untrodden with each new day. The established early routes were gone, and every morning brought about stunning new surroundings and experiences. We had to remain flexible in our planning to ensure all team members successfully navigated the long stretches and often inconsistent descents.

Finally, we reached a much-welcomed rest stop and drove up to the Jotunheimen mountain range to attempt to ski up and

DIRECTIONS

Best time to go // February to April.
Gear required // Waterproof shell jacket and trousers; thermals (top and bottom); lightweight insulated jacket; warm down jacket for evenings; hat, gloves (inner and outer) and socks; sunglasses and goggles; rucksack (25-35L).
Nearest town // Rjukan.
Getting there // Fly to Oslo Airport, from where it's a 2.5-hour drive to Rjukan.
Where to stay // Thon Hotel Rosenkrantz Oslo. While touring there are DNT huts (or camping if you prefer). In Spiterstulen, go for the Spiterstulen Mountain Lodge.
Things to know // It's recommended that you join the Norwegian Trekking Association (DNT) to get membership prices at the 550 DNT huts across Norway.

MORE LIKE THIS
AMBITIOUS MULTI-DAY SKI-TOURS

THE HAUTE ROUTE, FRANCE

The Classic! The Haute Route is on every ski-tourer's bucket list because it's the most famous in the world. And it's a classic for good reason. Connecting the two Alpine centres of Chamonix and Zermatt, the 6- to 8-day route offers stunning scenery, traverses glaciers and includes tough climbs and big descents. Each mountain pass manages to provide even greater views than the last. Starting near Mt Blanc and ending up in the shadow of the Matterhorn, this famous journey is one that will live long in the memory.
Nearest town // Chamonix

THE GRAN PARADISO, ITALY

Circumnavigating the Gran Paradiso massif, this hut-to-hut tour is another stunner. Set in a national park, it feels like a true wilderness with a wide variety of wildlife and plants. Generally culminating with a summit attempt at Gran Paradiso itself – the highest mountain entirely in Italy – it will certainly test your skills and stamina throughout, but no specific technical mountaineering experience is required. The quiet trails, combined with Italian hospitality at its finest – including fine wines, food and coffee – make this a special and highly satisfying venture.
Nearest town // Turin

GREENLAND

Greenland is the most sparsely populated country on the planet. For those seeking tranquillity, remoteness and escapism, this is it. The flight from Copenhagen to Kangerlussuaq alone will have your eyes peeled to the airplane window. The Greenland ice sheet below you is the biggest ice mass in the Northern Hemisphere and covers 80 percent of the world's largest island. From Kangerlussuaq, there are numerous options, including flights to Nuuk, Ilulissat, Sisimiut and others, all offering a wide variety of multi-day excursions well off the beaten path. Alternatively, head to the island of Kulusuk in eastern Greenland, embrace the local fishing and hunting communities, and be treated to a special combination of hospitality and sublime scenery. A ski-touring venture to this country is a truly unforgettable experience.
Nearest town // Kangerlussuaq

Clockwise from top: Italy's Gran Paradiso National Park; Kulusuk village in eastern Greenland; Argentière Glacier near Zermatt, along France's famed Haute Route

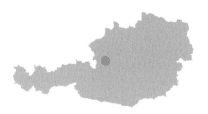

DEEP INSIDE EISRIESENWELT

*High in the Austrian Alps, the world's largest accessible ice cave enthrals
with its riot of spectacular formations and fascinating geological origins.*

I t's a sweltering summer day in the Austrian Alps, but where
I'm headed it is always winter. Dark clouds bubbling up in
the distance herald a thunderstorm. From the cable-car top
station I can see the scree-strewn trail leading upwards and the
limestone turrets and spires of the Tennengebirge range, which
tower some 6000ft (1800m) above the river-woven Salzach Valley
like the rocky ruins of a fantasy fortress.

Scenes from *The Sound of Music* were filmed in the wildflower-
freckled pastures near the town of Werfen below, but there is
nothing gentle about the geography up here at 5200ft (1600m).
The near-vertical cliffs have been starkly eroded by wind and
weather over millennia, and the karst plateau that rises above
them is pitted with crevices, sinkholes and caves. Suddenly, I see it:
a vast gash in the rock, more than 60ft (18m) wide and nearly 60ft
high. It looks like the entrance to another world.

This is Eisriesenwelt ('World of the Ice Giants'), billed and much-
hyped as the world's largest accessible ice cave. Stepping inside
is like opening a freezer. A blast of cold air hits me like a crisp
left hook. Still wearing just a T-shirt, I lunge for my backpack and
pull out a fleece and jacket. Each of us in our group is handed an
old-fashioned carbide lamp – the only thing that will illuminate our
passage through the pitch-black icy underworld.

Even on the hottest day outside, the temperature in the cave
can dip below freezing. It's eternally winter here. In *actual* winter,
the caves are off-limits, completely iced-in from late October to
April. With our lamplights dancing mysteriously across the ice, we
slowly pick our way through tunnels and passageways, where I'm
floored by the scale and beauty of the ice. The cave's altitude and
its precarious position on ragged cliffs means it has never been

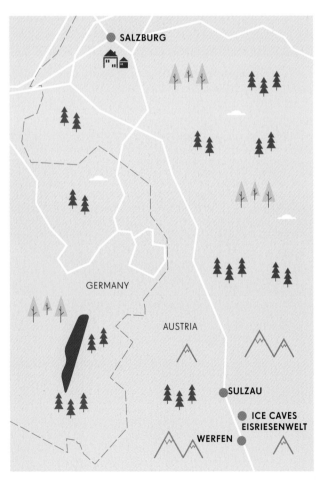

TAKING SHAPE

Research published in 2021 has revealed more about the unusual origins of Eisriesenwelt. Although you might expect water to flow downhill, scientific studies have proven that the ice caves were created when extreme pressure forced water 460ft (140m) *uphill* millions of years ago. When the caves were formed, they were completely filled with water, and swirling eddies created shell-shaped depressions in their walls.

From left: the ice caves were discovered by accident in 1879; guides are mandatory in the 26-mile maze. Previous page: 'World of the Ice Giants'

possible to install electric lighting, so to walk in these caves today is precisely as it was when they were discovered. In the dim light, our guide points out glittering ice formations as clear as blown glass and as delicate as cut crystal. There are smooth walls of ice rippled through like marble, waterfalls of ice and great forests of frozen stalactites. There is ice resembling enormous waves about to break, and a huge ice mountain that we ascend in quiet wonder via a long flight of wooden steps and metal handrails.

The origins of the cave are fascinating. Imagine how Anton von Posselt-Czorich, a naturalist from Salzburg, must have felt when he discovered them by accident in 1879. Before then, God-fearing locals were aware of the caves, but they never dared set foot in them, believing them to be the entrance to hell. I imagine that if our torches were suddenly extinguished, the total darkness and bitter cold would indeed be hellish – those locals had a point. Posselt-Czorich went alone but didn't get beyond the first 600ft (200m), before a solid ice wall blocked his path. Nevertheless, he published his findings a year later in the *Alpenverein* magazine and sowed the seeds for future exploration.

It was in 1913 that the big breakthrough came, our guide tells me, as we duck through an ice tunnel that shimmers an ethereal shade of blue in the half-light. Armed with crampons and pickaxes, pioneering Austrian cave explorer Alexander von Mörk and his team launched a proper expedition, using brute force to hack out steps to reach the top of the ice wall. What they found was beyond their wildest dreams: a 26-mile (42km) maze of tunnels burrowing deep into the icy heart of the mountain.

Tales of these intrepid early explorers propel me deeper through the caves, as I feel my way in the chilly darkness, through tunnels, chambers and up and down flights of steps that have been expertly hacked and bored out of the solid ice. Our guide holds his lamp up to some ice columns, frozen falls and sculptures emerging from the shadows, one shaped like a polar bear, another like an enormous elephant. In the Eispalast – or 'Ice Palace', a space as vast and echoing as a cathedral – there are curtains of icicles as big as organ pipes and walls of veined ice in every fathomable shade, from pearl white to sapphire blue.

Eisriesenwelt is a 'paradox', explains our guide. Even in the

© Eisriesenwelt

*"There is ice resembling
enormous waves about
to break, and a huge ice
mountain that we ascend
in quiet wonder"*

DIRECTIONS

face of climate change, when glaciers are rapidly retreating and ice caps are melting elsewhere, the amount of ice in the caves has grown. Ironically, hot and dry summers in the Alps in recent years have led to earlier snow melt, which seeps into the caves and freezes, whereas more rain would make the ice melt. However, climatologists have conducted studies deep in the warren of the caves, beyond the area visited by the public, and found tiny crystals that indicate the ice once covered a much greater area than it does now, proving that on a very long-term scale, the amount of ice is shrinking. These crystals have also been instrumental in helping to determine the age of the caves; estimates range between 50 and 100 million years old.

This ice is ancient and I can feel the weight of history and scientific endeavour pressing down upon me as we come to the end of our tour, following a tunnel to a flight of 700 steps, which descends back to the entrance. I blink in the bright daylight like a rabbit caught the headlights as I pass back through the hole and into the mountains that for so long kept these ice caves and their giants a secret. **KC**

Best time to go // Eisriesenwelt opens daily from late April to late October. The last cave tour departs at 3.45pm.
Gear required // Wear solid, grippy shoes and bring layers: a fleece, hat and thick padded jacket are recommended.
Nearest town // Werfen is the nearest village, where frequent trains connect to Salzburg, a 50-minute journey.
Getting there // The bus from Werfen station to the visitor centre departs every two hours until 2.18pm. It's then a short uphill hike to the cable car that hauls you up the mountain. The last descent is at 5.32pm. If you'd prefer to hike, it takes 1.5 to 2 hours to climb from the valley to the cable car.
Where to stay // Werfen's Hotel Obauer offers appealing digs as well as one of the region's finest restaurants. There are other simple guesthouses in the village, while the caves are also doable on a day trip from Salzburg.
Things to know // No filming or photography is permitted in the caves. For more details, visit www.eisriesenwelt.at

MORE LIKE THIS
ICE CAVES OF EUROPE

LANGJÖKULL, ICELAND

All is dazzlingly white as far as the eye can see at Langjökull, or the 'Long Glacier', Iceland's second largest ice cap. Around 40 miles (64km) long, 15 miles (24km) wide and 395 sq miles (1025 sq km) vast, its frozen glory spreads across the Highlands. Dark nunataks and volcanic cones rise like shark fins above the swirling, crevassed ice. However, like many glaciers, it is shrinking fast due to global warming.

If the glacier is compelling from above, its ice cave beggars belief. Designed and built by celebrated Icelandic geophysicist, explorer and mountaineer Ari Trausti Guðmundsson, the world's longest man-made ice tunnel reaches almost 1000ft (300m) into the solid glacier ice, 100ft (30m) below the surface. Slip on crampons for a walk through the surreal blue passageway. There's even a tiny ice chapel where couples can tie the knot.

Tours by 4WD are plentiful and the closest point of access in western Iceland is the village of Húsafell (longer day tours from Reykjavík can also be arranged).

Nearest town // Húsafell

DACHSTEIN GIANT ICE CAVE, AUSTRIA

High above ravishingly pretty Hallstätter See in Austria's lake-spattered Salzkammergut region, Dachstein Giant Ice Cave offers a frosty reception at 4770ft (1455m) above sea level. A cable car wings you up the mountain to Schönbergalm, then it's a short uphill trudge to this glittering ice empire, one of the showpieces of the Hallstatt-Dachstein Unesco World Heritage Site. Here, water has trickled down from a karst plateau and frozen, forming an 'ice mountain' some 26ft (8m) high – twice as tall now as it was when the caves were first explored in 1910. There is a touch of theatre here thanks to the rope bridge that traverses the ice, getting you thrillingly close to the impressive formations. Lights in vivid blues and reds illuminate the ice, which takes on eerie and strange shapes.

The cave is open from late April to early November and can only be visited on a 50-minute guided tour. Wear sturdy shoes and warm clothes as the temperature hovers around -2°C (28°F).

Nearest town // Obertraun

SCĂRIȘOARA, ROMANIA

The limestone mountains that pucker up in Transylvania's Apuseni Nature Park in western Romania are utterly wild. Honeycombed with caves and blanketed in thick, ferny forest, they hide the magnificent Scărișoara ice cave, which wows with one of Europe's largest underground glaciers, formed some 3500 years ago and glimmering with 75,000m³ of ice.

You have to earn your ice viewing here, however. At 3822ft (1165m) above sea level, the cave is remote. Reaching it feels like a proper adventure, especially if you approach it on foot from the commune of Gârda de Sus, 5.6 miles (9km) away.

Flights of steps weave down past mossy, craggy cliffs into the bat-filled cave, like something from a Tolkien fantasy. They lead deep into a glacial forest, stippled with ice formations; some as delicate as wax candles, others colossal stalagmites towering 20ft (6m). Temperatures range from 1°C (34°F) in summer to a teeth-chattering -7°C (19°F) in winter, so dress accordingly. Tours depart frequently.

Nearest town // Cluj-Napoca

Clockwise from top: the Scarisoara Glacier shelters the largest underground ice caves in Romania; Dachstein Ice Cave near Hallstatt, Austria; exiting the mouth of an ice cave in Langjökull, Iceland

WINTER TRADITIONS IN THE TATRAS

In Poland's Podhale region, a cradle of seasonal customs, vivid reminders of the living Górale Highlander culture are around every corner.

Snow is falling on Jaszczurówka Chapel, outside the town of Zakopane, Poland, 60 miles (100km) south of Kraków. Fat flakes bank on the wooden roof and the boughs of surrounding coniferous trees, adding to the seven or so inches already piled on the ground. The turn-of-the-20th-century building is full of reminders that, historically, locals couldn't wait to see the back of winter. Decorations hint at a longing for winter's end, with rays of sunlight carved above a doorway and a recurring motif of crocuses and violets. When these flowers bloom, it signals spring and no snow for another year. These days, however, visitors flock to the Podhale region in the south largely *for* the snow.

Like a lot of the traditional mountain towns at the base of the Tatras, Zakopane is a year-round resort. In summer, it offers hiking, mountain biking, mountain vistas and fresh air. In winter, mountain vistas transform into snow playgrounds and Podhale becomes a popular base for hitting the slopes at various ski resorts, including Kasprowy Wierch and Nosal. The most unique adventure in Podhale, however, may be to immerse yourself in the annual winter Highlander Carnival, held every February in the village of Bukowina Tatrzańska, a short drive east of Zakopane.

It's a wonderful occasion, one that enables visitors to experience this living culture first-hand. As well as a parade, there are carols

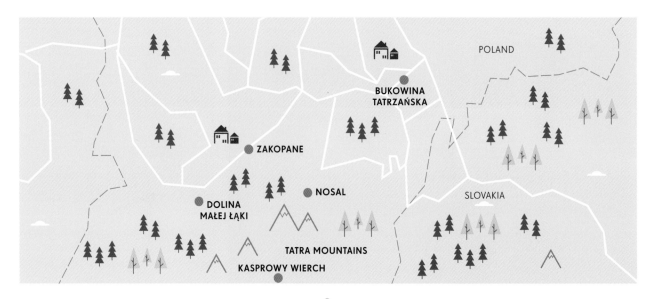

POLAND

BUKOWINA TATRZAŃSKA

ZAKOPANE

DOLINA MAŁEJ ŁĄKI

NOSAL

SLOVAKIA

TATRA MOUNTAINS

KASPROWY WIERCH

and dancing; demonstrations of *kumoterki* (sleigh-racing) and horse-drawn skiing; and a Polish Tatra sheepdog show. It's also a great place to pick up souvenirs, with expert craftspeople displaying work including embroidery and wood carving.

The festival is a celebration of all things Górale, or 'Highlanders', the ethnic group whose hard task it has been to farm these mountain pastures. The Zakopane chapel is a reflection of a typical Górale home with its wooden construction and elaborately carved interior. Craftsmanship is still at the heart of Highlander culture, and there's a dazzling array of wares displayed on Krupówki, Zakopane's main street. Among stalls selling everything from wooden bowls to embroidered slippers are those offering slices of oscypek cheese; its halloumi-like density and smoky richness cut through by the accompanying dollop of cranberry preserve. Made with sheep's milk, the cheese acquires its distinctive patterns from hand-carved sycamore moulds – each Highlander family has its own design.

Upon arrival at the festival, I meet the best-dressed man I have ever encountered. 'It took me two weeks of solid work to make these trousers,' says Jan Kubik, proudly running his fingertips along the colourful stitching. Made from naturally insulating fabrics such as wool and sheepskin, Highlander clothing is distinctive for its lavish embroidery. 'I was a baker for more than 40 years,' Jan continues. 'But in secret I learned how to sew and embroider clothes. When I was a child, my parents, like most Highlanders, were poor and wanted me to spend any spare time working on the land. But this is my passion – this and music!'

Jan gets out his *trombita*, a large, wooden alpine horn, and plays a loud and ominous note that sounds like a call to war. 'In the past, before mobile phones, shepherds used these to communicate,' he explains. 'And to scare deer from the potato and cabbage crops, and warn off wolves and bears.' Highlander know-how is passed down within families and you can't claim to be a Highlander unless you can trace your Górale heritage back at least three generations.

Podhale Highlanders used to keep sheep in meadows all over the mountains, but the creation of Tatra National Park in 1954 aimed to protect endemic species by limiting grazing to just a handful of pastures. One of those pastures claimed by the park is Dolina Małej Łąki, which I reach by following a path uphill through spruces, larches and pines. The snow deadens all sound; the dense silence is punctured only by the occasional burst of laughter when my legs disappear into a thigh-high drift.

It's no trouble for Agnieszka Szymaszek, though. Seven years of guiding walks in the Tatras have taught her how to avoid such pitfalls. She steps smoothly across the snow using walking poles for balance, white light glinting off her official pin-badge. It features the edelweiss flower, which grows on the limestone that's a characteristic of these mountains, which include Rysy, Poland's highest peak at 8205ft (2501m). 'It's beautiful, but, because it's the biggest, everyone goes there,' laments Agnieszka. 'For me, it's more important to be alone with nature. I seek out the quietest parts of the park.'

The path passes more trees, a brook filled with snowmelt and

HIGH LIFE

One of the first local explorers, around 1890, was Klemens Bachleda, a Highlander who, as a boy, earned his living shepherding high in the Tatras. He later used his knowledge of the terrain to become one of Poland's most highly regarded alpine guides and a founding member of the Tatra Volunteer Search and Rescue service. But it speaks of the mountains' many dangers that even someone of his experience was fallible – he died during a rescue attempt in 1910.

"Craftsmanship is still at the heart of Highlander culture"

Clockwise from left: traditional Podhale highlander clothing; Jaszczurówka Chapel, near Zakopane; Podhale's 'winter games'. Previous page: cheese being prepared in Zakopane

a moss-covered stump with a foot-high hat of snow, before emerging onto a plain where the only evidence of life is a trail of human footprints. We follow them until the path opens out onto an idyllic winter scene: families in brightly coloured snowsuits tow children on sledges. This is precisely why most people visit this region, to ski or otherwise play in the abundant fresh powder, partaking in winter activities that include snow tubing and husky sledding.

Nowhere can the power of the mountains be felt more keenly than at the top of the nearest ski resort, Kasprowy Wierch. Most reach the 6512ft (1985m) summit by cable car, gliding over miles of forest and sparkling snow, criss-crossed with ski trails. Still tucked into the mountainsides are old shepherd's huts and a nunnery encircled by trees. At the top, the air is thin, the sun so bright I'm squinting behind shades. Some people strap on skis and descend immediately, but many stand, stunned, gazing on jagged white rocks stretching to Slovakia.

Making their way along the exposed ridge, hikers with poles and crampons seem small and precarious; a row of ants tightrope-walking at the top of the world. What gives Kasprowy Wierch its potency is its a sense of nature untamed. It is a place where few but the Highlanders could feel truly at home. **OT**

DIRECTIONS

Best time to go // Reach Kraków by train, then transfer onto a local bus or train to Zakopane.

What to pack // There is generally snow all winter, but visit in February for the Highlander Carnival, or March to avoid peak ski season.

Where to stay // Villa Dorota or Hotel Sabala, Zakopane.

Where to eat // Karczma Przy Młynie, Zakopane.

Tours // Bazatatry offers excursions to learn about Highlander life, as well as ski lessons, sleigh rides and snowshoeing. www.bazatatry.com

Things to know // It's fairly straightforward to explore this region without a car, as there are many city buses, private mini buses and taxis serving the area.

MORE LIKE THIS
INDIGENOUS EXPERIENCES

THE AINU OF HOKKAIDŌ, JAPAN

The indigenous people of the country's northernmost island, the Ainu are now largely integrated into Japanese society, but it's still possible to experience aspects of their traditional culture if you visit Hokkaidō today. Ainu Kotan is the largest community on the island, and residents make a living selling foods such as *pochie* (fermented potato dumplings) as well as wood and leather crafts. The Ikor theatre hosts regular performances of dance and song, while above the village the Ainu Folklore Museum is also worth exploring. Elsewhere, Ainu-run guesthouses on the island offer an opportunity to learn about indigenous culture in a more informal setting. In Shiretoko National Park, Shūchō no Ie is an Ainu chief's house, doubling as an inn with basic rooms and a restaurant serving home-cooked cuisine. And at Marukibune, beside Kussharo Lake, you can be treated to recitals by its owner, an Ainu musician.

Nearest town // Sapporo

THE SÁMI OF NORWAY

The Sámi are the descendants of the nomadic indigenous peoples of northern Scandinavia, but today their biggest population lives in Norway, predominantly in the county of Finnmark. Here, the Varanger Sámi Museum offers an interesting overview of the community's history and culture. Reindeer husbandry has long been central to their existence, and there are ample opportunities to try reindeer meat at regional restaurants. The most famous dish is *bidos*, a slow-cooked stew. Across Norway's far north are companies offering a more hands-on experience of Sámi life. Tromsø Arctic Reindeer is run by a family of Sámi reindeer herders who offer sledding trips with their flock as well as excursions to see the northern lights. Alternatively, arrange an overnight stay in a traditional *lavvu* (a Sámi herdsman's tent) with Tromsø Lapland. You'll sled to camp and hear the stories of Sámi guides over a shared meal around the fire.

Nearest town // Tromsø

CANADA'S INDIGENOUS PEOPLES

The First Nations, Métis and Inuit indigenous peoples were Canada's first inhabitants, and today communities across this enormous country offer some unforgettable winter experiences. On Baffin Island in the far north, Arctic Bay Adventures works with Inuit guides on a range of immersive tours, including wildlife safaris to see polar bears, plus a five-day igloo-building trip where guests can meet community elders. But visitors needn't travel quite so remotely in search of a proper adventure. Just outside Québec City you can explore the Huron-Wendat Museum, overnighting at its wood and bark-built Iroquoian longhouse (or at the more modern hotel attached), before setting out on snowshoes. Recently opened in Alberta, Métis Crossing is an indigenous-owned hotel and cultural interpretive centre. As well as guest rooms curated by a local artist, it offers activities including a course in Métis winter survival skills and a storytelling programme taking in dark skies and cross-country skiing.

Nearest town // Québec City

Clockwise from top: Sámi woman in northern Norway; a local Hokkaido wood carver; traditional Sámi reindeer-skin tents beneath the northern lights

ASIA

CENTRAL ASIA'S SNOW HEARTLAND

If it wasn't for its complicated past, Kyrgyzstan would be a ski destination on par with Verbier or Jackson Hole. In the meantime, one outfitter holds the key to the castle.

I t's said that 'thieves oil' dates back to the bubonic plague, when four industrious robbers concocted the brew to protect themselves from illness as they snatched gold from fresh corpses. Slide-stepping woozily among the peaks of Kyrgyzstan's Terskey Ala-Too mountain range, I was starting to think the miracle serum could actually bring people *back* from the dead.

Hours earlier, I had been doubled over in a thick woollen yurt, my stomach turning an uneasy, fever-pitched dance. There was probably decent medical attention down in Bishkek, but that was a six-hour drive away. With a crackling woodfire as my sole companion, I'd spent 12 hours in agony, until Ptor Spricenieks poked his head through the entry flap. A former professional big-mountain skier from Canada who had travelled the world before settling in La Grave, France, the pony-tailed skier with a flair for the eccentric offered me his personal stash of thieves oil, squeezing a few drops on my tongue and handing me a bottle of water. Over the next 30 minutes, my stomach unclenched and my fever subsided. I threw on my ski pants and lifted the flap of the yurt, feeling just alive enough to click-in at least one more time.

And there I was, tipping my skis over the edge of a line called Yahtzee, feeling invigorated in the cold mountain air, looking out over a vertical expanse of snow and jutting rock. I dropped into velvety powder bliss, ready to roll the dice once more in Kyrgyzstan's high alpine.

Known primarily for walnuts, wool, and gold and uranium deposits, Kyrgyzstan is in many ways an afterthought in the global economy (in Central Asia, only Tajikistan is poorer, according to the World Bank). Skiing, though, has become the keystone in attracting foreign interest and investment to the nascent winter tourism industry. One

of my guides on this trip, Ryan Koupal, caught that wave on the upswing. After years of leading educational trips throughout Central and Western Asia, the Colorado native landed in Kyrgyzstan in 2009 with his splitboard in tow, anxious to explore ski terrain that had long been off the map for Westerners. Since Uzbek militants began waging a clandestine war against the country in the late 1990s – the same conflict that resulted in the kidnapping of American climber Tommy Caldwell – many travellers had shied away from the region. Although governments worldwide continue to issue travel advisories for the country's southern border, Koupal quickly found peace in the alpine, of which there is no shortage in Kyrgyzstan.

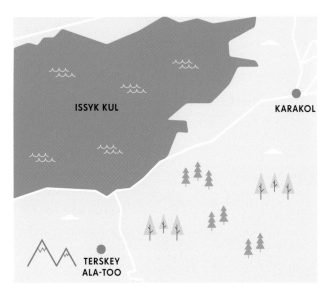

RIVAL CAMPS

"The skeletons of the Soviet regime linger throughout the landscape"

Up until a few years ago, Kyrgyzstan was the only country to house both a Russian and a US military base at the same time. While Russia has continued to operate a base in the country since the fall of the Soviet Union, the US opened Manas Air Base in 2001 as a staging ground for the war on terror in Afghanistan. The US handed over the base to Kyrgyzstan in 2014.

From left: 40 Tribes' Kyrgyzstan expeditions are one of a kind; gear and people are brought into the mountains by any means necessary. Previous page: yurt life in the Terskey Ala-Too mountains

The country is made up of 158 mountain ranges covering 94 percent of its area, roughly the size of Nebraska. Frigid Siberian storms blow off Lake Issyk Kul, the world's second largest alpine lake, creating a microclimate similar to Salt Lake City, Utah, burying nearby lines like Yahtzee under a blanket of fresh on a near weekly basis. The country has about 20 ski resorts, remnants of the Soviet Union. Unchanged for several decades, they still cater mostly to Russian tourists. But Kyrgyzstan's inbounds laps don't even begin to scratch the surface of the country's real ski potential.

Kyrgyzstan has long been at the Central Asian crossroads. In 1936, the Soviet Union absorbed the country as the Kirghiz Soviet Socialist Republic and united the ethnically diverse population under one flag. Although the Iron Curtain lifted in 1991, the skeletons of the Soviet regime linger throughout the landscape: town squares with life-size Stalin and Lenin statues, Russian signage dominating the capital, Bishkek, and, high on the hills, ski bases. The Soviets were in fact the first to realise the region's alpine potential, setting up these ski areas during the 1970s and 1980s. One, Karakol Mountain Ski Base, served as the Soviet Olympic team's official training ground during the USSR's alpine push through the 1980s. It was here outside Karakol in the Terskey Ala-Too – part of the Tien Shan range – that Ryan Koupal saw a chance to explore Kyrgyzstan's untapped backcountry. After a few years of scouting terrain and making the right local connections, the Coloradan established 40 Tribes

Backcountry, a yurt-serviced freeride touring experience among some of the most landlocked mountains on the planet.

Those first years were a crash course in cultural dynamics and perseverance. After linking up with local villager Nurbek Kasym-Uulu near the rural area outside Jalpak Tash, Koupal set about levelling ground for a yurt in the autumn of 2010, outfitting the campsite with materials from the bazaars in and around Karakol. That first winter, in 2011, Koupal and 40 Tribes hosted only one group, but the seed had been planted in the fertile Kyrgyz soil.

Koupal brought in Ptor Spricenieks that same year, and together they have grown the operation far beyond Kyrgyzstan, with something of a unique vision in the ski world. 40 Tribes now runs trips in Georgia, Svalbard, Chile, Greenland and the Russian island of Kamchatka, among other destinations. Renowned international guides, including Eric Layton, Ty Mills and Jessica Taylor, have helped that expansion, so much so that, in recent years, 40 Tribes has started operating something called the Mystery Trip, a ski and splitboard adventure fully planned by the team, but only revealed to the guests after they land – in 2022, a group flew into Istanbul before learning that they were headed to Georgia.

For me, linking up with Koupal and his band of locals had been anything but a heli-connected, surf-and-turf-fuelled luxury experience – and that was kind of the point. Stripped down Soviet UAZ-452 vans shuttled us over miles of rutted country roads, rumbling through

© 40 Tribes X 3

the mud in low gear. At the trailhead, we loaded our gear onto two packhorses before schlepping to a small collection of yurts. Up at basecamp, Nurbek cooked us meals ranging from a rich borscht to a Central Asian beef-and-noodle dish known as *laghman*. We rolled cigarettes in the fading afternoon light and sipped vodka as smoke from evening cooking fires wafted up from the valley below.

Kyrgyzstan also holds some of the most uncommon snow on Earth. As I cut my way down Yahtzee, the cold, dry snow slid downhill like granules of sand. Unlike the Continental Divide brand of powder in places like Colorado and Utah, the Kyrgyz variety is heavy enough to stay on top, making for fast, buttery descents among small rivers of slough. Around the valley, point release avalanches (with wet, loose snow) scarred the otherwise pristine amphitheatre, reminders that even this dreamy surface should come with a warning label. I navigated right across the slope, away from a convoluted terrain trap and towards my moraine rendezvous with Spricenieks. Rounding the guide, I slowed to a stop, waiting for gravity to catch up.

Spricenieks beamed through his patchwork of scraggly beard. 'I guess the thieves oil worked then?' quipped the alpine-tanned veteran, referencing the remarkably potent blend of, as it turns out, just oregano, rosemary, eucalyptus, clove and cinnamon, that had brought me back from the brink. 'I mean, you're alive.' Taking a deep breath of frigid mountain air, I looked up at my tracks and managed a smile. I certainly was. **KK**

DIRECTIONS

Best time to go // 40 Tribes runs expeditions from January through March when temperatures are coldest and precipitation is most consistent.

Gear required // Beacon, shovel, probe and an AIARE Level 1 (avalanche safety course) certification. A standard AT setup will work wonders and binoculars can scout lines.

Nearest town // Karakol (40 minutes from the trailhead).

Getting there // The trailhead is about a six-hour drive from Bishkek. International flights land in Bishkek throughout the day (they can be interrupted by Russian military air traffic) There are also flights from Bishkek to Karakol.

Where to stay // Before settling at the yurts, rest at Karakol's Matsunoki, a beautiful guesthouse close to one of the largest open-air animal markets in the world.

Things to know // You can stay in Kyrgyzstan for up to 60 days without a tourist visa. The two official languages are Kyrgyz and Russian; the latter is spoken widely in Bishkek.

Opposite, from top: skinning past traditional nomad yurts at Shymbulak ski resort near Almaty, Kazakhstan; ripping it up at Gudauri in Georgia

MORE LIKE THIS
BACK IN THE USSR

KAZAKHSTAN

Often confused with its southern neighbour, Kazakhstan is another ski destination that flies under the international radar. Like Kyrgyzstan, Kazakhstan is split by the mighty Tien Shan (a range that stretches from China through Central Asia to the Himalaya), but the former Soviet republic is also home to the Ural and Altai mountains, giving the country an underappreciated alpine pedigree. In fact, Kazakhstan has been so quiet about its mountains, that when Almaty, the former capital, made the shortlist to host the 2022 Winter Olympics (a Games that was eventually given to Beijing), most adventurous skiers were sent scrambling for their mapping apps. Currently, the country is home to seven ski resorts and only 28 miles (45km) of on-piste skiing, but those numbers belie a much deeper (and more powdery) truth. Shymbulak offers 3000ft (920m) of inbounds vertical just 17 miles (28km) from Almaty, but because of Kazakhstan's convoluted array of mountain terrain, some of its most adventurous skiing is best accessed by helicopter – an approach that costs fractions of its North American equivalent. Heliski KZ offers four-day midwinter flight packages, and when things heat up, birds from Kan Tengri Expeditions shuttle skiers higher into the Tien Shan.

Nearest town // Almaty

GEORGIA

Sitting in Russia's southern shadow, Georgia has emerged as an unlikely player in the global ski scene. Though the country is blessed by cold winters and big storms blowing off the Black Sea, Georgia had just a few ski areas and a trickle of ski tourism (mainly from Russia) before the late 2010s. That's when the oligarchs moved in, bringing with them enough capital infusion to turn Georgia's Caucasus Mountains into a worldwide destination. Gudauri may be the best representation of that evolution. A harrowing 75-mile (120km) drive from Georgia's capital city, Tbilisi, Gudauri's car park sits at a dizzying 7200ft (2200m) above sea level and the resort offers over 4000ft (1200m) of vertical relief. The area has increased in size in recent years, but prides itself on cheap lift tickets and uncompromised access to the backcountry. Even with its recent rise, Georgia's ski scene maintains a days-of-old charm, and it's not uncommon to see backcountry skiers dropping off-piste and staying the night in snowbound mountain villages before skiing back over to the resort the following day.

Nearest town // Tbilisi

AZERBAIJAN

Azerbaijan's ski scene might have been the least expected to emerge from behind the Iron Curtain, but the cradle of crude oil has found a new calling in its multitude of mountain ranges. Topped by 14,652ft (4466m) Mt Bazardüzü, this Caspian nation is 60 percent mountainous, and its high regions receive snowfall from mid-December through to March. However, the ski scene is very much in its infancy here, as only three resorts spin lifts in the country. Unlike Kyrgyzstan, many of these resorts are new and were built with the modern consumer in mind. Shahdag Mountain Resort, for example, offers luxury spas, a high-rise five-star hotel and paragliding lessons in place of the wild backcountry adventures you'd expect in other Central Asian locales. Azerbaijan has become a cost-effective alternative to the Alps for many throughout the Middle East, receiving easy daily flights from Dubai and Western Europe.

Nearest town // Quba

HOKKAIDŌ'S VOLCANO

Home to some of the best skiing in the world, this island off the north coast of Japan has mega-resorts and Zen-like backcountry sanctuaries. Mt Yōtei is the centrepiece.

I stood on the lip of a giant 6200ft/1900m-high, 2300ft/700m-wide teacup, which was filled with the lightest, driest Japanese powder. I turned to my mate, Chris 'Cones' Jones, then strapped into my snowboard and delivered the movie quote I'd been rehearsing throughout the six-hour hike to get here: 'Nobody knows anything. We'll take this leap and we'll see. We'll jump and we'll see. That's life.'

Before he had the chance to laugh – or, more likely, groan – at the Meg Ryan line from *Joe Versus the Volcano* (the film starring Tom Hanks that we'd watched far too many times at university a decade ago), I swooped into the crater of Mt Yōtei. The near-perfect, free-standing conical volcano in Japan's northernmost island of Hokkaido had been calling my name since I'd arrived in the famous powder ski town of Niseko two weeks before. My first frontside turn was 150ft (45m) long, as I scythed through knee-deep powder. The second backside arc was double the length.

In this part of Hokkaidō, Mt Yōtei is gloriously unavoidable. Also known as Yōtei-zan ('sheep-hoof mountain') and Ezo-Fuji (due to its resemblance to Mt Fuji), the semi-active volcano, which last erupted in 1050 BCE, rises out of the flatlands to the east of the bustling Niseko ski resort area. No matter which of the four main Niseko ski resorts you ride – collectively known as Niseko Mt Resort Grand Hirafu – the volcano will be there in the distance, catching your eye and blowing powdery kisses in your direction.

Although all Niseko ski resorts have incredible off-piste skiing that funnels back to the lifts, Mt Yōtei is much less crowded and is a pure backcountry adventure. There are no marked or maintained winter routes on the mountain. Nor is there any avalanche control. It is an entirely different kind of Hokkaidō ski experience.

That day, we had our guide, Owain Bassett, with us. The Welshman is a long-time Niseko resident and founder of the Island Snowboards brand. While there are five established routes up the eastern side of the volcano, which provide the best access and quality of snow, Bassett had picked out the Jinja-no-sawa Route (also known as the Cemetery Route) as our best option. We'd met near the Makkara cemetery in the dawn light at 6.30am, which provided an eerie, almost spiritual start, giving way to a beautiful 90-minute hike through the forest of Japanese birch that covers the foothills. At the upper edge of the forest, the terrain opened into a series of incredible glades – and untracked powder – that

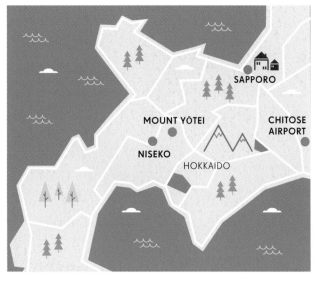

THE NISEKO EXPRESS

Niseko's snow isn't a result of storms, but comes from clouds formed when cold Siberian air meets the warm maritime air of the nearby Sea of Japan. Known as the 'Niseko Express', this can create daily snowfalls for weeks on end. Despite the low altitude, this natural snowmaking machine provides an average of 50ft (15m) of snow every year, twice that of the French Alps, and 80 to 100 days of snowfall. Deep, not steep, is the mantra in Japan.

"It was only at the summit that I could truly appreciate the grand scale and epic dimensions of the volcano"

we would be riding through on the way back down. As we gained elevation, the view revealed a patchwork of forests, farmland and villages that gave way to the waters of Lake Tōya and the Sea of Japan glistening under the just-risen winter sun.

There were no marked trails, so we followed the boot tracks of skiers who had made an even earlier start to the day. Just before the treeline ended, around 4250ft (1300m) above sea level, we sat down for a rest and some lunch. We had already spent a week riding the groomed trails and endless powder tree runs in the Niseko resorts, but the three-hour hike was still arduous. The triangle-shaped, salmon and beef short-rib rice balls, or onigiri, were both utterly delicious and desperately needed.

Bassett explained to us that since the best snow lies below the 4000ft (1200m) mark, most of the locals will descend from here and lap the glades. The climb to the top, he warned, would be cold, steep and windy, and there would more scrambling than hiking during the final section. But we wanted the top.

As we carried on, we watched as a pair of Japanese snowboarders dropped in from a gully just up ahead. Riding short, swallow-tailed boards, they worked around Yōtei's obstacles with style, grace and flow, drawing long arcs that were generating huge clouds of white smoke at each turn. Immediately, we recognised the inherent Japanese style of riding known as snowsurfing, incorporating elements of surfing and skating, pioneered by local legend Taro Tamai.

Tamai, born in Tokyo in 1962, had grown up in a skiing-mad family. In his late teens, he had also become an avid surfer, and when he saw footage of a skier in Utah riding a surfboard-like shaped board, he knew what he wanted to do with the rest of his life. He first snowboarded in the 1980s and would go on to become Japan's first professional snowboarder and national champion. That same decade, he pioneered numerous peaks inside and outside Japan, including Mt Yōtei and others in Alaska, Mongolia, Russia, Ecuador, Uzbekistan, Peru and Argentina. In the late 1990s, he started his snowboard brand, Gentemstick. The handmade approach and the boards' wider, shorter designs changed the way people approached powder. 'I feel there are no boundaries in snowsurfing,' Tamo has said about his methods. 'I head to the mountains when it snows and to the ocean if there are swells. It's just as simple as that.' As it happens, Bassett's snowboards are also hand-crafted, from Hokkaidō honoki wood, and specifically designed to shred Japan powder, known as JaPow.

Seeing the snowboarders carve the snow provided us with just the inspiration to set off for the last section of the hike. Bassett was right – it was tough going. With no trees, the Siberian wind cut through our jackets. Yet it was only at the summit that I could truly appreciate the grand scale and epic dimensions of the volcano.

Bassett explained to us that if we were to drop into the crater itself, it would require hiking back up to the rim to drop the line that led to our cars. With clear skies and time on our side – and my *Joe Versus the Volcano* quote in my locker – it seemed madness

to not ride the crater. But was my minute of unbridled joy worth the subsequent half hour of additional painful leg burn on the hike back out? Once I was safely back on top of the teacup, the answer was obvious.

The following half hour remains one of the best I've had on a snowboard in my life. Although the top, treeless section was a little crusty, as soon as we passed our lunch spot the conditions were beyond perfect. Bassett led the way, allowing us to carve a wide swathe, but always within sight of the boot track. He had stories of skiers overcome with the endless powder and carried away, ending in dead-end gullies that required more hiking. Bassett knew his way around and, eventually, after more faceshots than anyone had a right to receive, we made it back to the cemetery and the car.

Within 10 minutes, we'd secured two cold, giant, silver cans of Sapporo beer from the vending machine and were lowering ourselves into the outdoor *gensen kakenagashi* (naturally sourced hot spring) at Makkari Onsen.

'I wonder where we'll end up?' said Cones, quoting the penultimate line from *Joe Versus the Volcano*. I supplied the response: 'Away from the things of man, my love. Away from the things of man.' **BM**

Clockwise from top: Paper birch trees on the slopes of Niseko ski resort; an onsen (hot spring). Previous page: contemplating the crater on Mt Yotei

DIRECTIONS

Best time to go // Niseko receives consistent light-powder snowfall from December to May. The best conditions for ski touring in Mt Yōtei are in the late season: April and May.

Gear required // A jacket with a high windproof rating, warm gloves and a face cover. An avalanche beacon, probe, shovel and skins or snowshoes are mandatory. Niseko Village has dozens of ski rental shops if you don't have the gear. Pack a pair of swimmers for the hot spring afterwards.

Nearest town // Niseko Village.

Getting there // Niseko is a two-hour drive from Hokkaidō's New Chitose Airport. The Hokkaido Resort Liner bus runs regularly to the resorts. From Niseko, you can drive to the car park at the base of Mt Yōtei.

Where to stay // The Green Leaf Niseko Village is an unbeatable spot right at the base of Mt Niseko Annupuri.

Things to know // A Niseko United All Mountain Pass provides access to all four of the Niseko resorts.

Opposite, from top: catching air at Furano; Lake Toya, as seen from the summit of the Isola slope at Rusutsu

MORE LIKE THIS
THE BEST OF JAPAN

WHITE WORLD OZE IWAKURA

Only 105 miles (170km) from Tokyo, the White World Oze Iwakura ski resort near Katashina is surprisingly good for how accessible iot is. It has fun and easy-going off-piste terrain that is a little steeper than its Niseko cousins, yet it hasn't yet been discovered by the overseas masses. With most local skiers and snowboarders sticking to the piste, and no midweek crowds, there are generally plenty of freshies on offer. Additionally, the terrain layout allows an abundance of off-piste powder lines with easy exits back to the lifts. There's no terrain park and facilities are basic for beginners or families, so this is a hill for advanced and expert skiers and snowboarders who live for the dry powder days skiing among the pine and white birch trees.

Nearest town // Tokyo

FURANO

Furano is one of Japan's largest ski resorts, which means it can fill days and days of exploring. The groomed runs are some of the best in the country for beginners and families, but the off-piste terrain and side-country, for those with avalanche gear and know-how, is world-class. The town of Furano also offers a more authentic Japanese experience compared with Niseko's very Westernised resorts. It is also one of the few Japanese ski resorts that has a wider variety of accommodations, including self-contained apartments, as well as hotels, pensions and a couple of backpackers hostels. It does receive a little less snow than Niseko – averaging a piddling 27ft (9m) a year – but the Furano weather is generally more pleasant, with more days of sunshine.

Nearest town // Furano

RUSUTSU RESORT

Hokkaidō's biggest resort, which has an average annual snowfall of 43ft (13m), is a nirvana for experienced powder hounds, as well as providing the best possible conditions for those who are learning how to ski or ride pow. Only a 30-minute drive from Niseko, Rusutsu has a more scenic mountain backdrop to accompany its 37 runs across 420 acres (170 hectares) of on-piste terrain. However, the tree runs and ample off-piste skiing are its biggest draw cards. The town itself is a charming, explorable mix of traditional and Western restaurants, shops and hot springs, and is one of the few Hokkaidō resorts where you can ski-in, ski-out. Its proximity to the non-skiing attractions of Sapporo, Otaru and Lake Tōya seals the deal for one of Japan's best skiing experiences.

Nearest town // Rusutsu

IN DEEP IN INDIA

*Skiing in Gulmarg may not look or feel like anything you
are used to at home – but that's the whole point.*

It was the winter of 1987. The snow kept falling, and the macarons and chai kept coming, as I huddled, shawl around shoulders, next to a tiny wood heater in a small, cheap hotel that was sinking ever deeper below a white blanket. I'd been in Gulmarg, India almost a week, but had hardly skied at the country's premier resort, so thick and heavy was the snow. During that winter of 1987, I had been on my first ski mountaineering trip to the Indian Himalaya. Then, with my companions having headed home, I'd taken rickety buses and rattling trains west to Kashmir to experience Gulmarg, with its short, old chairlift and a couple of struggling pomas.

But what a difference 30 years makes. 'Your robe, Mr Kingston,' smiled the attendant in 2019 as I emerged from the pool, which had a wall of clear glass looking out onto snow-capped peaks. I returned to my warm room in the luxurious Khyber Resort & Spa, promising myself a massage in the day spa later in the week.

Although it was my first visit back to Gulmarg itself, over the intervening decades I'd fallen totally for the Himalaya in winter. Indeed, I'd fallen time and again under heavy packs on numerous backcountry ski tours through those epic mountains. It was a love affair that reached its peak with a 360-mile (580km) ski traverse from Kashmir, through Kishtwar, Zanskar, Lahaul and finally into Kulu.

But back to Gulmarg, back to 2019. Before that soothing swim I'd skied down through fresh powder from the top of a modern gondola which, at nearly 13,000ft (4000m) above sea level, is the highest lifted point in the world. My thighs had packed in, my lungs still suffered from the altitude. Only days earlier I'd been below sea level, scuba diving in Kerala, more than 2000 miles (3200km) away at the opposite end of India.

Gulmarg, home to the Indian Institute of Skiing and Mountaineering, sits at 8700ft (2650m). Across it are scattered numerous hotels and lodges of all standards, and a clutch of poma lifts offering what the Indians call their bunny or beginner slopes. A network of narrow roads links it together; when snow covered, the roads make for interesting driving. Gulmarg is the only ski area in the world where you can see one of the world's 26,000ft (8000m) peaks: Nanga Parbat, the ninth highest mountain in the world.

In the late 1980s, a militant separatist movement emerged in Kashmir and, in response, the Indian government stationed thousands of troops there. Although this presence is still

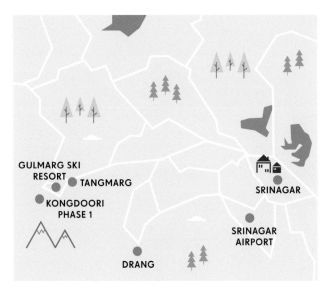

GULMARG SKI
RESORT
TANGMARG

KONGDOORI
PHASE 1

DRANG

SRINAGAR

SRINAGAR
AIRPORT

© Amjed / Shutterstock

noticeable, the impact on tourists is negligible and isn't felt at all in Gulmarg. Blocking the view to the west, 5000ft (1500m) above Gulmarg, is the Apharwat ridgeline. The top station of the gondola sits here, at 13,000ft (4000m) and the ridge itself runs for miles. This easy access from the gondola means that Apharwat now attracts experienced off-piste skiers from around the world to make the most of its dozens of lines.

On a fine day, the Kongdori station area is bustling. A long row of cheap restaurants, *dhabas*, are set up for winter, offering biryanis and bhel puris. Sled wallahs cry out for business, offering tows on their chunky wooden sleds. Skidoos zoom by with their cargo of pleasure-seeking Indians screaming in unison. Snowball fights are everywhere. You see, most people who come to Gulmarg don't come to ski. As the Indian economy has boomed, so has domestic tourism. Millions are looking for ways to spend their new wealth and thousands come to Gulmarg just for the snow experience.

This leaves the skiers and boarders among us with slopes that are often near deserted. I'd teamed up with Aadil, an apprentice motor mechanic from Tangmarg, whose engine was decades younger than mine. In turn we skied with Ashama and Jayan, outdoor enthusiasts spending a month honing their ski skills. Grooming is minimal – a line from the top of the chair back to Kongdori and one down through the trees back to Gulmarg. Signage, too, is scarce.

We met again later that evening at the Gulmarg Avalanche Centre's weekly talk, packed into a small room at Hotel Pine Palace Resort. It's one of the few places in Gulmarg where you can buy an après ski beer (Kashmir is predominantly Muslim).

Snow was bucketing down and there wasn't a breath of wind as I bought my last full-day ski pass. For head-scratching reasons, the ticket office at Gulmarg was in a little hut. You could hardly see the ticket wallah through the tiny window and, at times, had to tightly grip the window security bars to stop yourself slipping down the icy steps. It was all so typically Indian and beautifull when the gondola bottom station, 100 metres away, was a spacious building with loads of room for a large ticket office.

After too much fun, we lunched at the Kong Posh restaurant below the gondola mid-station. It must the only ski restaurant anywhere in the world built with neither windows nor terrace to take in the mountain views. But on this cloudy, snowy day, it mattered little.

'I'm 52, but I've had a hard life,' said our ski guide, Wali, as if to explain his grizzled appearance. There was one more ski to enjoy, the eponymously named Wali's World, a backcountry run down to the village of Drang and then to Tangmarg. When Wali introduced himself, I recalled the shop sign I'd seen in Kashmir decades ago, proudly proclaiming the store was run by 'Useless Wali'. His namesake, however, would turn out to be more than useful as we plunged into a cloud sea from the top of the gondola and descended a series of ridges and bowls for some 6000ft (1800m) into the Drang Valley. Once in the valley, we came across a couple

THE HUMAN SKI LIFT

Years ago, in India's Solang ski area, there was a single 300ft/90m-long poma lift that rarely worked. No problem. Indian women in saris, men in turbans, all in fur jackets, would rent skis and boots, usually many sizes too big, and then hire a couple of porters. These wiry porters would, with some difficulty, push their charges uphill, turn him or her around at the top and let go. Repeat and repeat again. But that did not deter eager locals from skiing.

Clockwise from top: sledding for everyone at Gulmarg ski resort; firing up a snowmobile; Hazratbal Shrine. Previous page: the Gulmarg gondola, one of the world's highest operating cable cars

"Most people who come to Gulmarg don't come to ski. This often leaves us skiers and boarders with near-deserted slopes"

of soldiers hiking to a military camp, a reminder of just how close we were to the actual Line of Control between India and Pakistan.

After a chai at Drang village, we skied through snow-covered apple orchards to a waiting vehicle at Tangmarg. Two hours later, I was enjoying lunch on the India Palace houseboat, floating on Nagin Lake in Srinagar, the main city of Kashmir. I'd stayed on the same houseboat ahead of that Kashmir-to-Kulu ski traverse back in 1991. In 2019, the same barber, Bashir, gave me a shave and head massage as the sun went down across the lake and the muezzin called the faithful to prayer. What little difference 30 years makes. **HK**

DIRECTIONS

Best time to go // January to March. Gulmarg isn't high by Himalayan standards, so often has a relatively short season.
Gear required // If you're staying inbounds, regular alpine or boarding gear will be fine. Venturing further afield, with a guide, will require a full touring set up – ski or splitboard. Reasonable kit can be hired at Kashmir Alpine Ski Shop.
Nearest town // Tangmarg is the jumping-off point. Srinagar, Kashmir's capital, is 30 miles (50km) away.
Getting there // Fly into a major Indian city such as Mumbai or Delhi then take an internal flight to Srinagar. Taxis will take you from there to Tangmarg, where 4WD taxis jostle for business to get you up to Gulmarg.
Where to stay // Five-star hotels like the Khyber will satisfy those with the dollars. Highlands Park and its cottages offer a more authentic experience. Cheaper hotels are plentiful too.
Things to know // Don't get too frustrated if things aren't working 100 percent. Relax and drink another chai.

Opposite: Mt Rishi Pahar (left) and Mt Kalanag in the dramatic Garhwal region of India

MORE LIKE THIS
CENTRAL ASIA'S SKI GEMS

MANALI AND SOLANG, INDIA

At the head of the Kullu Valley, in Himachel Pradesh, the mountains of the Pir Panjal range sit just below the main Himalaya. Although there is a gondola-served, ungroomed ski area at Solang, it is the easy access to skiable peaks and touring that has made Manali a popular destination (in relative terms) and it's an experience melded with the endless charms and challenges of India. Skin up the slopes of Patel Su or those around Bhrigu Lake, or head over Rhotang La or Hampta passes into the trans-Himalayan region of Lahaul. Or take a week-long tour up the Jagatsukh valley, over the near 16,000ft (5000m) Goru pass, and drop into the Malana valley, heading out via the unusual ancient and isolated village of Malana. Manali, a major summer hill town, has dozens of hotels and restaurants or, alternatively, base yourself in a room in one of the surrounding villages.
Nearest town // Ludhiana

KALANAG PEAK, INDIA

There are endless ski-mountaineering objectives across the vastness of the Indian Himalaya. The Garhwal region, in particular, is full of options, including an ascent of Kalanag (21,000ft/6390m) from an approach up the Tons Valley to Ruinsara. Requiring full ski-mountaineering gear for glacier travel and full acclimatisation due to the altitude, Kalanag is a relatively straightforward ascent, albeit one with a steep, generally non-skiable kick for the final summit approach. Ensure you check in with the Indian Mountaineering Foundation about status and requirement for peak permits.
Nearest town // Dehradun

FANN MOUNTAINS, TAJIKISTAN

The Stans, that jigsaw of former Soviet Republics amid the vastness of Central Asia, offer a huge canvas on which to paint your snow experiences. Tajikistan is the smallest and most mountainous. In the east of the country rise the Pamirs, comprising giant 23,000ft (7000m) peaks. Further west are the Fann Mountains, reaching a mere 18,000ft (5500m). Just beyond the outskirts of Dushanbe – the capital of Tajikistan – is Safed Dara, the country's sole ski resort. With a gondola and a T-bar, it's a good place to get your post-flight ski legs. This alpine range still offers many unridden slopes. You might be able to persuade Eraj to open his Artuch summer mountain camp early to start your tours. Beware the vodka, though.
Nearest town // Dushanbe

CHINA'S BIG POWDER DREAM

Snow sports are exploding in China. Although the resort experience is like nothing else on Earth, there is backcountry to be explored that will make powder lovers feel right at home.

S o... are we in North Korea right now?' asks pro skier Chad Sayers as he sets our winding skin track.

'Honestly, guys,' replies our guide, Jeff Oliveira. 'There's no way of knowing.'

Although it's only a two-hour flight from Beijing, Changbaishan in China couldn't feel any further from the nation's capital. Unlike the arid climates to the south, the volcanic peak sits directly in the path of Siberian systems spinning towards Japan, picking up buckets of wind-whipped, dry snow from December through to March. Changbaishan is a popular national park during the summer, but a small area within its borders, known as Powder Paradise Changbaishan, started running a fleet of snowmobiles over a decade ago, shuttling China's most adventurous skiers and boarders up a thin flank of the sprawling volcano. In 2015, the operation introduced China's first cat skiing, running up against North Korea's northern border. On my visit, the border is buried under 8ft (2.5m) of snow. It's hard to believe that something like

this exists after a week of man-made chaos around the Chongli resorts, but here we are, 750 miles (1200km) from Beijing, scoring face shots on China's border with North Korea.

Oliveira has spent more than a decade exploring ski zones across China, becoming the go-to Western resource for skiing in the Far East. But now he's faced with the reality that the only real distinguishing barrier between North Korea and not North Korea is a picket fence and a white stone border marker somewhere beneath our feet. It's a far cry from the armed guards and demilitarised zones we see on TV, and today there is not a single clue to keep us from skiing our way into international headlines.

Thanks to a 946 CE eruption, Changbaishan is now an atoll of skiable peaks and a high-consequence backcountry skiing destination. At its centre lies a deep blue crater lake and, according to North Korean legend, its highest point is the birthplace of the hermit nation's former dictator, Kim Jong-il. Even though our day began in China, we're now not entirely sure whether or not we're side-stepping on his side of the fence.

Despite its expanse of skiable terrain, Powder Paradise Changbaishan's boundaries remain limited to a few groomed strips and a pair of high alpine bowls, something the area's general manager assures us will change 'as demand increases'. But that move is likely to be years off, as adventure skiing, and powder skiing in general, are in their infancy in China. For the most part, skiers stick to their netted slopes and there isn't any managed avalanche control – much less any off-piste skiing – at any of the resorts we visited on the trip.

Just across the valley, on a separate igneous blip, Wanda Changbaishan International Resort is a stark foil to the wilds of untapped volcano skiing. Operated by Wanda Group, one of the largest real estate companies in the world, the resort is on a butte no bigger than a small community ski hill, but it has nine hotels (including Holiday Inns, Hyatts and a Westin), a resort village, a separate spa resort and an indoor water park. In just a few years, Wanda has turned this small farming community into a bustling Western-style destination. Justin Bieber pumps from the heated six-pack chairlift speakers and the base village offers KFC, McDonald's and Pizza Hut. Wanda has even overhauled the airport to prep for the forecasted flow of winter sports enthusiasts from Beijing and Shanghai, adding a shuttle bus directly to the slopes.

The skiing at Wanda is a return to China's usual ski experience: short, icy shots with bone-chattering leg burn and piles of granular moguls. As Chinese skiing slowly begins its push into bigger and bigger terrain, resorts like Wanda and the 2022 Olympic venues around Chongli provide the packaged 'ski experience', selling Chinese president Xi Jinping's vision of a countrywide ski explosion. They are the entry point, an escape from the stresses of city life and the long working week, and a welcome step in a society rewriting its script from the ground up.

When Beijing won the bid for the 2022 Winter Olympics back in 2015, Jinping accompanied the victory with a decree,

promising that China would have 300 million winter sports participants by the start of the Games. Although the number of actual participants by 2022 was unclear, the boom is visible. A country that had six ski areas in 1996 is now home to around 800, including Harbin Wanda Indoor Ski and Winter Sports Resort, the largest indoor ski centre in the world, offering patrons 365 days a year on the snow.

With that continued growth, it's only a matter of time before the freestyle scene and places such as Changbaishan challenge the boundaries of what's possible on snow.

There are very few foreign skiers seeking out China's far reaches, but domestic skiers have already started migrating from the park to the backcountry. Still, on a cold day in March, it's just our small group skirting empty ridgelines at Changbaishan into deep tree pockets. Each bottomless turn recalls Hokkaidō rather than the hardpack that we've experienced at China's traditional resorts.

Higher up on the volcano, a stack of sheer fins drops into Changbaishan's crater – 1500ft (460m) exposed faces built for eye-catching dorm-room posters – but wind loading and

*"A country that had six ski areas in 1996
is now home to around 800"*

Although Norway has laid claim to being the land where skiing was invented, a growing group of international historians have traced its origins back to China's Altai Mountains, where a cave painting depicting early skiers has been dated to over 10,000 years ago. It's taken 10,000 years to make a comeback here.

From left: six-pack of snowboarders at Changbaishan ski resort; self-drive snow-buggy touring. Previous page: Wanda resort, at the base of Changbaishan

DIRECTIONS

Best time to go // The best combination of snow and weather at Changbaishan is from mid- to late-March, when snow has filled in and the bone-chilling cold starts to wane.

Gear required // Beacon, shovel, probe (and an AIARE Level 1 certification). An AT setup isn't necessary, but will help to explore some of the further reaches of the area.

Nearest town // Donggangzhen, 20 miles (33km) away, is the nearest town, though Wanda Changbaishan International Resort is close and comes to life during winter.

Where to stay // Wanda Changbaishan International Resort has a modern alpine village with all of the amenities: restaurants, spas and a slew of well-equipped hotels.

Things to know // Changbaishan is still an active volcano. There have been no eruptions for centuries, but the area has registered earthquakes ranging from magnitude 4 to 6 over the past decade. The last sizable quake, a magnitude 6.3, temporarily closed the resort in 2017.

an uncertain snowpack force our party over to more stable terrain and the promise of deep turns.

As we skin along the buried border, the steps become a little more calculated. On one side of the ridgeline, cornice drops and endless bowls beckon; on the other, we're tempted by 1200ft (365m) of steep, shaded birch. Half enthralled, half terrified, we opt for the line back towards Powder Paradise. After a few minutes munching fish-flavoured rice cakes, adjusting packs and taking one last look over our shoulders, we drop towards the forest, back into China and the welcome thwap of untouched powder turns.

Deep in the folds of the north-facing fall line, we throw shimmering rooster tails into the mid-afternoon sun. Low-lying birches cast gnarled shadows across the slope, the only contrast along an uninterrupted pitch of fresh snow. Despite warnings of fines and jail time for skiing out of bounds along the volcano, the worries are washed away with a fist bump from the snowmobile operator scoping our line from below. His smile is stuck wide open. We are the first he's ever seen 'ski the trees', but we know our tracks won't be the last. **KK**

Opposite, from top: anticipating a perfect day on the slopes; Genting Olympic resort, which hosted skiing and snowboarding events at the 2022 Winter Olympics

MORE LIKE THIS
CHINA'S FINEST SKI RESORTS

GENTING RESORT SECRET GARDEN

One of a handful of ski resorts that had a major upgrade ahead of the 2022 Beijing Olympics, Genting Resort Secret Garden is the crown jewel of the Chongli region, outside Beijing. The 42-piste resort has nearly 1300ft (400m) of vertical, accessed by seven lifts, including a gondola, and has become one of China's freeskiing epicentres with two sizable terrain parks. In 2022, the area hosted the freestyle skiing and snowboard events for the Beijing Games. In many ways, Genting exemplifies the Chinese ski experience. Located in Hebei province in the lower ranging Dama Mountains, the resort relies mainly on an extensive system of man-made snow, so powder is consistent, but delegated for on-slope skiing, rather than adventures off-piste. The resort rounds out a typical ski day with off-ski offerings including five-star lodging, a full-service fitness centre and piping-hot noodle bars outdoors.
Nearest town // Beijing

THAIWOO SKI RESORT

If skiing along North Korea's border isn't your idea of a good time, China offers a series of novelty ski experiences that are unlike any in the world. Try Thaiwoo Ski Resort, for example, an area that is not only in view of the Great Wall of China, it shares its northwest border with the historic fortification. One of the skiing venues for Beijing 2022, Thaiwoo currently has over 12 miles (20km) of ski trails, with plans to expand four-fold over the next few years. Also situated close to Chongli, Thaiwoo runs lifts from late November through to late March. The resort is well-equipped for overnight visitors, with a smattering of four-star hotels and a youth hostel. Plans for a Euro-style ski village are already underway.
Nearest town // Beijing

HARBIN WANDA INDOOR SKI AND WINTER SPORTS RESORT

One of the five biggest ski resorts in China, Harbin Wanda Indoor Ski and Winter Sports Resort is also the site of largest indoor ski centre in the world. Offering around two miles (3km) of ski terrain spread across six slopes, this fully contained ski resort allows for year-round skiing in China's northernmost province, Heilongjiang. While outside temperatures can dip below -30°C (-22°F) in winter, this refrigerated ski slope hovers around -6°C (42°F) year-round, providing skiers and boarders with consistent conditions, lap after lap. In addition to a full-size terrain park with lanes for jumps and rails, the 861,113 sq ft (80,000 sq m) centre is home to a separate beginner area as well as intermediate and expert terrain accessed by six surface lifts and two chairlifts that rise alongside facades of painted mountains and frosted trees. When legs get weary, guests can grab a hot coffee or bao bun at the ski area's mid-mountain lodge or the gaudy summit restaurant and lounge, before heading out into the cold climes of China's great white north.
Nearest town: Harbin

INDEX

Epic Snow Adventures of the World
August 2023
Published by Lonely Planet Global Limited
CRN 554153
www.lonelyplanet.com
10 9 8 7 6 5 4 3 2 1

Printed in Malaysia
ISBN 978 183 869 603 0
© Lonely Planet 2023
© photographers as indicated 2023

Publishing Director Piers Pickard
Senior Editor Robin Barton
Commissioning Editor Will Cockrell
Designer Kristina Juodenas
Mapping Daniel di Paolo
Picture Research Heike Bohnstengel
Editors Nick Mee, Joanna Cooke
Index Polly Thomas
Print Production Nigel Longuet

Lonely Planet Global Limited
Digital Depot, Roe Lane (off Thomas St),
Digital Hub, Dublin 8,
D08 TCV4
IRELAND

STAY IN TOUCH lonelyplanet.com/contact

Authors Amanda Canning (**AC**); Bianca Bujan (**BB**); Ben Mondy (**BM**); Becky Ohlsen (**BO**); Carolyn Heller (**CH**); Emily Matchar (**EM**);
Graham Averill (**GA**); Geordie Stewart (**GS**); Heather Hansman (**HH**); Huw Kingston (**HK**); Kerry Christiani (**KC**); Kade Krichko (**KK**); Lucy
Corne (**LC**); Luke Waterson (**LW**); Megan Michelson (**MM**); Marc Peruzzi (**MP**); Orla Thomas (**OT**); Stuart Kenny (**ST**); Stephanie Pearson
(**SP**); Steve Waters (**SW**); Scott Yorko (**SY**); Will Cockrell (**WC**).

Illustrations by Ross Murray (www.rossmurray.com).